PUBLISHER
DAMIAN A. WASSEL

EDITOR-IN-CHIEF
ADRIAN F. WASSEL

ART DIRECTOR
NATHAN C. GOODEN

MANAGING EDITOR
TAY TAYLOR

SALES /MARKETING - DIRECT MARKET
DAVID DISSANAYAKE

SALES /MARKETING - BOOK TRADE
SYNDEE BARWICK

OPERATIONS MANAGER
IAN BALDESSARI

EVP BRANDING/DESIGN
TIM DANIEL

PRINCIPAL
DAMIAN A. WASSEL, SR.

WRITER
DAVID
ANDRY

SKYLAR
PATRIDGE
ARTIST

COLORIST
JASON
WORDIE

DERON
BENNETT
LETTERER

CREATED BY DAVID ANDRY-SKYLAR PATRIDGE-ALEJANDRO ARAGON

SPECIAL THANKS TO:
LAUREN WINTERS-SHAWN KIRKHAM-SINA GRACE-DAN PETERSEN-TIM DANIEL AND BUSY BEE

VAULT

PRESENTS

RESONANT

VOLUME TWO

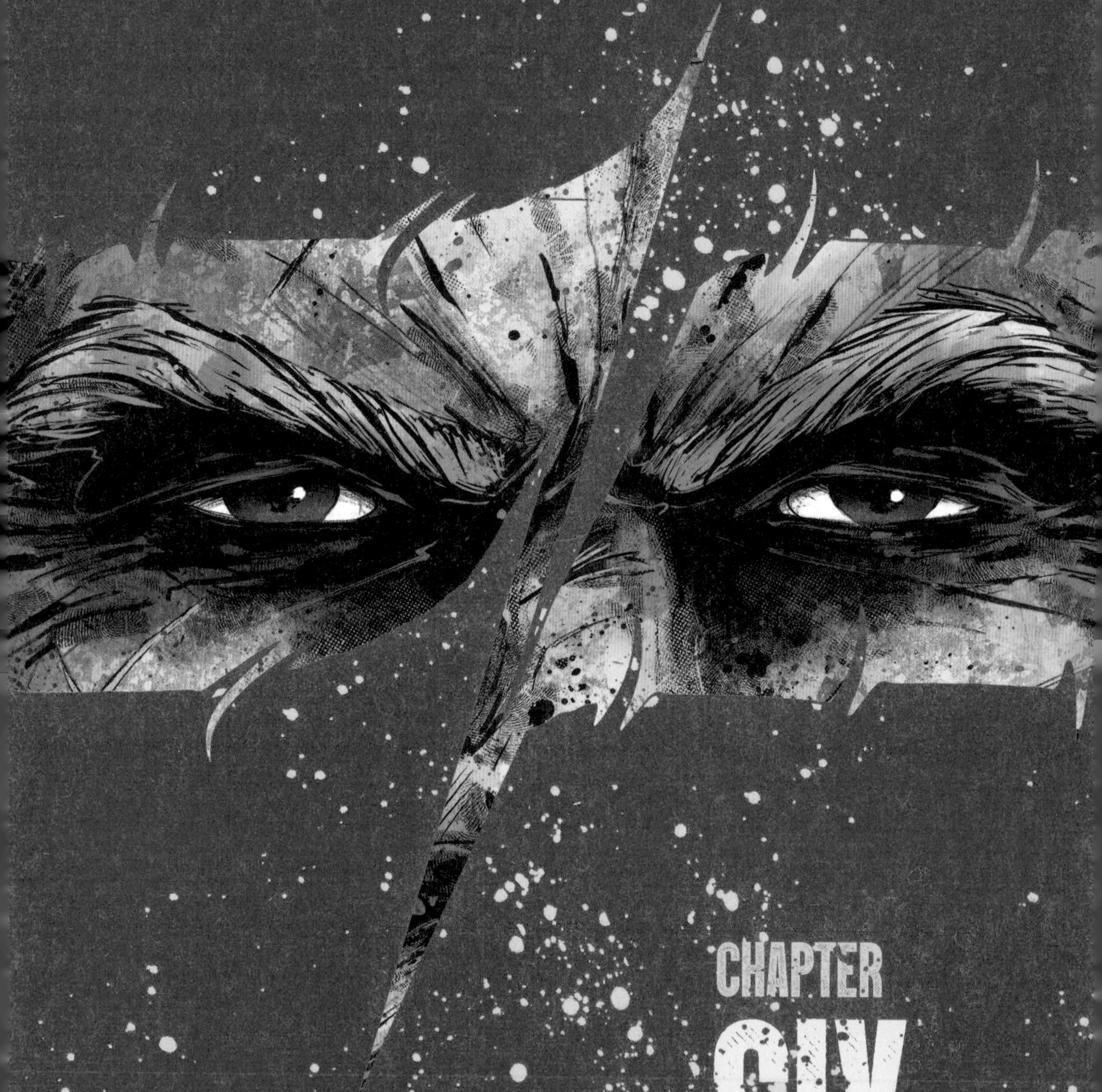

CHAPTER SIX

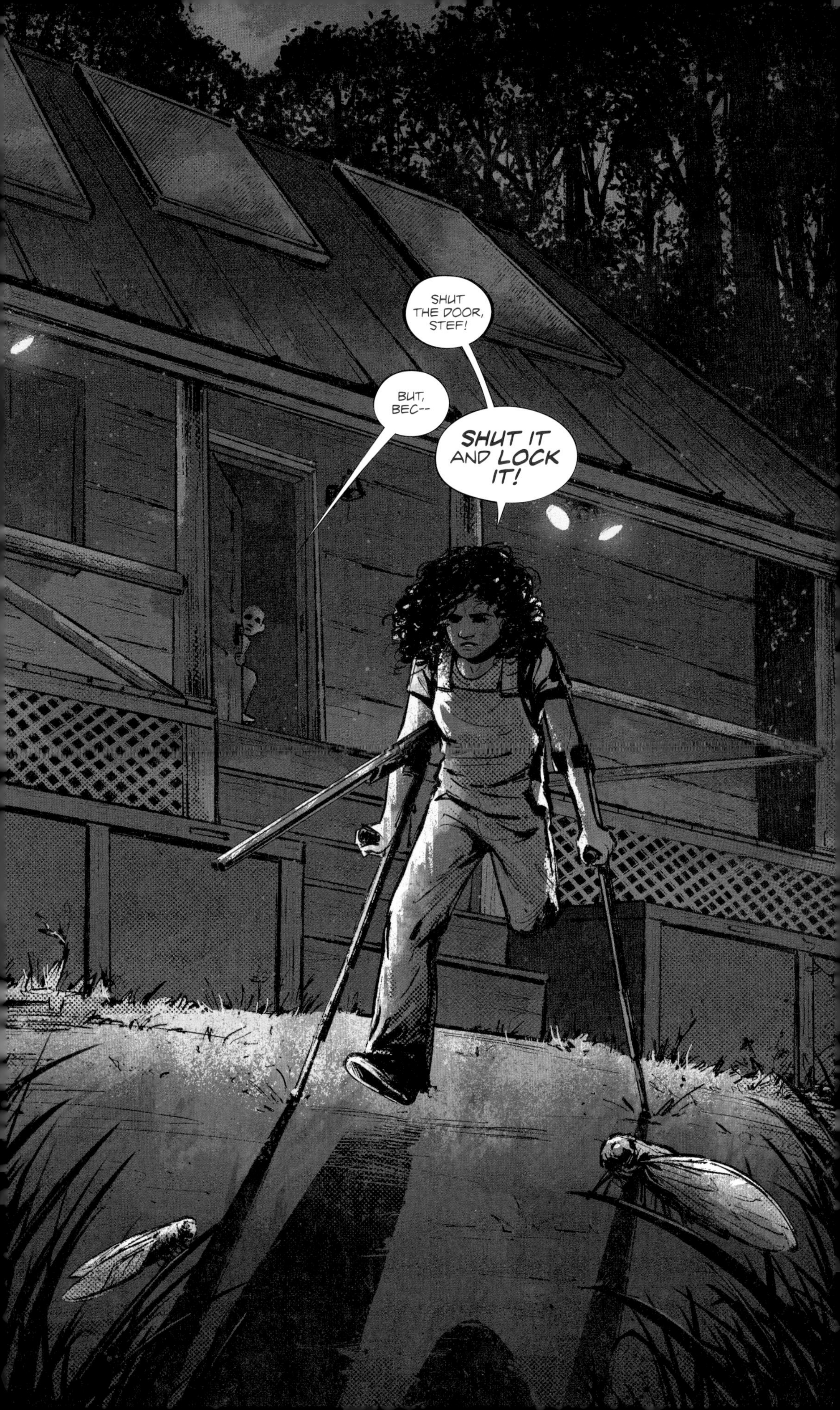
SHUT THE DOOR, STEF!
BUT, BEC--
SHUT IT AND LOCK IT!

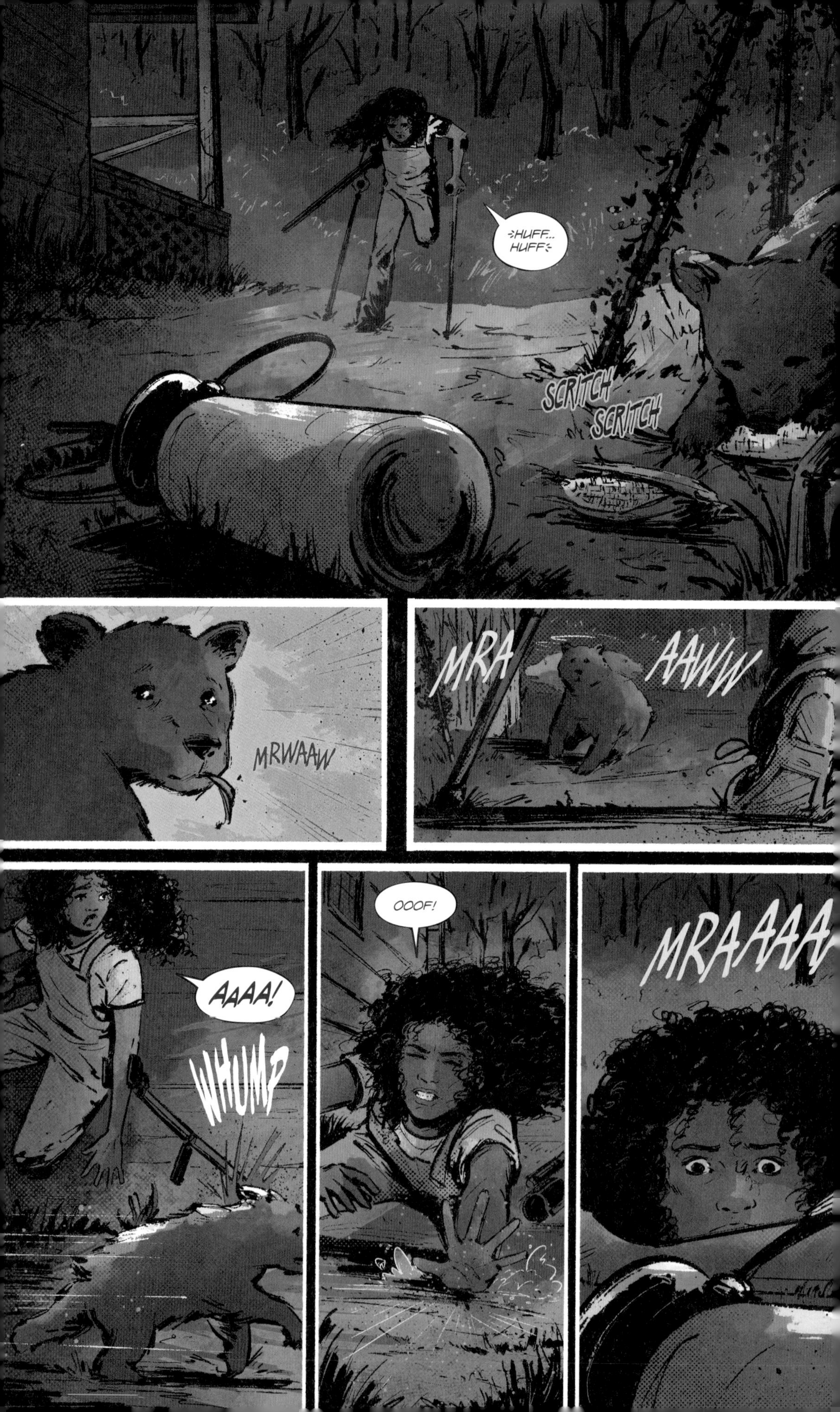
HUFF... HUFF
SCRITCH SCRITCH
MRWAAW
MRA AAWW
AAAA!
WHUMP
OOOF!
MRAAAA

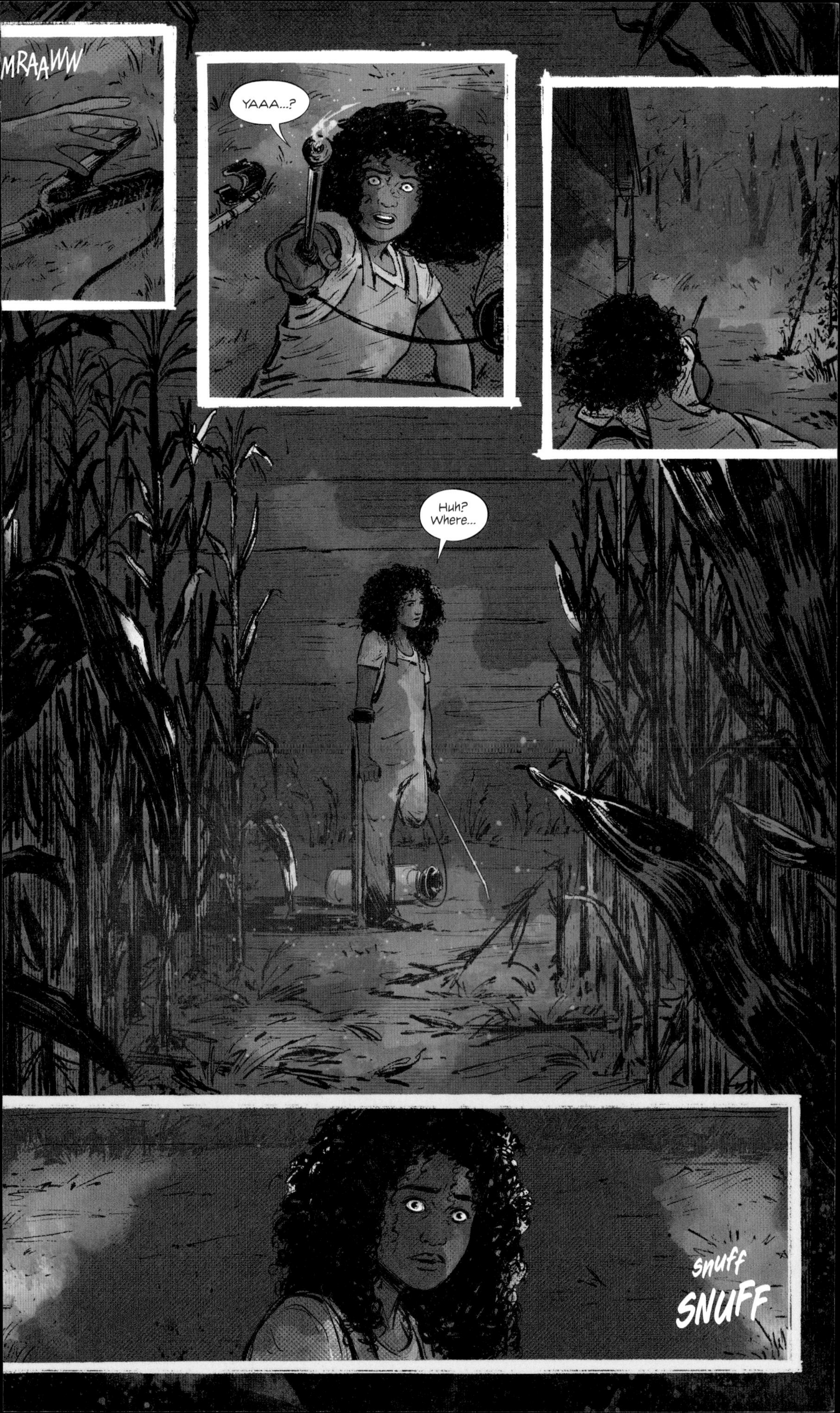
MRAAWW
YAAA...?
Huh? Where...
snuff
SNUFF

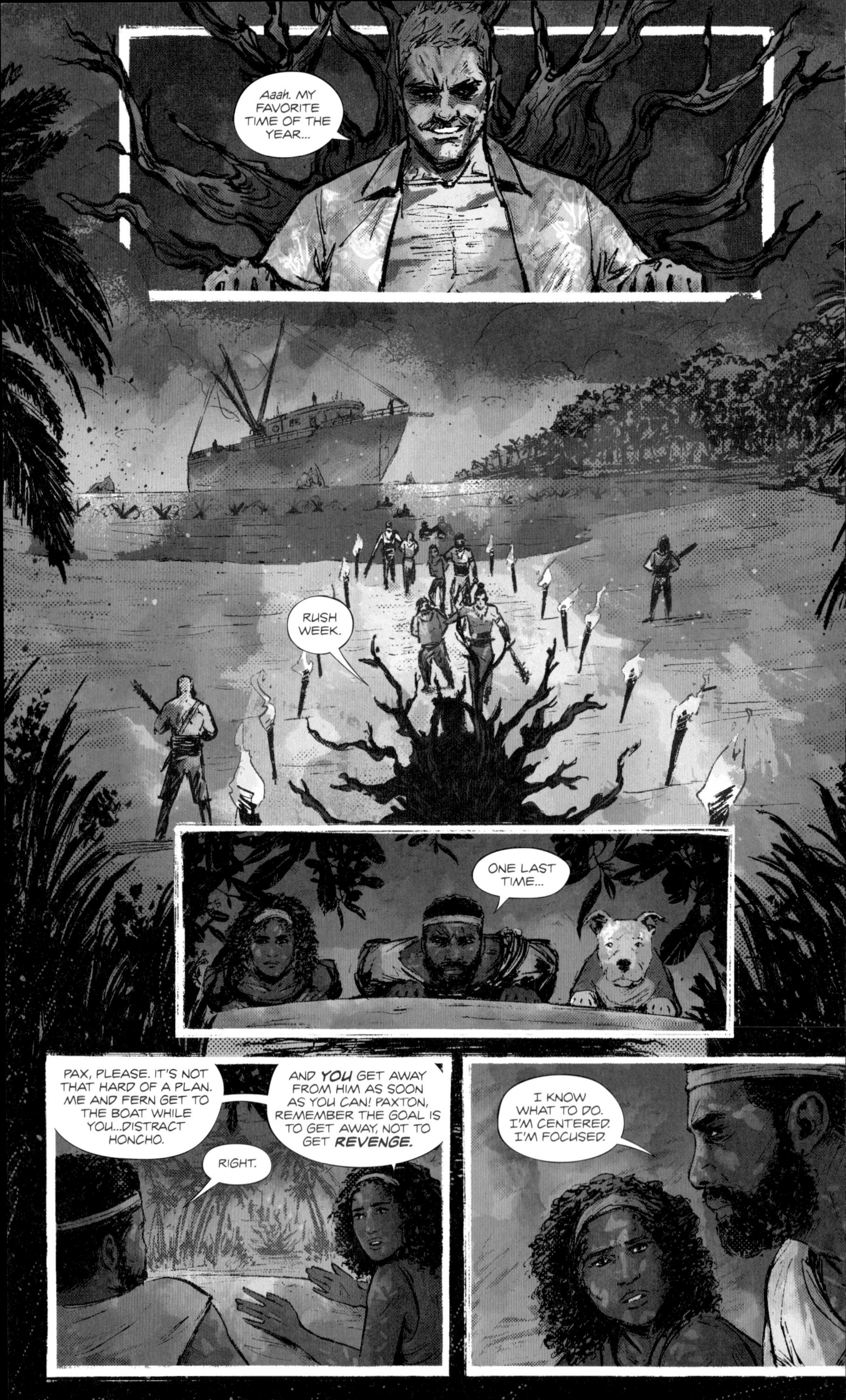
Aaah. MY FAVORITE TIME OF THE YEAR...
RUSH WEEK.
ONE LAST TIME...
PAX, PLEASE. IT'S NOT THAT HARD OF A PLAN. ME AND FERN GET TO THE BOAT WHILE YOU...DISTRACT HONCHO.
AND **YOU** GET AWAY FROM HIM AS SOON AS YOU CAN! PAXTON, REMEMBER THE GOAL IS TO GET AWAY, NOT TO GET **REVENGE.**
RIGHT.
I KNOW WHAT TO DO. I'M CENTERED. I'M FOCUSED.

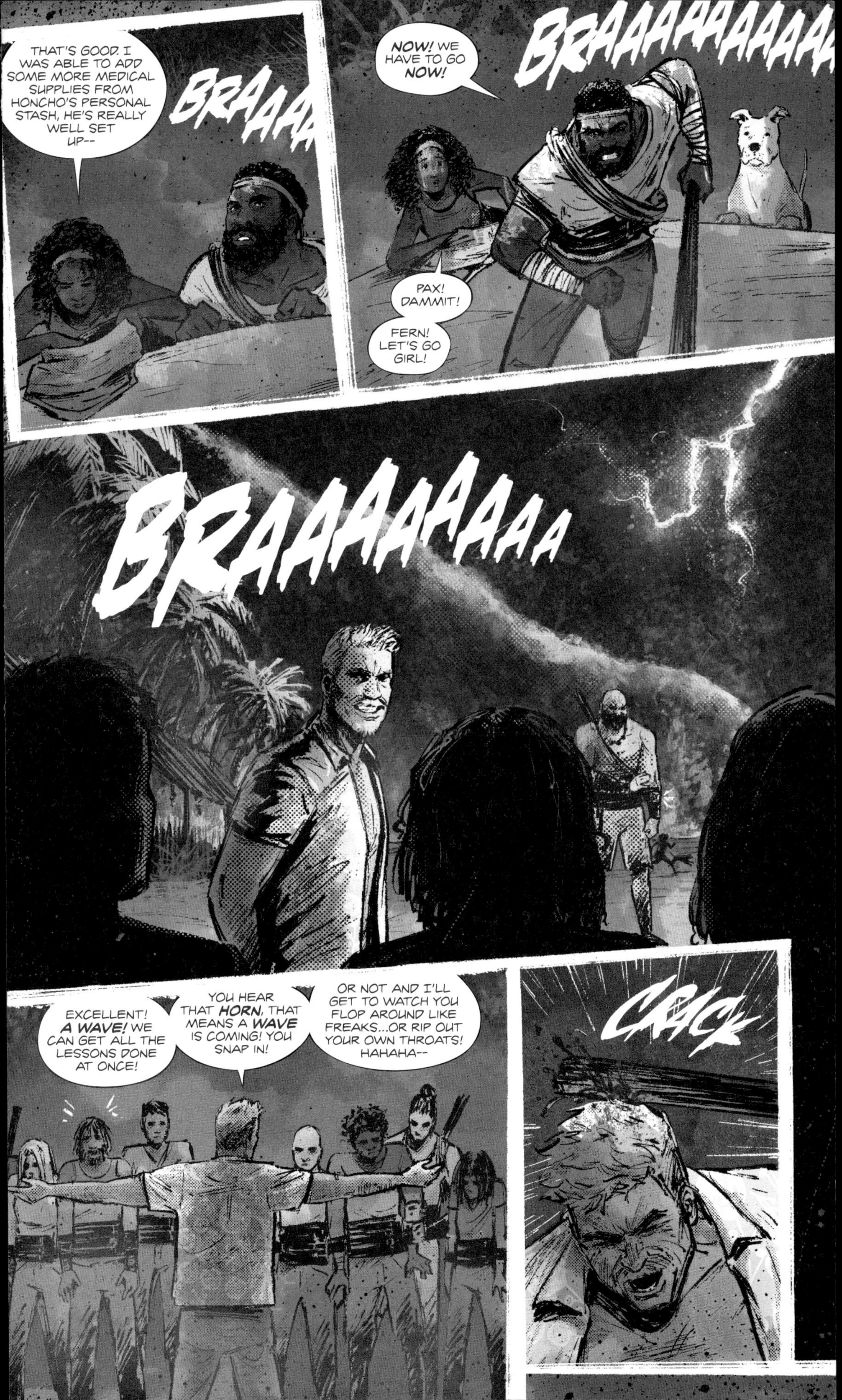
THAT'S GOOD. I WAS ABLE TO ADD SOME MORE MEDICAL SUPPLIES FROM HONCHO'S PERSONAL STASH, HE'S REALLY WELL SET UP--
BRAAAA
NOW! WE HAVE TO GO NOW!
BRAAAAAAAAAA
PAX! DAMMIT!
FERN! LET'S GO GIRL!
BRAAAAAAAAA
EXCELLENT! A WAVE! WE CAN GET ALL THE LESSONS DONE AT ONCE!
YOU HEAR THAT HORN, THAT MEANS A WAVE IS COMING! YOU SNAP IN!
OR NOT AND I'LL GET TO WATCH YOU FLOP AROUND LIKE FREAKS...OR RIP OUT YOUR OWN THROATS! HAHAHA--
CRACK

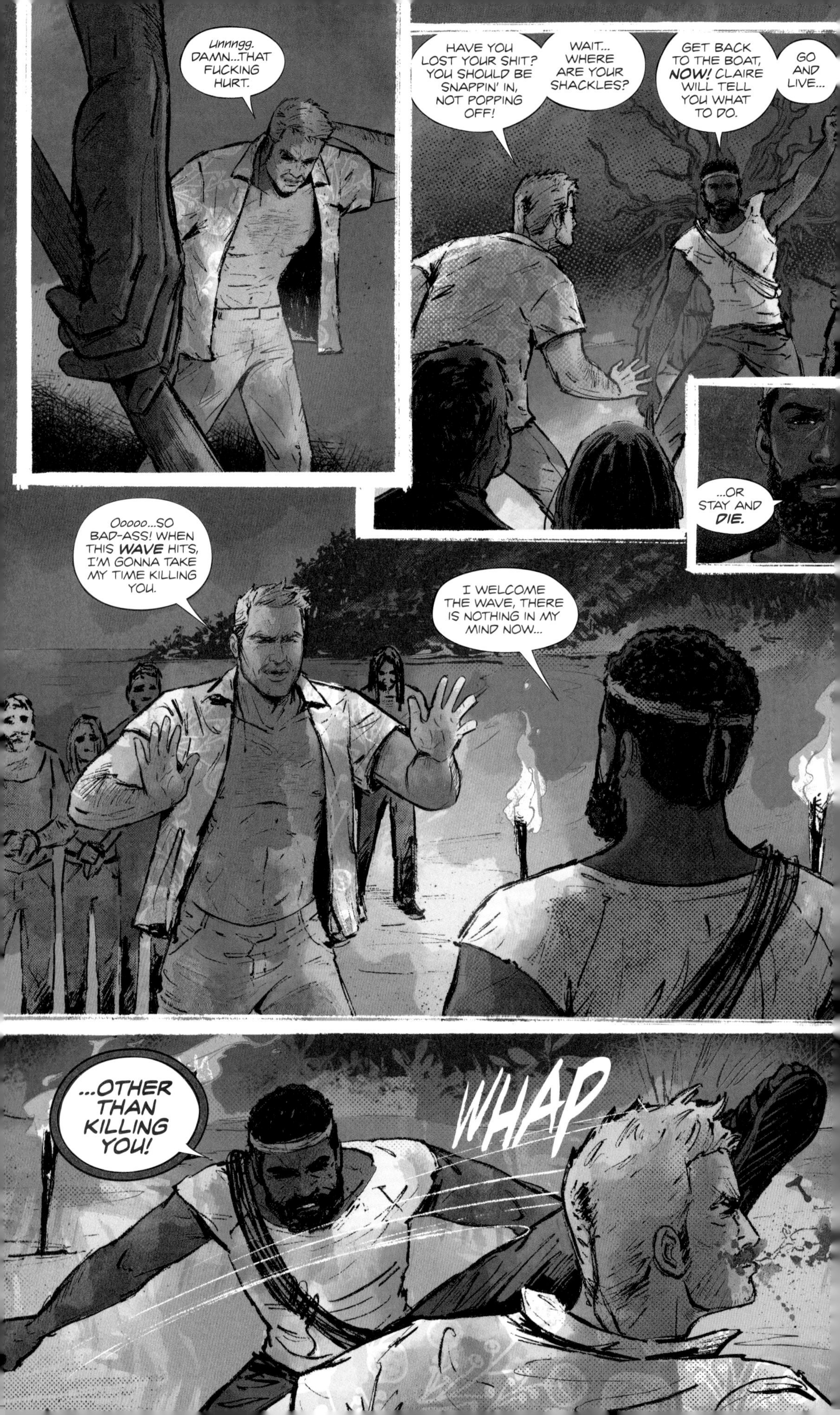
Unnngg. DAMN...THAT FUCKING HURT.
HAVE YOU LOST YOUR SHIT? YOU SHOULD BE SNAPPIN' IN, NOT POPPING OFF!
WAIT... WHERE ARE YOUR SHACKLES?
GET BACK TO THE BOAT, NOW! CLAIRE WILL TELL YOU WHAT TO DO.
GO AND LIVE...
...OR STAY AND DIE.
Ooooo...SO BAD-ASS! WHEN THIS WAVE HITS, I'M GONNA TAKE MY TIME KILLING YOU.
I WELCOME THE WAVE, THERE IS NOTHING IN MY MIND NOW...
...OTHER THAN KILLING YOU!
WHAP

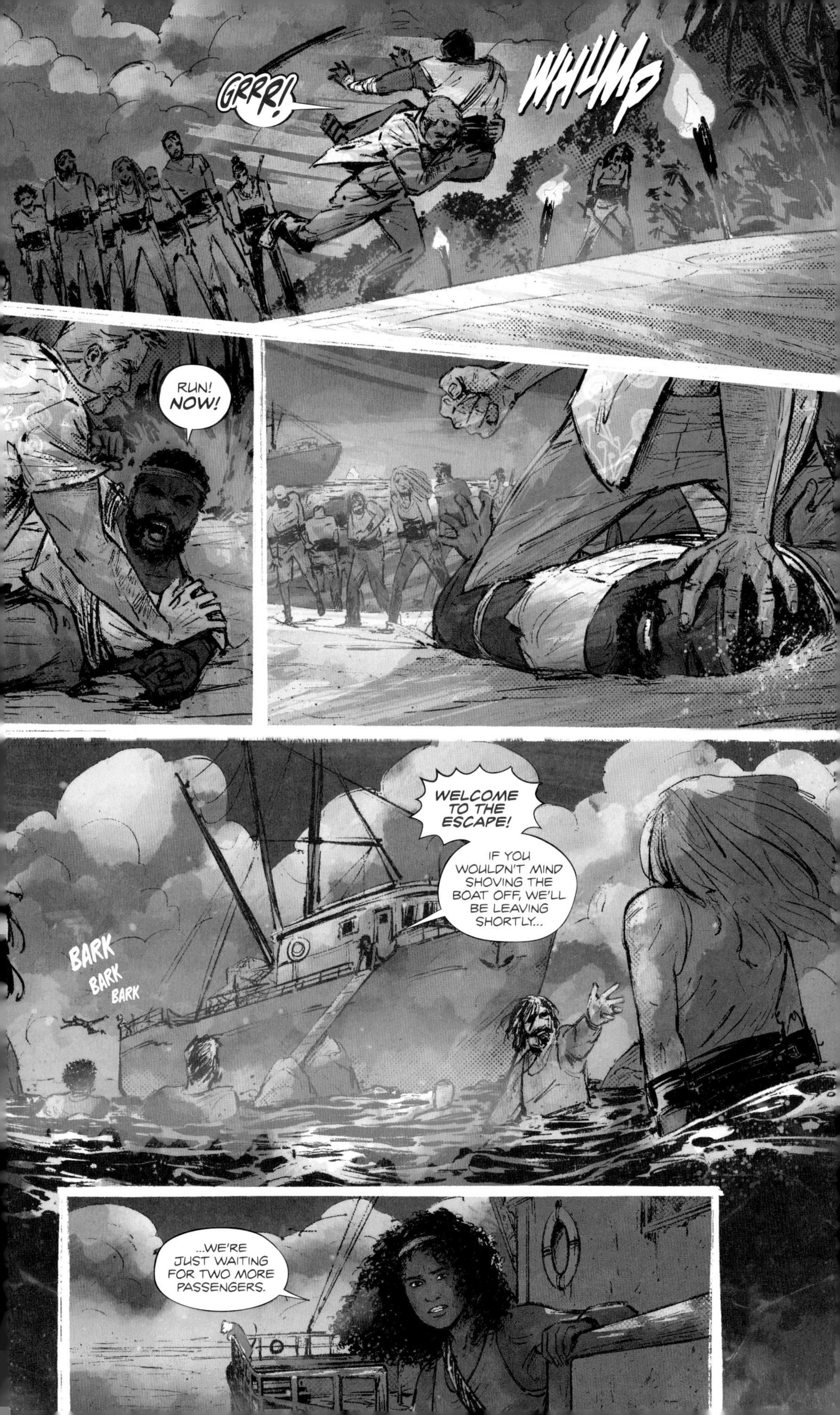
GRRR!
WHUMP
RUN! NOW!
WELCOME TO THE ESCAPE!
IF YOU WOULDN'T MIND SHOVING THE BOAT OFF, WE'LL BE LEAVING SHORTLY...
BARK BARK BARK
...WE'RE JUST WAITING FOR TWO MORE PASSENGERS.

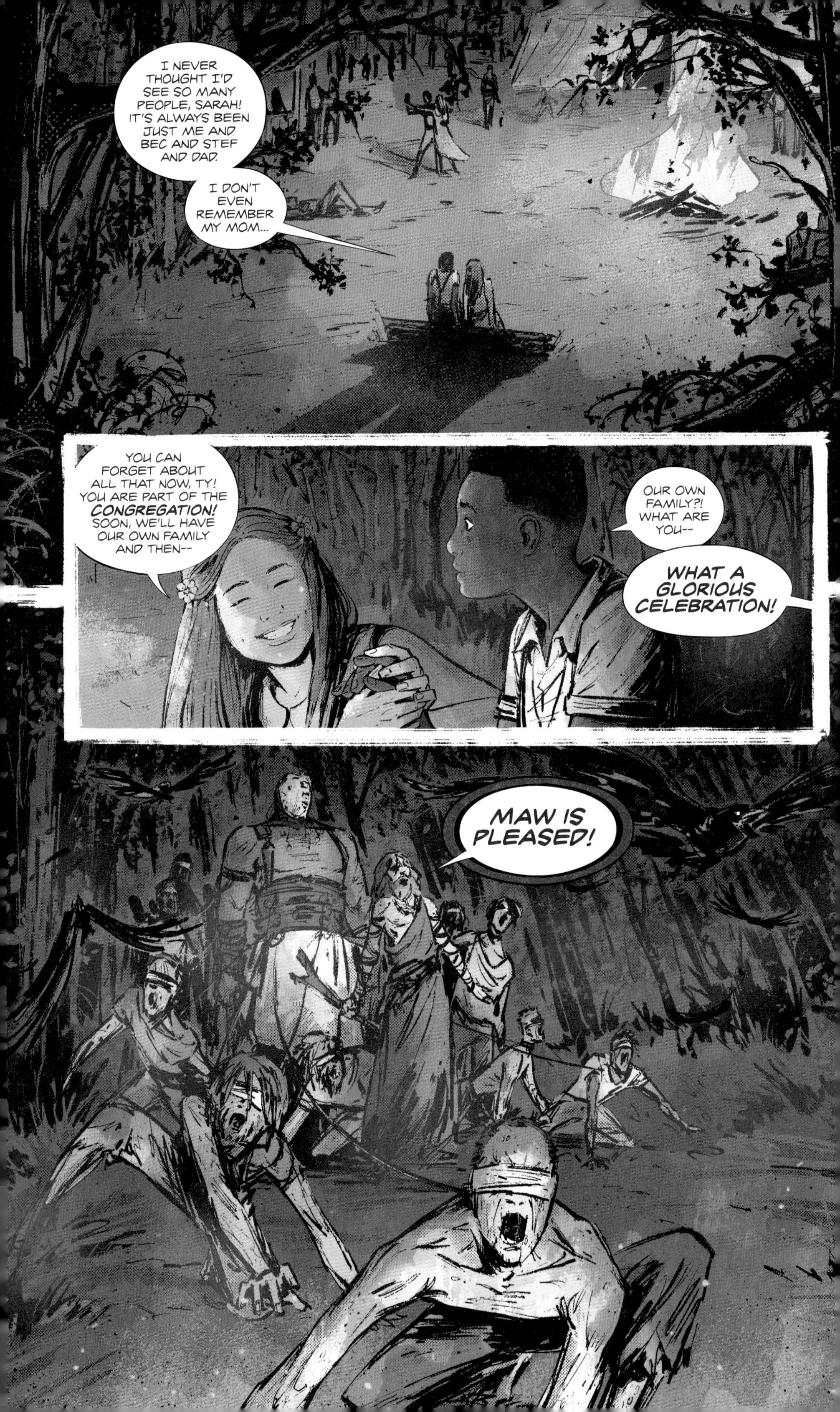

I NEVER THOUGHT I'D SEE SO MANY PEOPLE, SARAH! IT'S ALWAYS BEEN JUST ME AND BEC AND STEF AND DAD.
I DON'T EVEN REMEMBER MY MOM...
YOU CAN FORGET ABOUT ALL THAT NOW, TY! YOU ARE PART OF THE CONGREGATION! SOON, WE'LL HAVE OUR OWN FAMILY AND THEN--
OUR OWN FAMILY?! WHAT ARE YOU--
WHAT A GLORIOUS CELEBRATION!
MAW IS PLEASED!

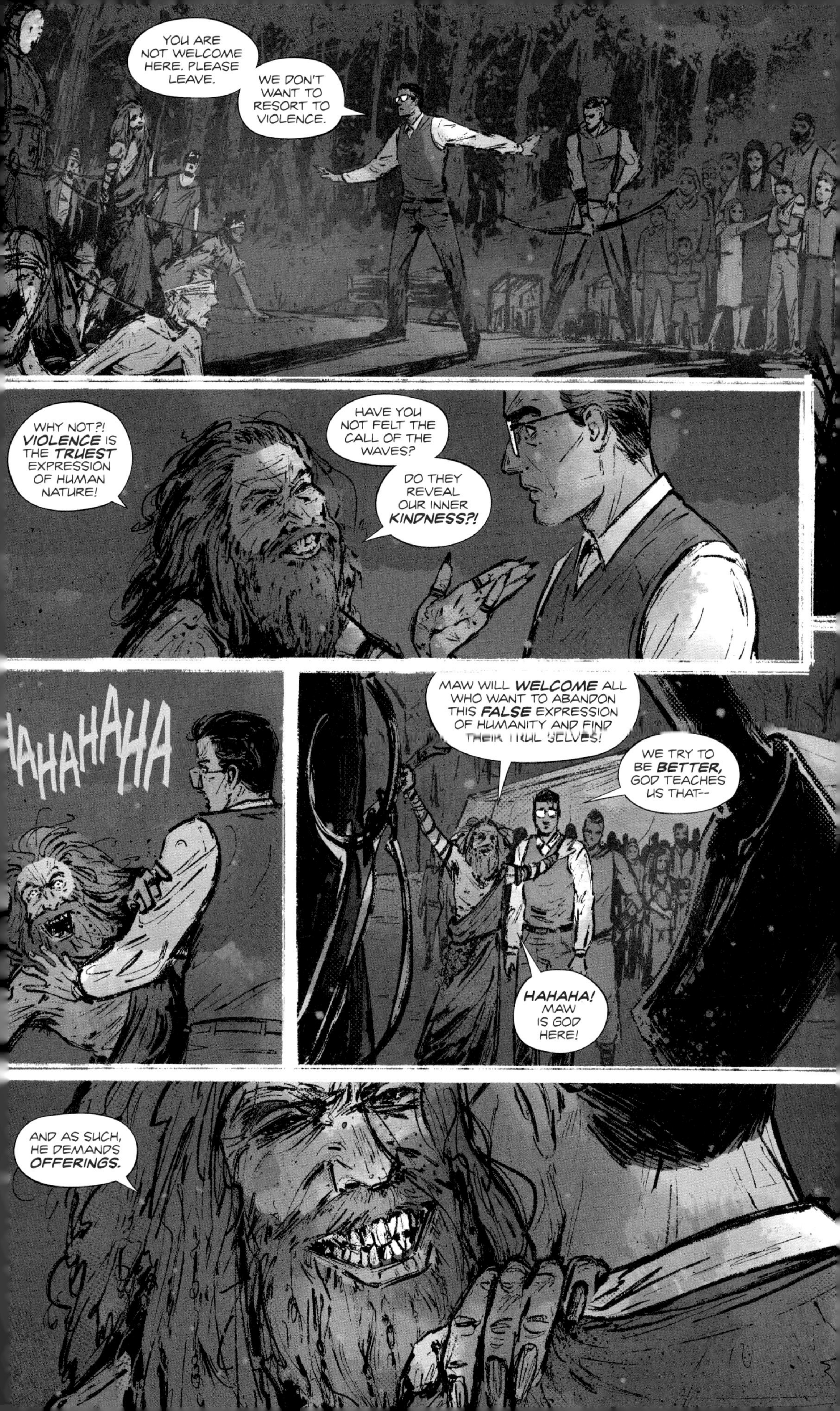

YOU ARE NOT WELCOME HERE. PLEASE LEAVE.
WE DON'T WANT TO RESORT TO VIOLENCE.
WHY NOT?! **VIOLENCE** IS THE **TRUEST** EXPRESSION OF HUMAN NATURE!
HAVE YOU NOT FELT THE CALL OF THE WAVES?
DO THEY REVEAL OUR INNER **KINDNESS?!**
HAHAHAHAHA
MAW WILL **WELCOME** ALL WHO WANT TO ABANDON THIS **FALSE** EXPRESSION OF HUMANITY AND FIND THEIR TRUE SELVES!
WE TRY TO BE **BETTER,** GOD TEACHES US THAT--
HAHAHA! MAW IS GOD HERE!
AND AS SUCH, HE DEMANDS **OFFERINGS.**

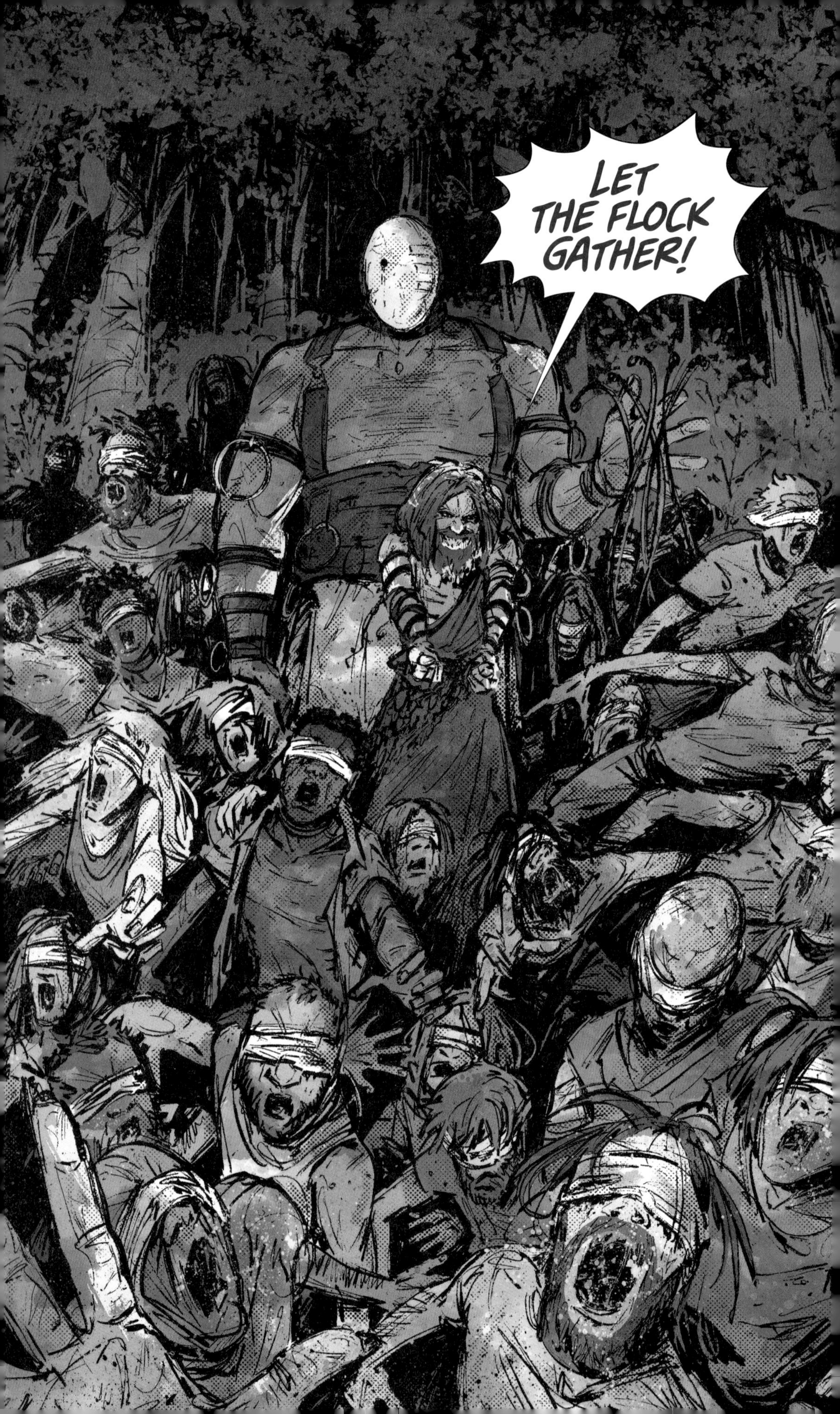
LET THE FLOCK GATHER!

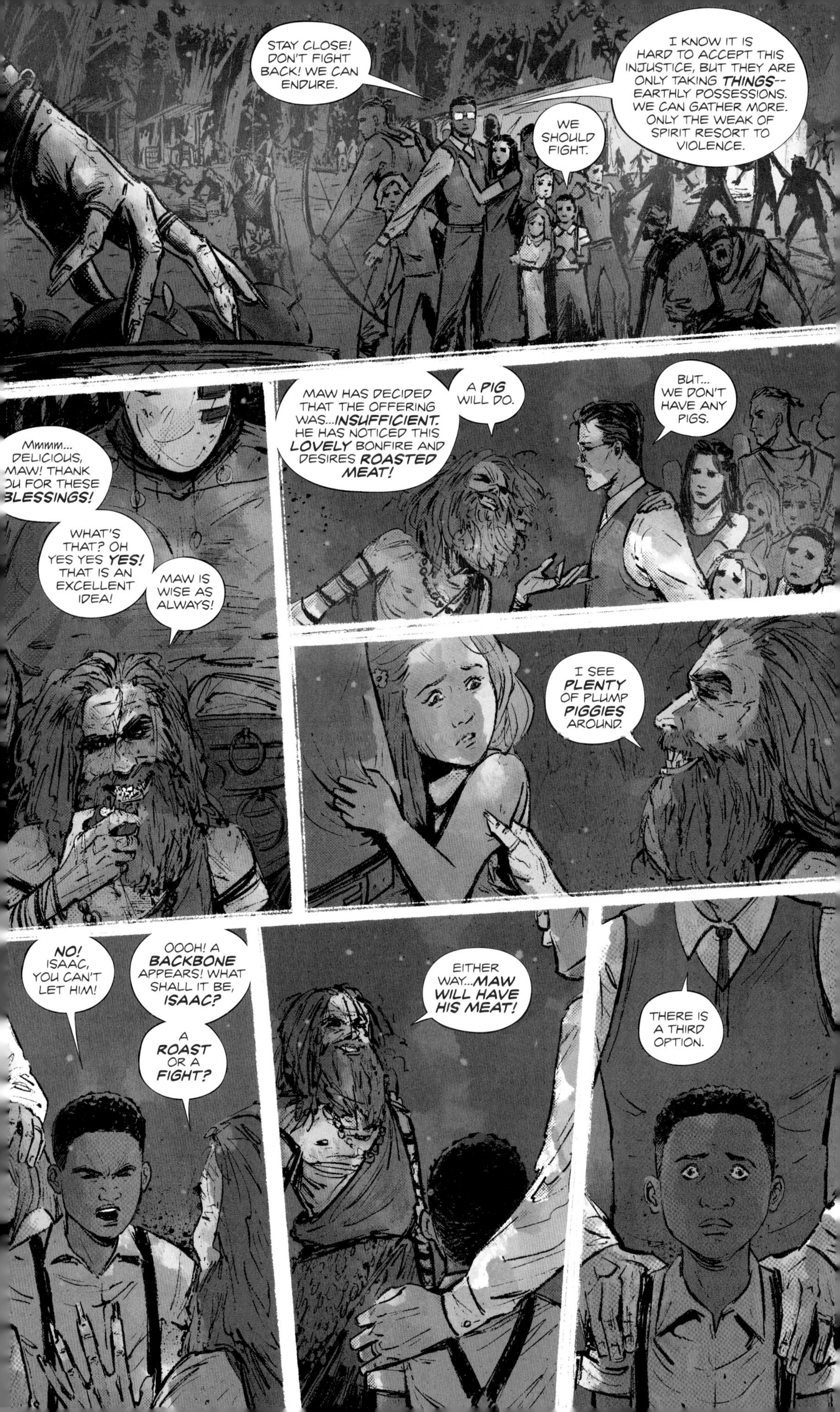
STAY CLOSE! DON'T FIGHT BACK! WE CAN ENDURE.
I KNOW IT IS HARD TO ACCEPT THIS INJUSTICE, BUT THEY ARE ONLY TAKING THINGS-- EARTHLY POSSESSIONS. WE CAN GATHER MORE. ONLY THE WEAK OF SPIRIT RESORT TO VIOLENCE.
WE SHOULD FIGHT.
Mmmm... DELICIOUS, MAW! THANK OU FOR THESE BLESSINGS!
WHAT'S THAT? OH YES YES YES! THAT IS AN EXCELLENT IDEA!
MAW IS WISE AS ALWAYS!
MAW HAS DECIDED THAT THE OFFERING WAS...INSUFFICIENT. HE HAS NOTICED THIS LOVELY BONFIRE AND DESIRES ROASTED MEAT!
A PIG WILL DO.
BUT... WE DON'T HAVE ANY PIGS.
I SEE PLENTY OF PLUMP PIGGIES AROUND.
NO! ISAAC, YOU CAN'T LET HIM!
OOOH! A BACKBONE APPEARS! WHAT SHALL IT BE, ISAAC?
A ROAST OR A FIGHT?
EITHER WAY...MAW WILL HAVE HIS MEAT!
THERE IS A THIRD OPTION.

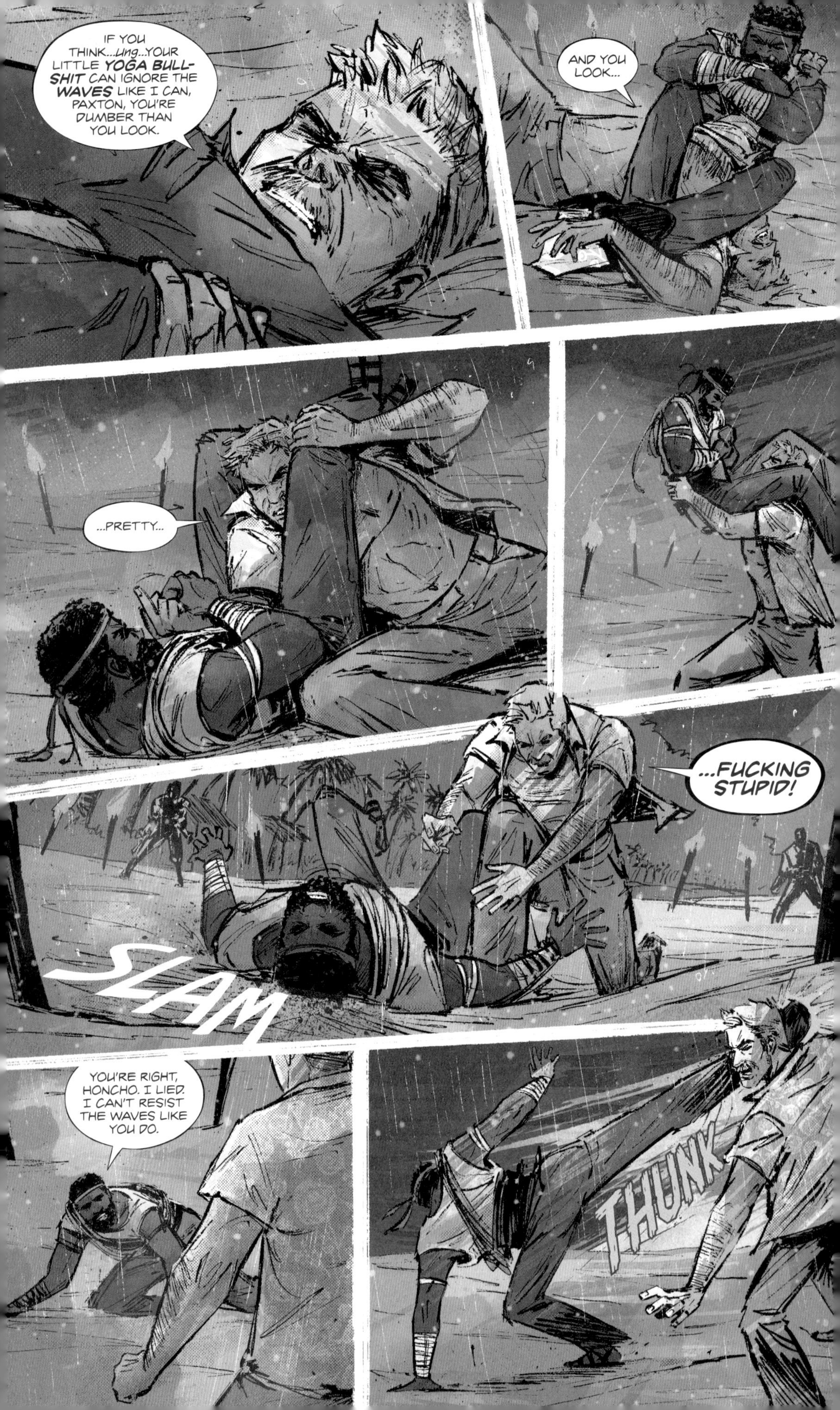
IF YOU THINK...*ung*...YOUR LITTLE **YOGA BULLSHIT** CAN IGNORE THE **WAVES** LIKE I CAN, PAXTON, YOU'RE DUMBER THAN YOU LOOK.
AND YOU LOOK...
...PRETTY...
...FUCKING STUPID!
SLAM
YOU'RE RIGHT, HONCHO. I LIED. I CAN'T RESIST THE WAVES LIKE YOU DO.
THUNK

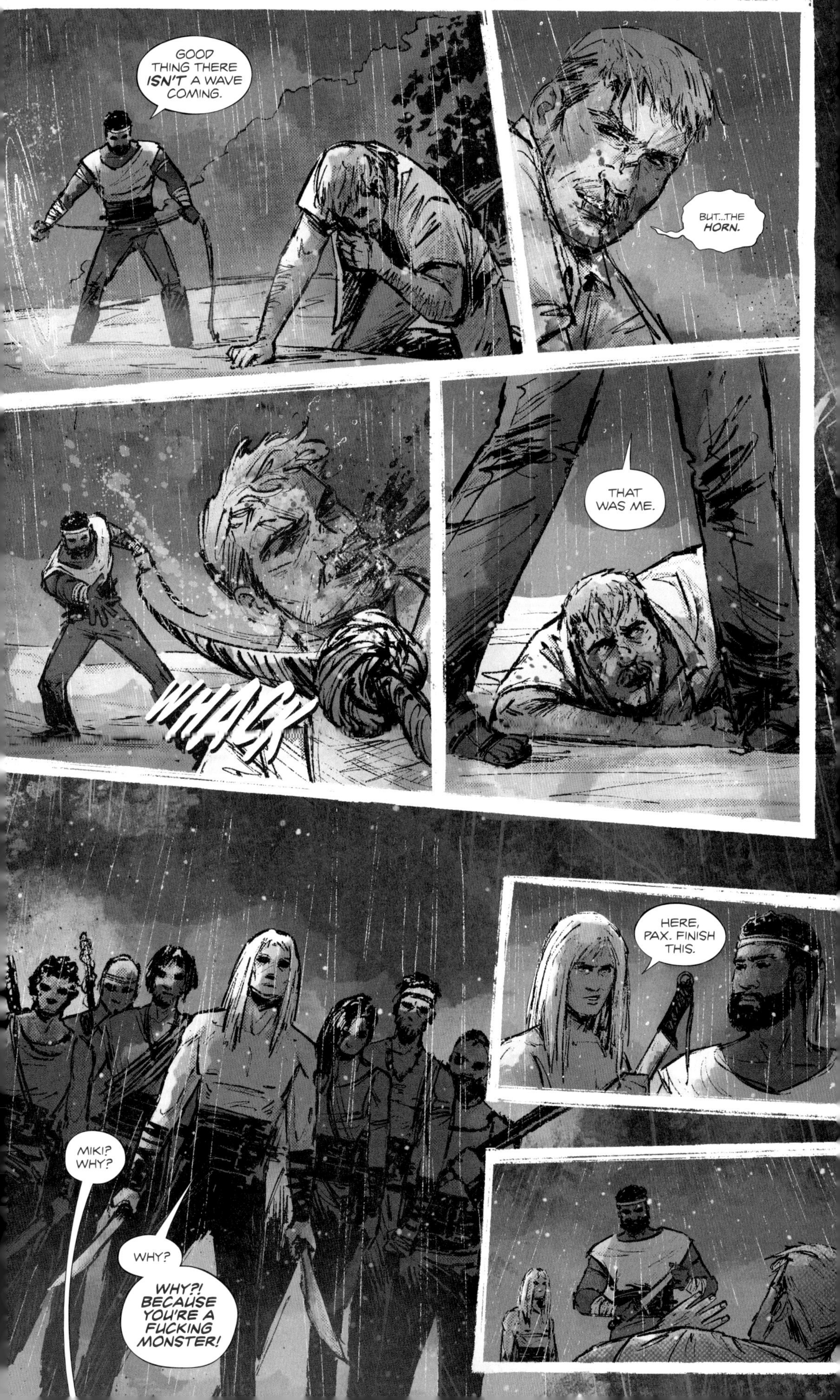
GOOD THING THERE ISN'T A WAVE COMING.
BUT...THE HORN.
WHACK
THAT WAS ME.
MIKI? WHY?
WHY?
WHY?! BECAUSE YOU'RE A FUCKING MONSTER!
HERE, PAX. FINISH THIS.

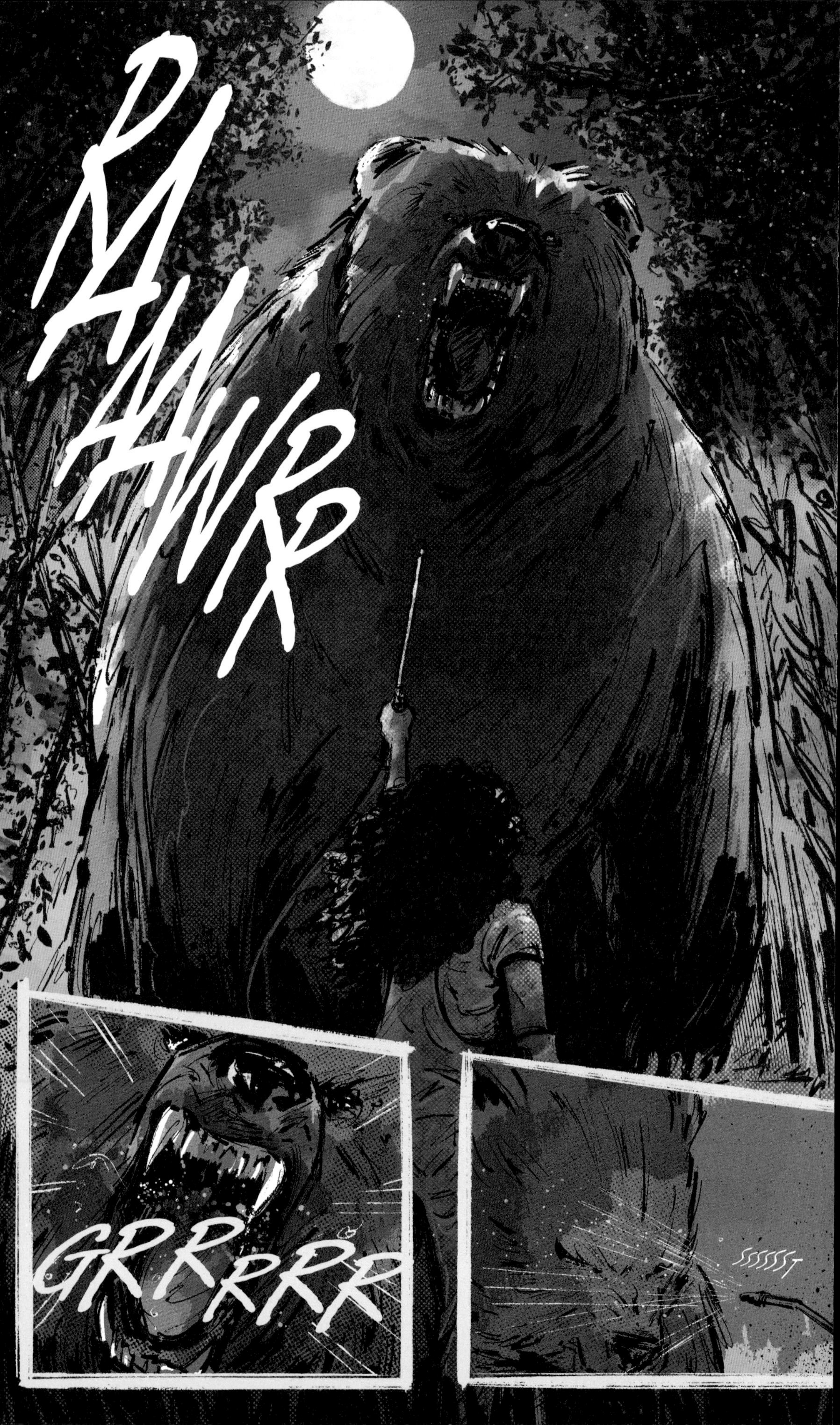
RAAWR
GRRRRR
SSSSSST

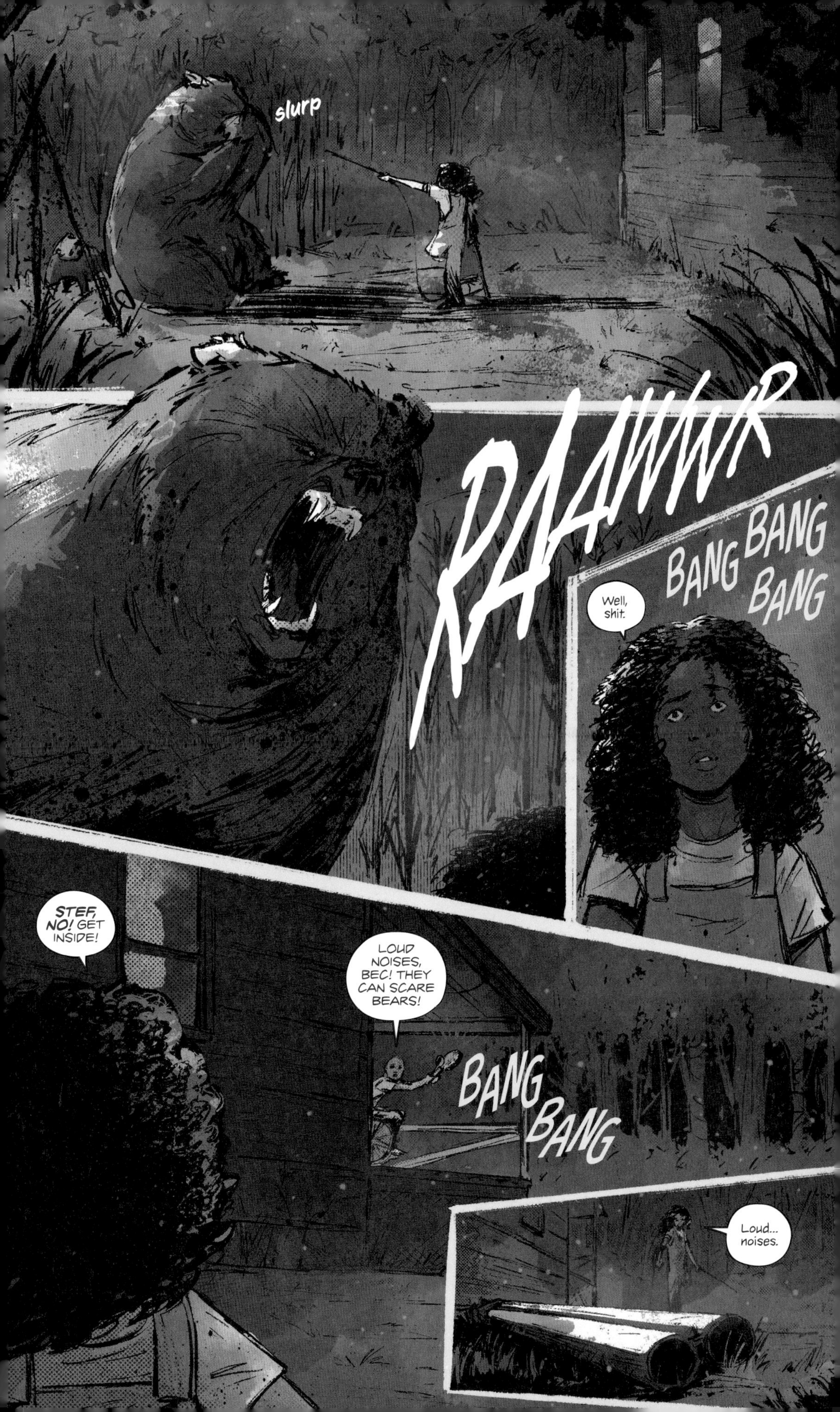
slurp
RAAWWR
BANG BANG BANG
Well, shit.
STEF, NO! GET INSIDE!
LOUD NOISES, BEC! THEY CAN SCARE BEARS!
BANG BANG
Loud... noises.

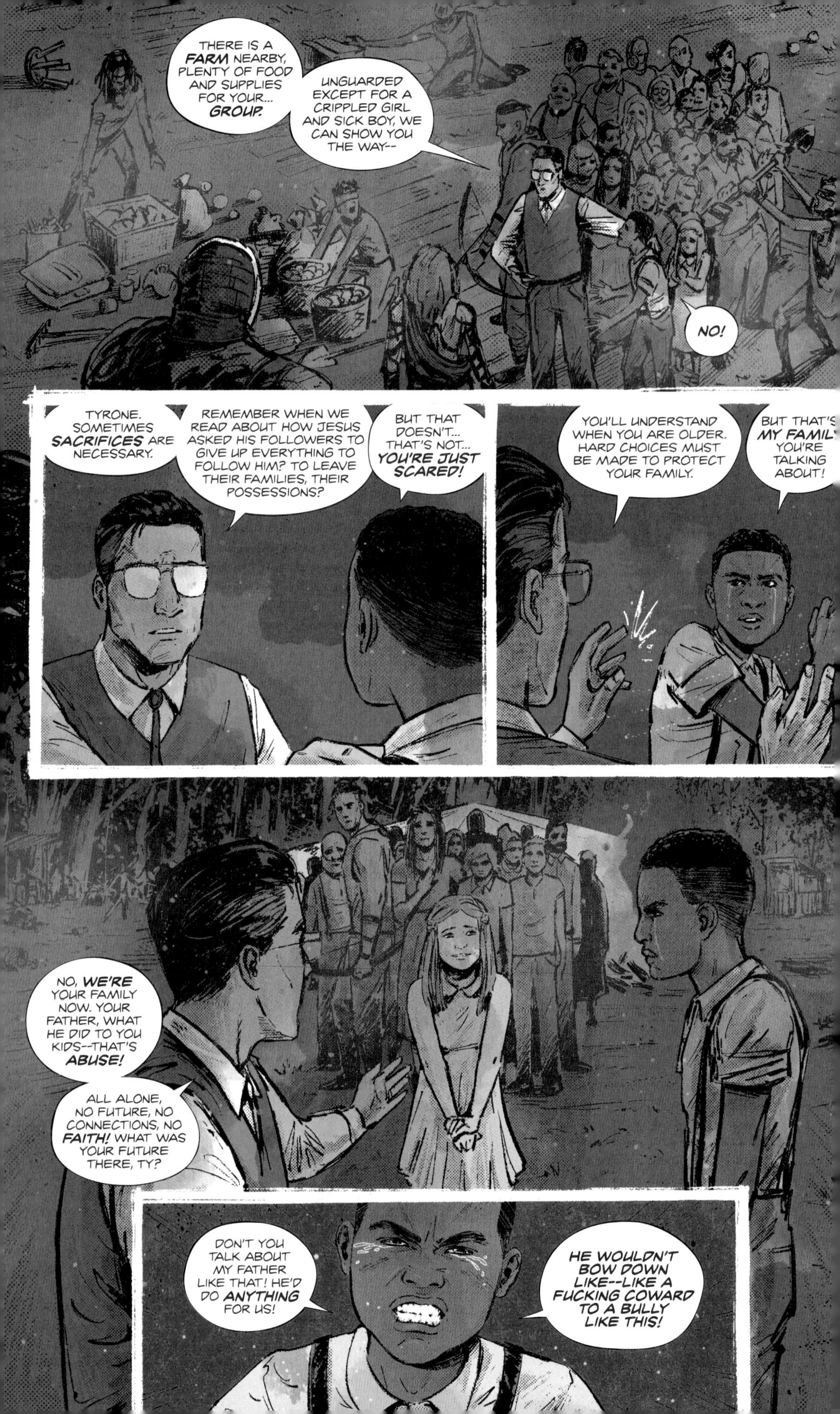
THERE IS A FARM NEARBY, PLENTY OF FOOD AND SUPPLIES FOR YOUR... GROUP.
UNGUARDED EXCEPT FOR A CRIPPLED GIRL AND SICK BOY, WE CAN SHOW YOU THE WAY--
NO!
TYRONE. SOMETIMES SACRIFICES ARE NECESSARY.
REMEMBER WHEN WE READ ABOUT HOW JESUS ASKED HIS FOLLOWERS TO GIVE UP EVERYTHING TO FOLLOW HIM? TO LEAVE THEIR FAMILIES, THEIR POSSESSIONS?
BUT THAT DOESN'T... THAT'S NOT... YOU'RE JUST SCARED!
YOU'LL UNDERSTAND WHEN YOU ARE OLDER. HARD CHOICES MUST BE MADE TO PROTECT YOUR FAMILY.
BUT THAT'S MY FAMIL YOU'RE TALKING ABOUT!
NO, WE'RE YOUR FAMILY NOW. YOUR FATHER, WHAT HE DID TO YOU KIDS--THAT'S ABUSE!
ALL ALONE, NO FUTURE, NO CONNECTIONS, NO FAITH! WHAT WAS YOUR FUTURE THERE, TY?
DON'T YOU TALK ABOUT MY FATHER LIKE THAT! HE'D DO ANYTHING FOR US!
HE WOULDN'T BOW DOWN LIKE--LIKE A FUCKING COWARD TO A BULLY LIKE THIS!

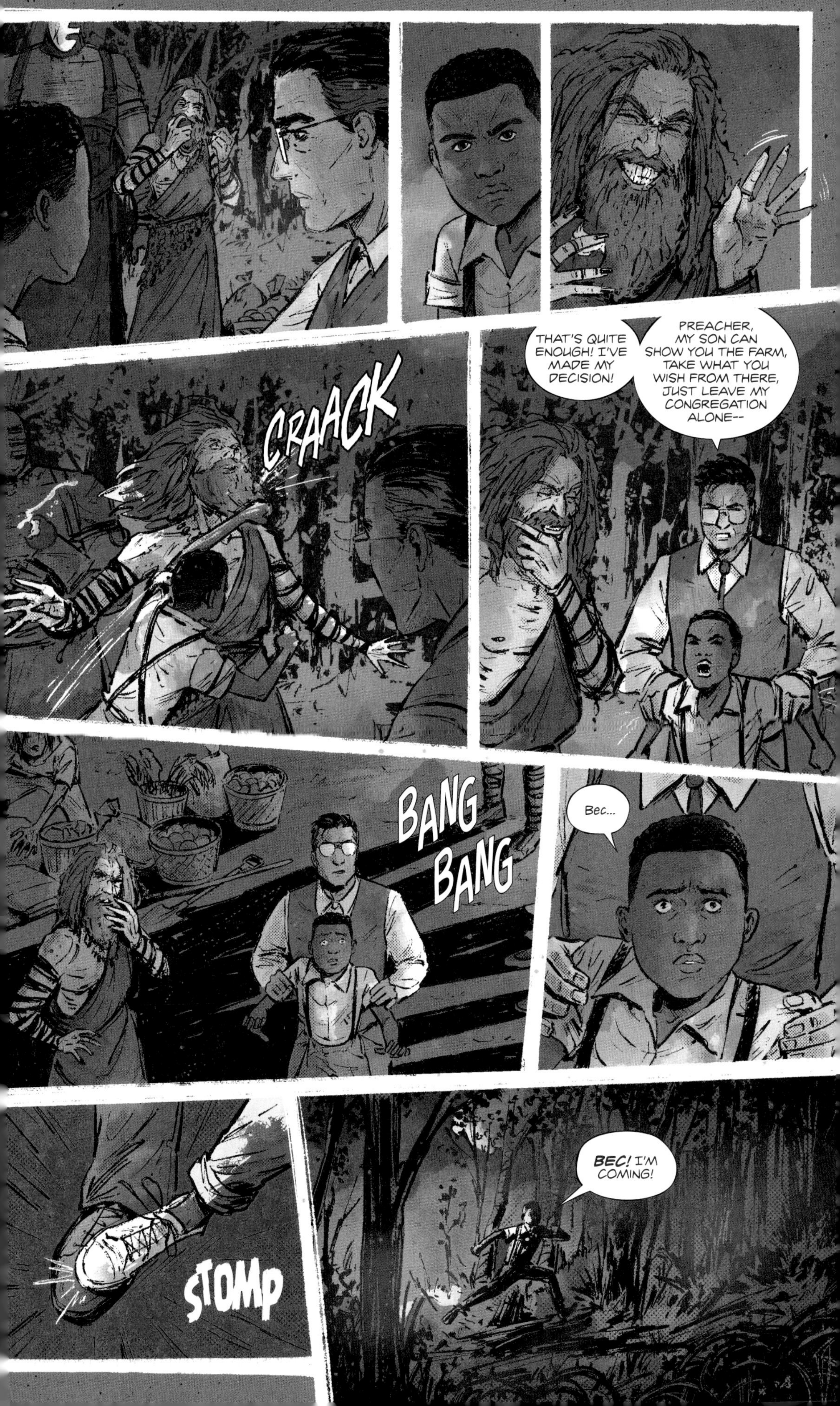
CRAACK
THAT'S QUITE ENOUGH! I'VE MADE MY DECISION!
PREACHER, MY SON CAN SHOW YOU THE FARM, TAKE WHAT YOU WISH FROM THERE, JUST LEAVE MY CONGREGATION ALONE--
BANG BANG
Bec...
STOMP
BEC! I'M COMING!

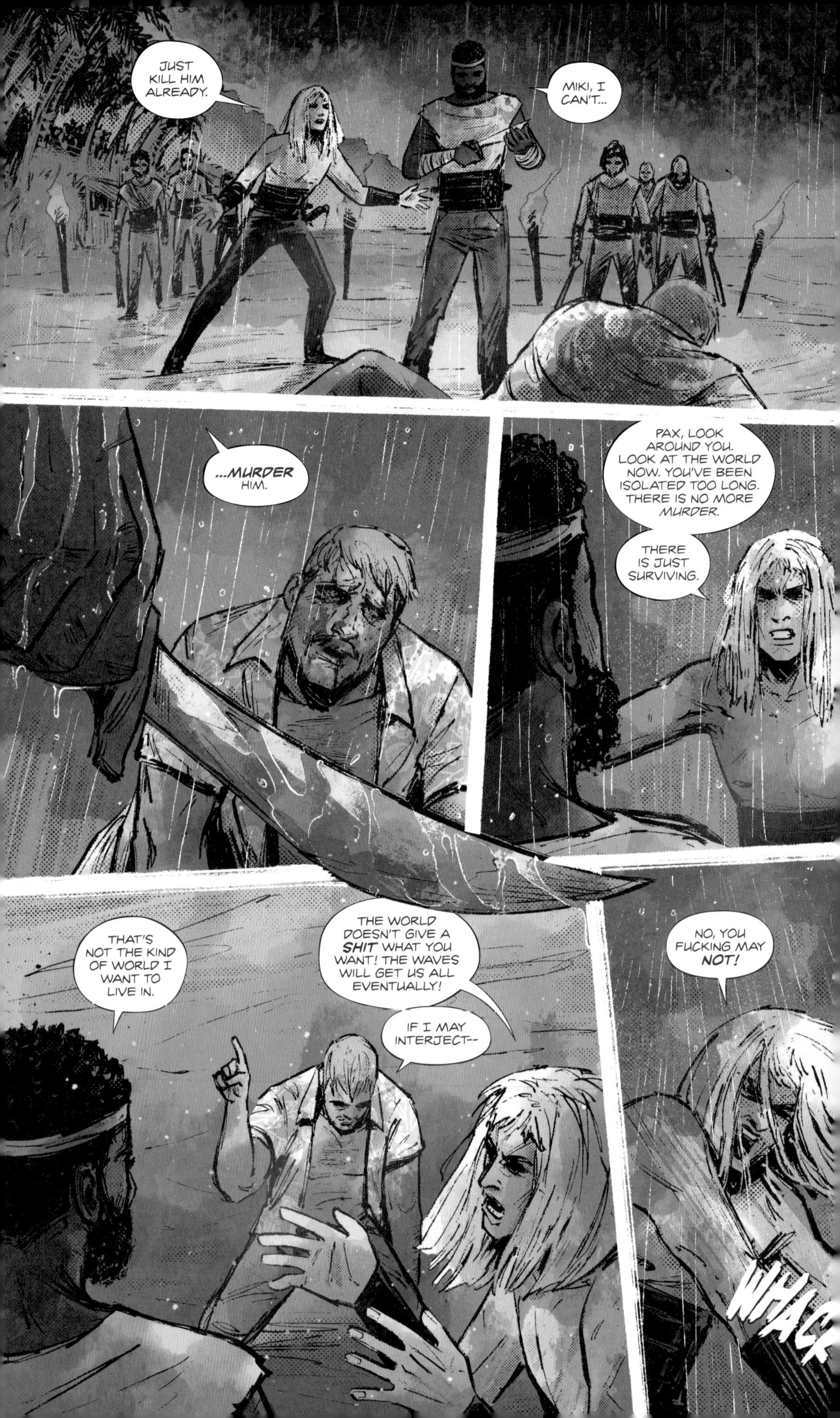
JUST KILL HIM ALREADY.
MIKI, I CAN'T...
...MURDER HIM.
PAX, LOOK AROUND YOU. LOOK AT THE WORLD NOW. YOU'VE BEEN ISOLATED TOO LONG. THERE IS NO MORE MURDER.
THERE IS JUST SURVIVING.
THAT'S NOT THE KIND OF WORLD I WANT TO LIVE IN.
THE WORLD DOESN'T GIVE A SHIT WHAT YOU WANT! THE WAVES WILL GET US ALL EVENTUALLY!
IF I MAY INTERJECT--
NO, YOU FUCKING MAY NOT!
WHACK

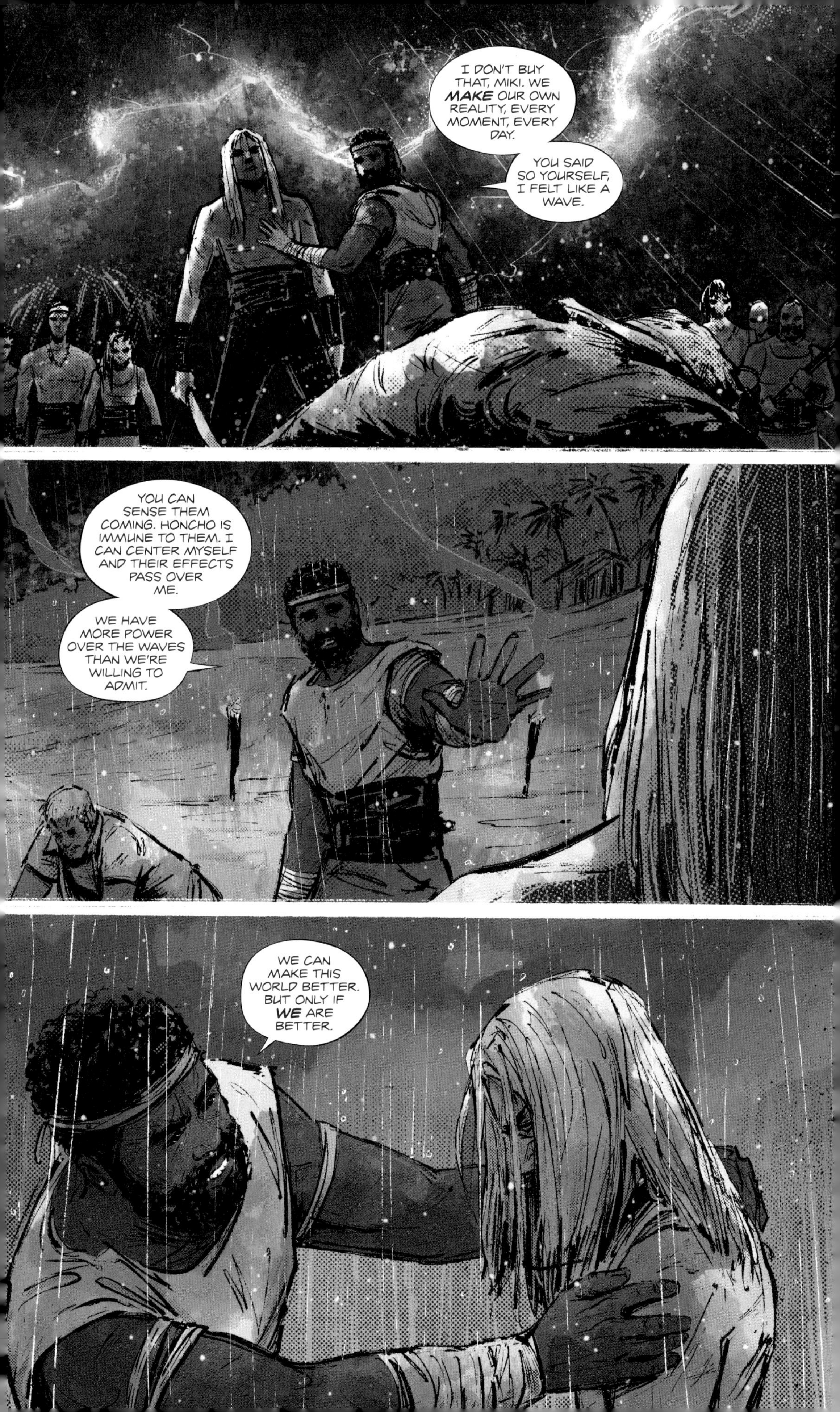
I DON'T BUY THAT, MIKI. WE MAKE OUR OWN REALITY, EVERY MOMENT, EVERY DAY.
YOU SAID SO YOURSELF, I FELT LIKE A WAVE.
YOU CAN SENSE THEM COMING. HONCHO IS IMMUNE TO THEM. I CAN CENTER MYSELF AND THEIR EFFECTS PASS OVER ME.
WE HAVE MORE POWER OVER THE WAVES THAN WE'RE WILLING TO ADMIT.
WE CAN MAKE THIS WORLD BETTER. BUT ONLY IF WE ARE BETTER.

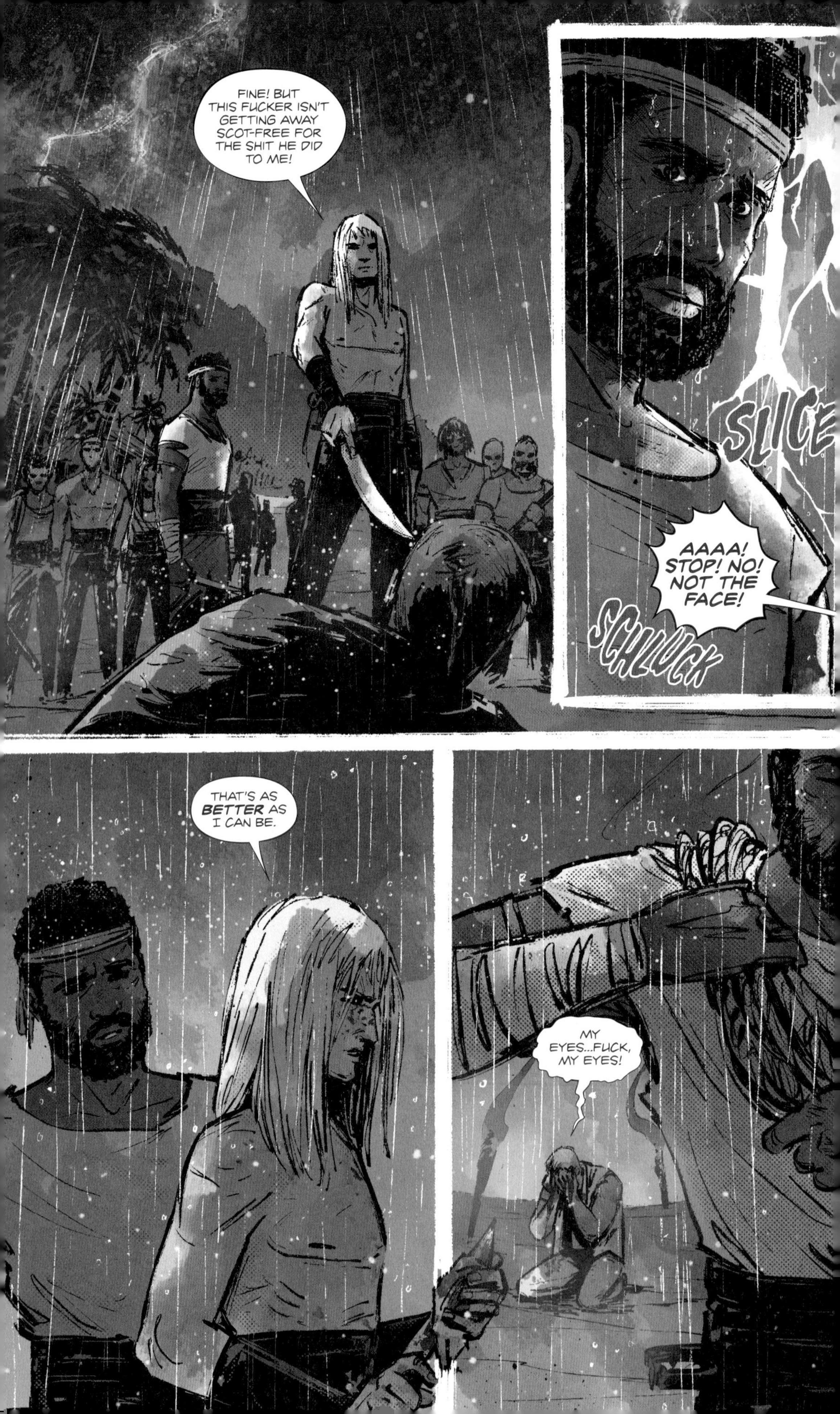
FINE! BUT THIS FUCKER ISN'T GETTING AWAY SCOT-FREE FOR THE SHIT HE DID TO ME!
SLICE
AAAA! STOP! NO! NOT THE FACE!
SCHLUCK
THAT'S AS BETTER AS I CAN BE.
MY EYES...FUCK, MY EYES!

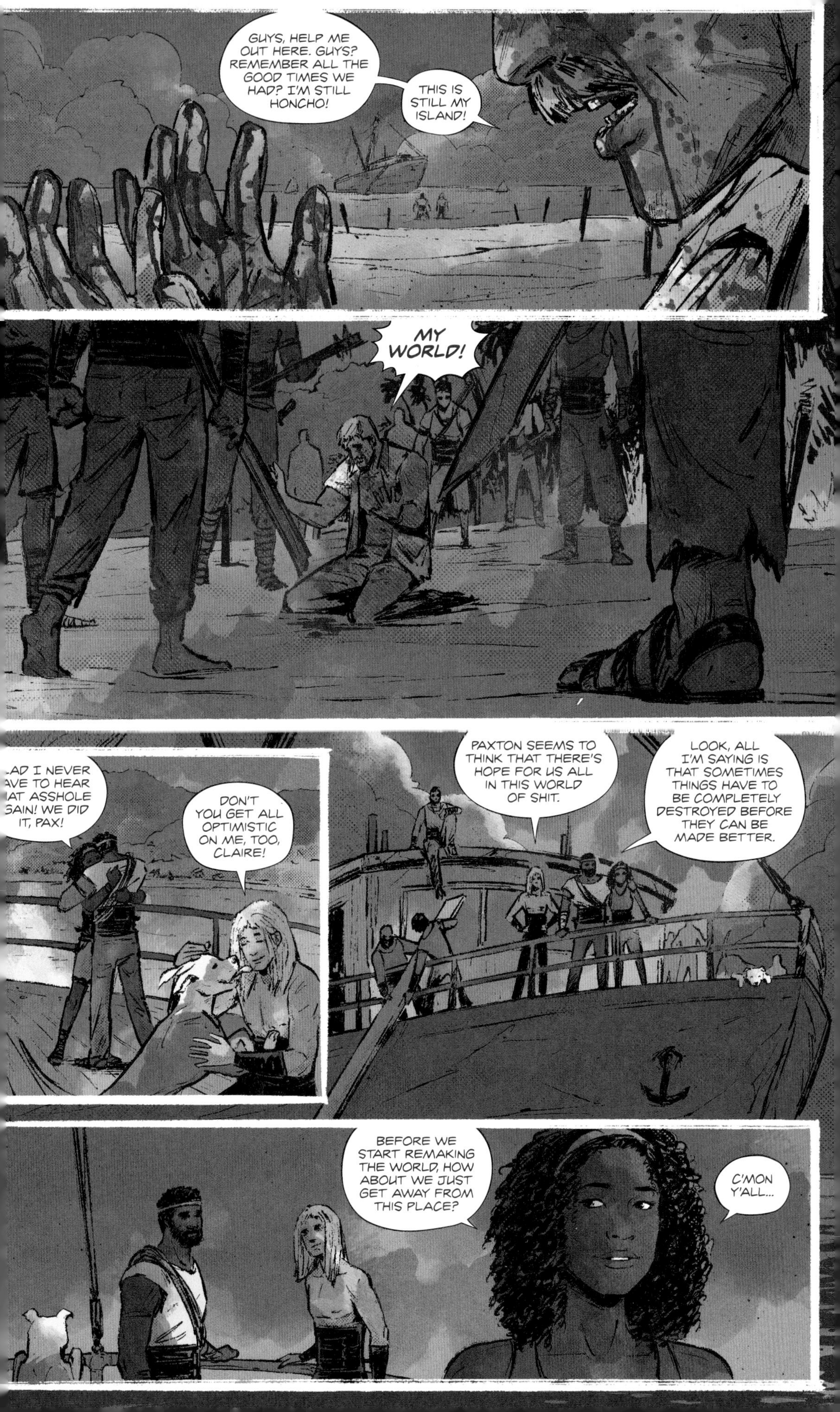
GUYS, HELP ME OUT HERE. GUYS? REMEMBER ALL THE GOOD TIMES WE HAD? I'M STILL HONCHO!
THIS IS STILL MY ISLAND!
MY WORLD!
LAD I NEVER AVE TO HEAR AT ASSHOLE GAIN! WE DID IT, PAX!
DON'T YOU GET ALL OPTIMISTIC ON ME, TOO, CLAIRE!
PAXTON SEEMS TO THINK THAT THERE'S HOPE FOR US ALL IN THIS WORLD OF SHIT.
LOOK, ALL I'M SAYING IS THAT SOMETIMES THINGS HAVE TO BE COMPLETELY DESTROYED BEFORE THEY CAN BE MADE BETTER.
BEFORE WE START REMAKING THE WORLD, HOW ABOUT WE JUST GET AWAY FROM THIS PLACE?
C'MON Y'ALL...

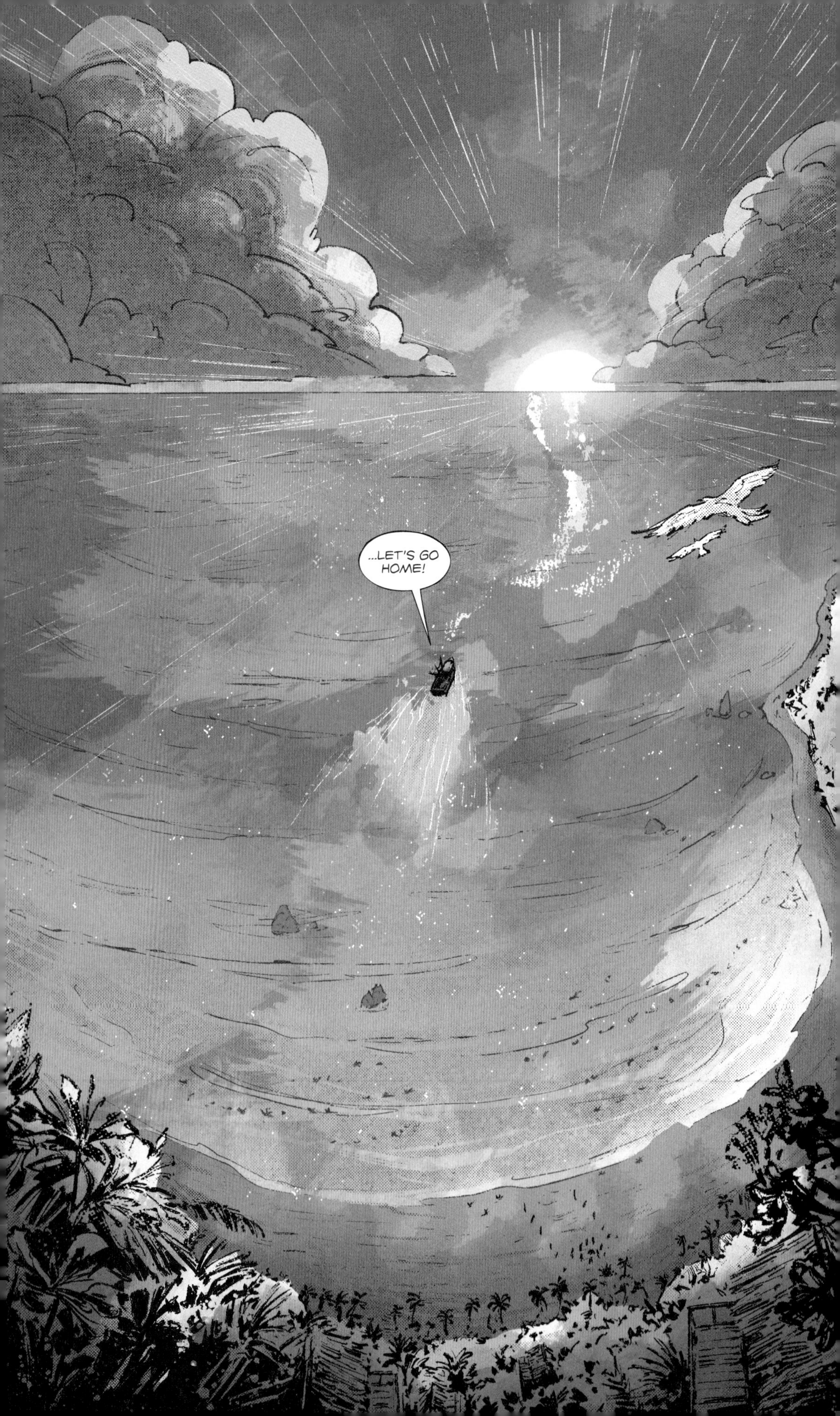
...LET'S GO HOME!

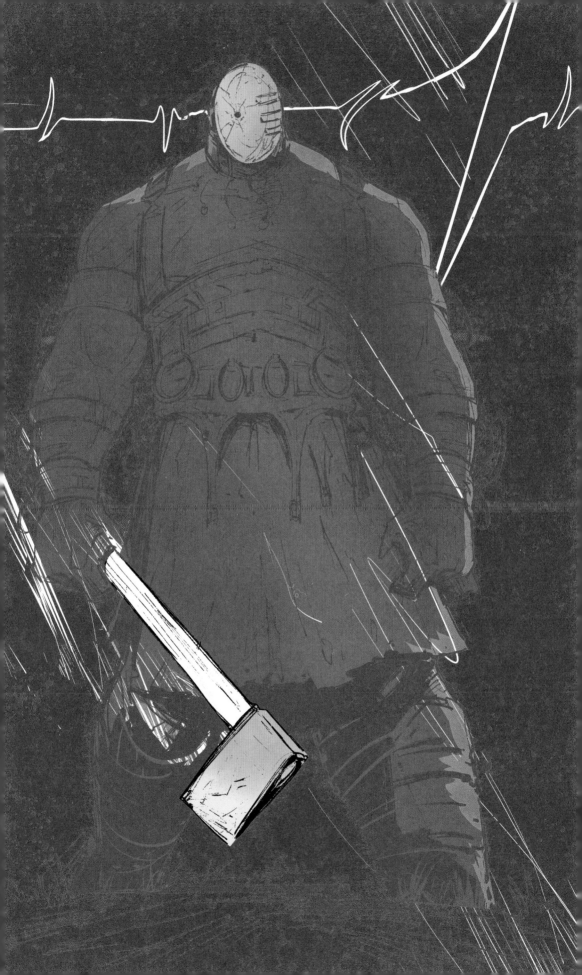

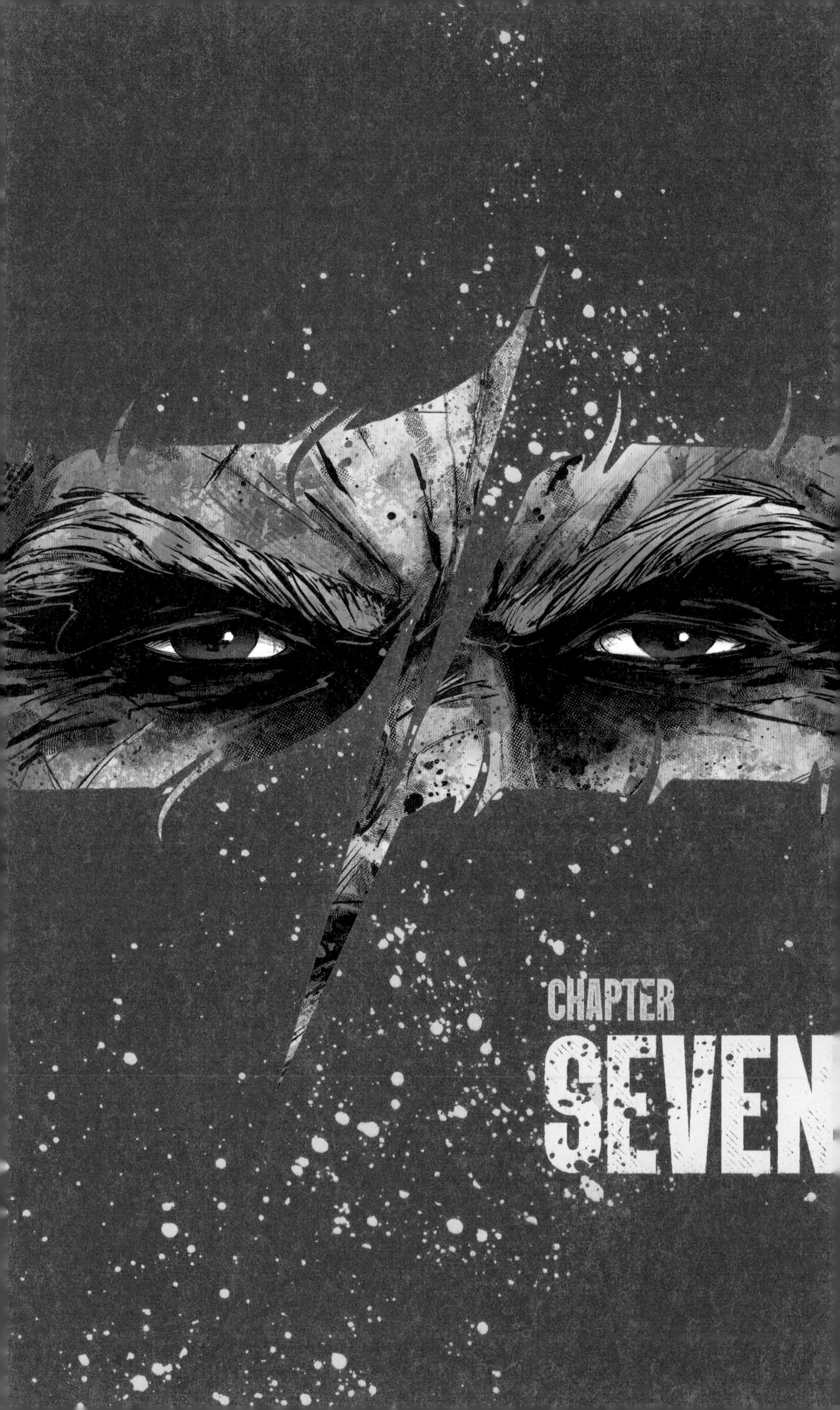
CHAPTER
SEVEN

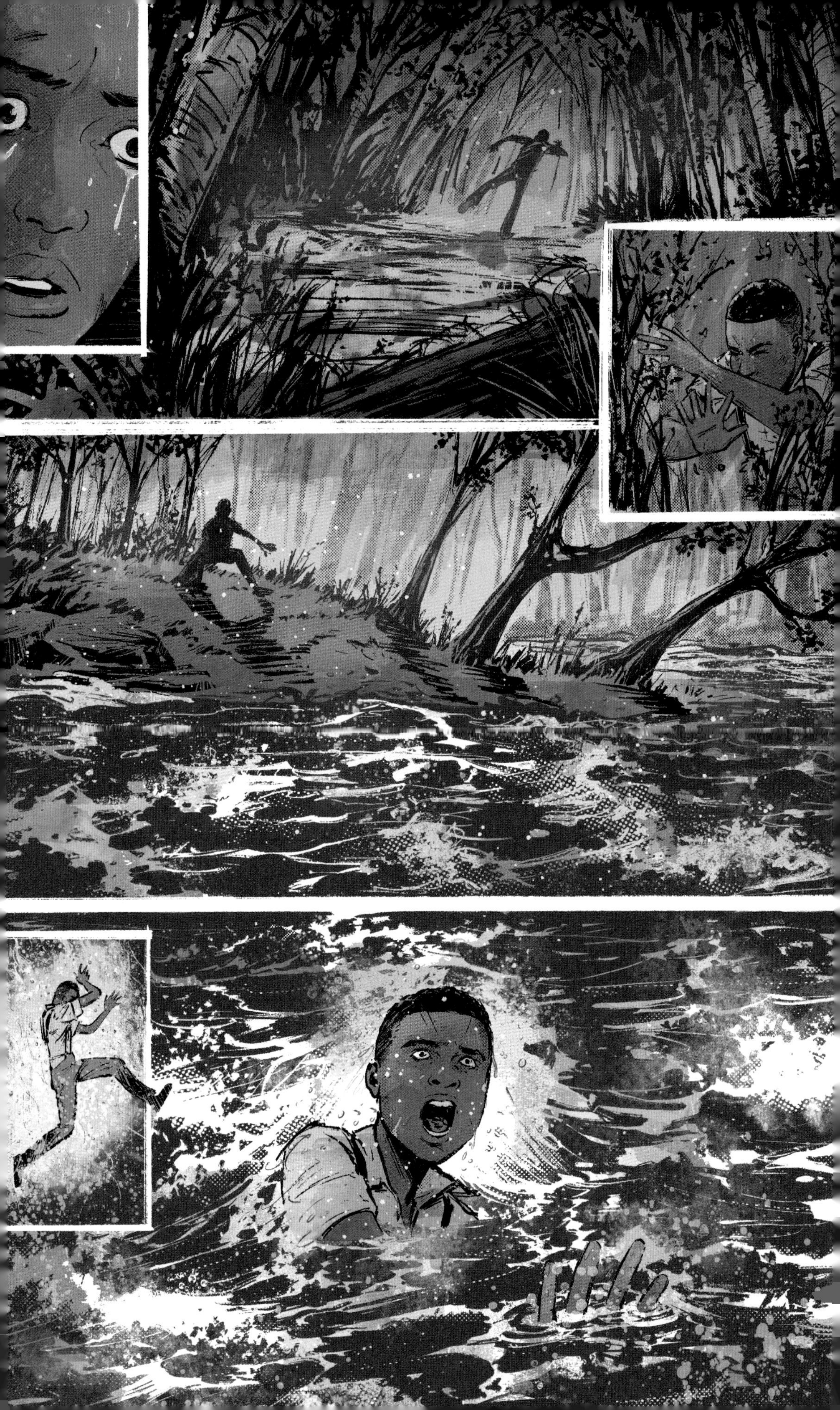

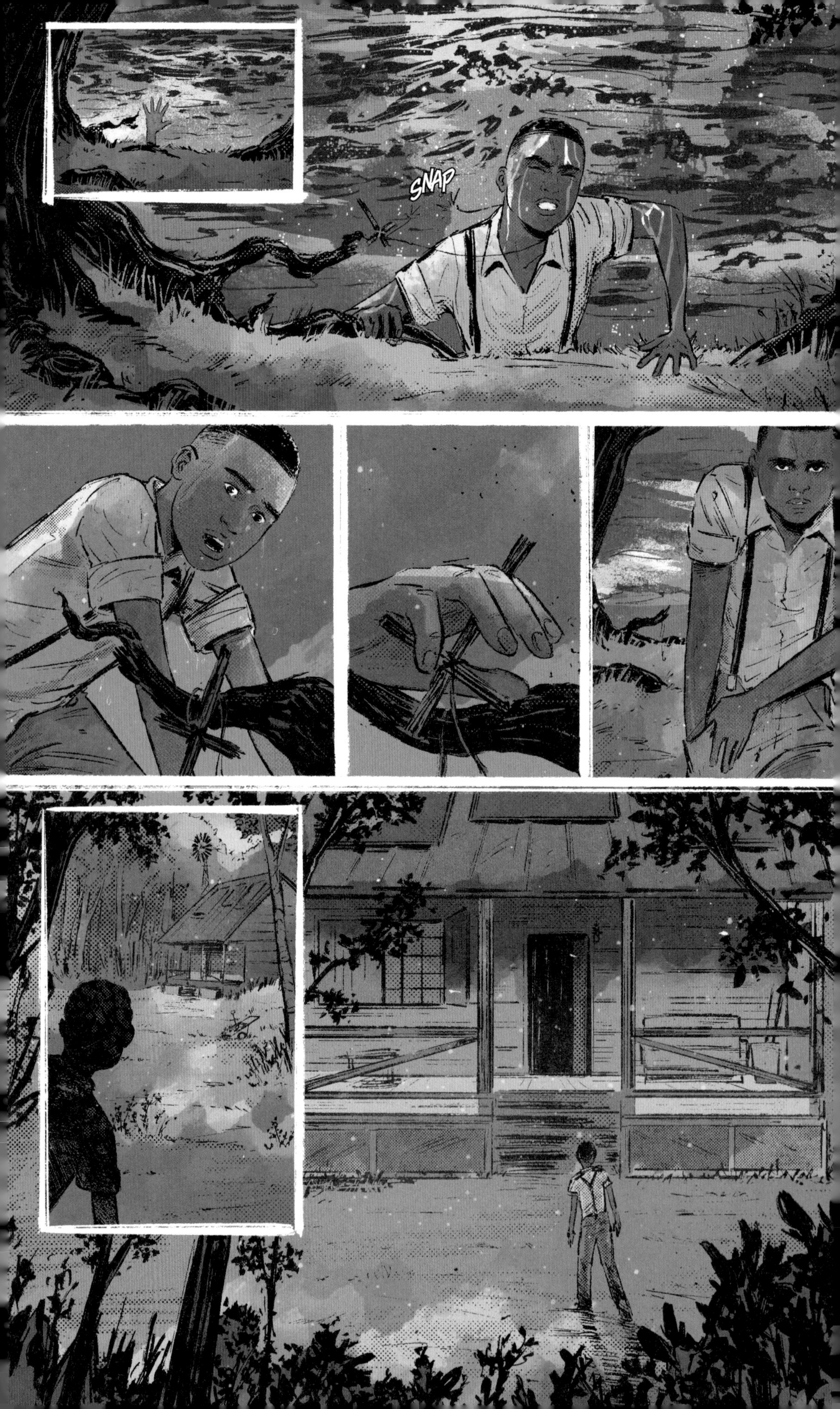
SNAP

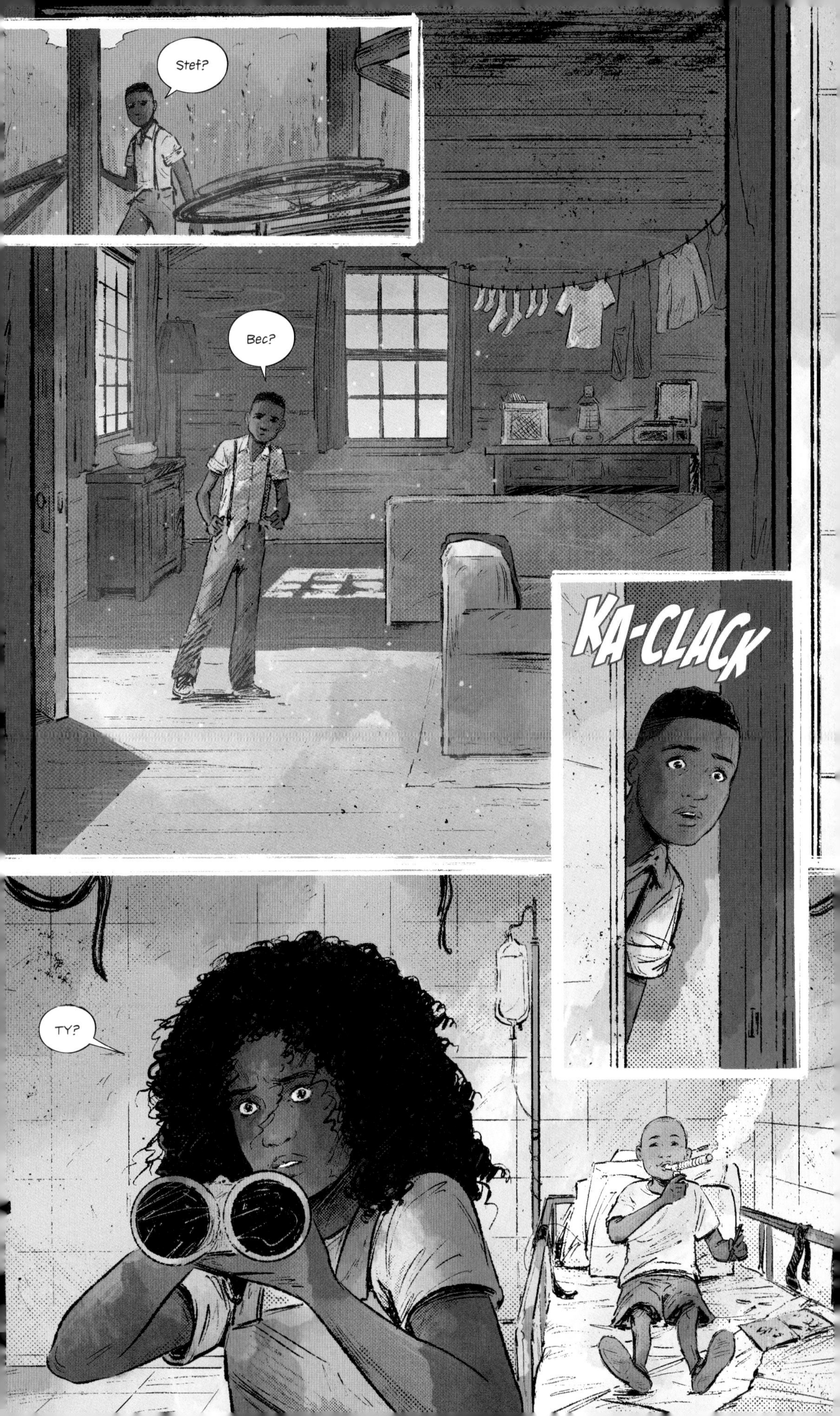
Stef?
Bec?
KA-CLACK
TY?

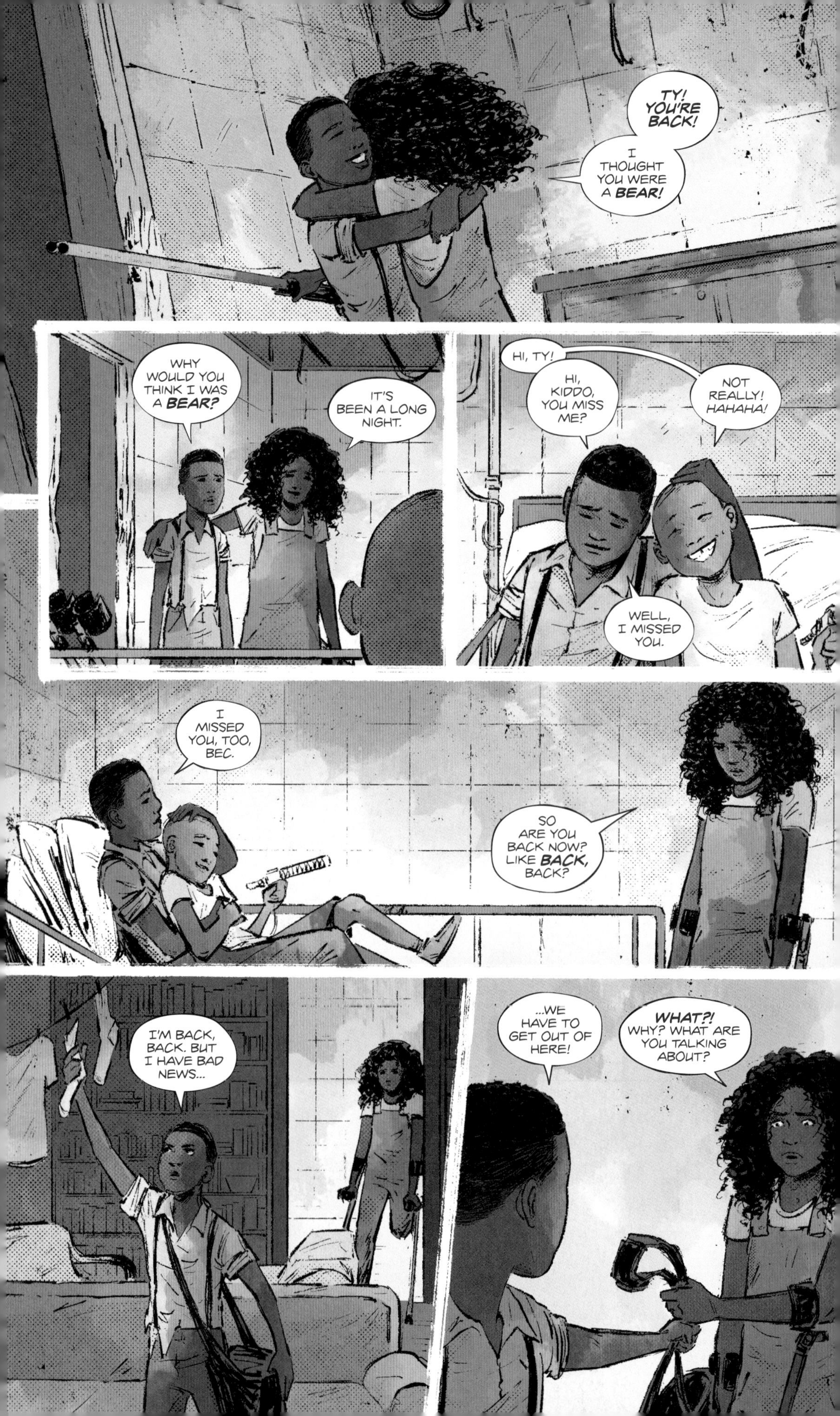
TY! YOU'RE BACK!
I THOUGHT YOU WERE A BEAR!
WHY WOULD YOU THINK I WAS A BEAR?
IT'S BEEN A LONG NIGHT.
HI, TY!
HI, KIDDO, YOU MISS ME?
NOT REALLY! HAHAHA!
WELL, I MISSED YOU.
I MISSED YOU, TOO, BEC.
SO ARE YOU BACK NOW? LIKE BACK, BACK?
I'M BACK, BACK. BUT I HAVE BAD NEWS...
...WE HAVE TO GET OUT OF HERE!
WHAT?! WHY? WHAT ARE YOU TALKING ABOUT?

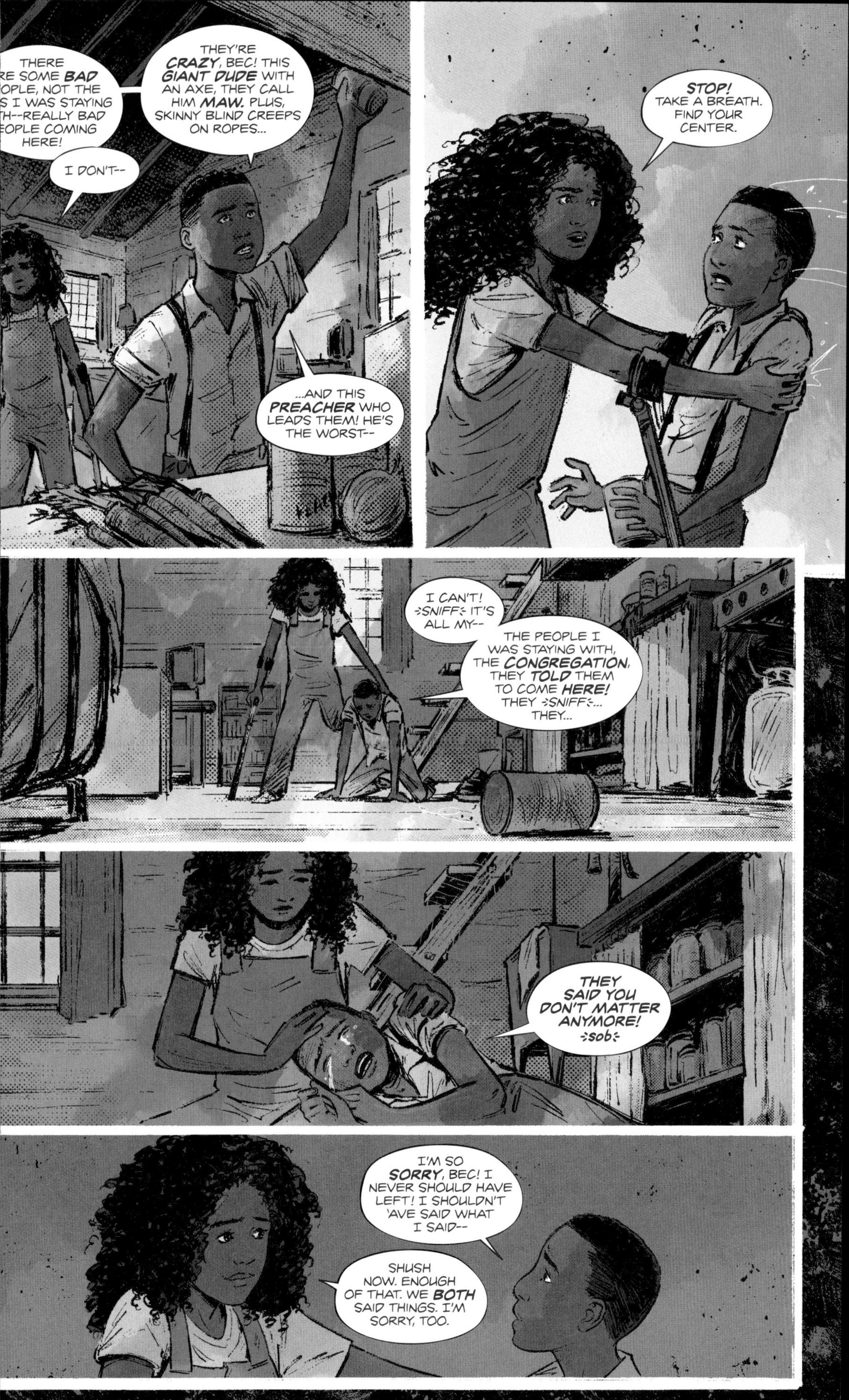
THERE RE SOME BAD OPLE, NOT THE S I WAS STAYING TH--REALLY BAD EOPLE COMING HERE!
I DON'T--
THEY'RE CRAZY, BEC! THIS GIANT DUDE WITH AN AXE, THEY CALL HIM MAW. PLUS, SKINNY BLIND CREEPS ON ROPES...
...AND THIS PREACHER WHO LEADS THEM! HE'S THE WORST--
STOP! TAKE A BREATH. FIND YOUR CENTER.
I CAN'T! -SNIFF- IT'S ALL MY--
THE PEOPLE I WAS STAYING WITH, THE CONGREGATION, THEY TOLD THEM TO COME HERE! THEY -SNIFF-... THEY...
THEY SAID YOU DON'T MATTER ANYMORE! -sob-
I'M SO SORRY, BEC! I NEVER SHOULD HAVE LEFT! I SHOULDN'T 'AVE SAID WHAT I SAID--
SHUSH NOW. ENOUGH OF THAT. WE BOTH SAID THINGS. I'M SORRY, TOO.

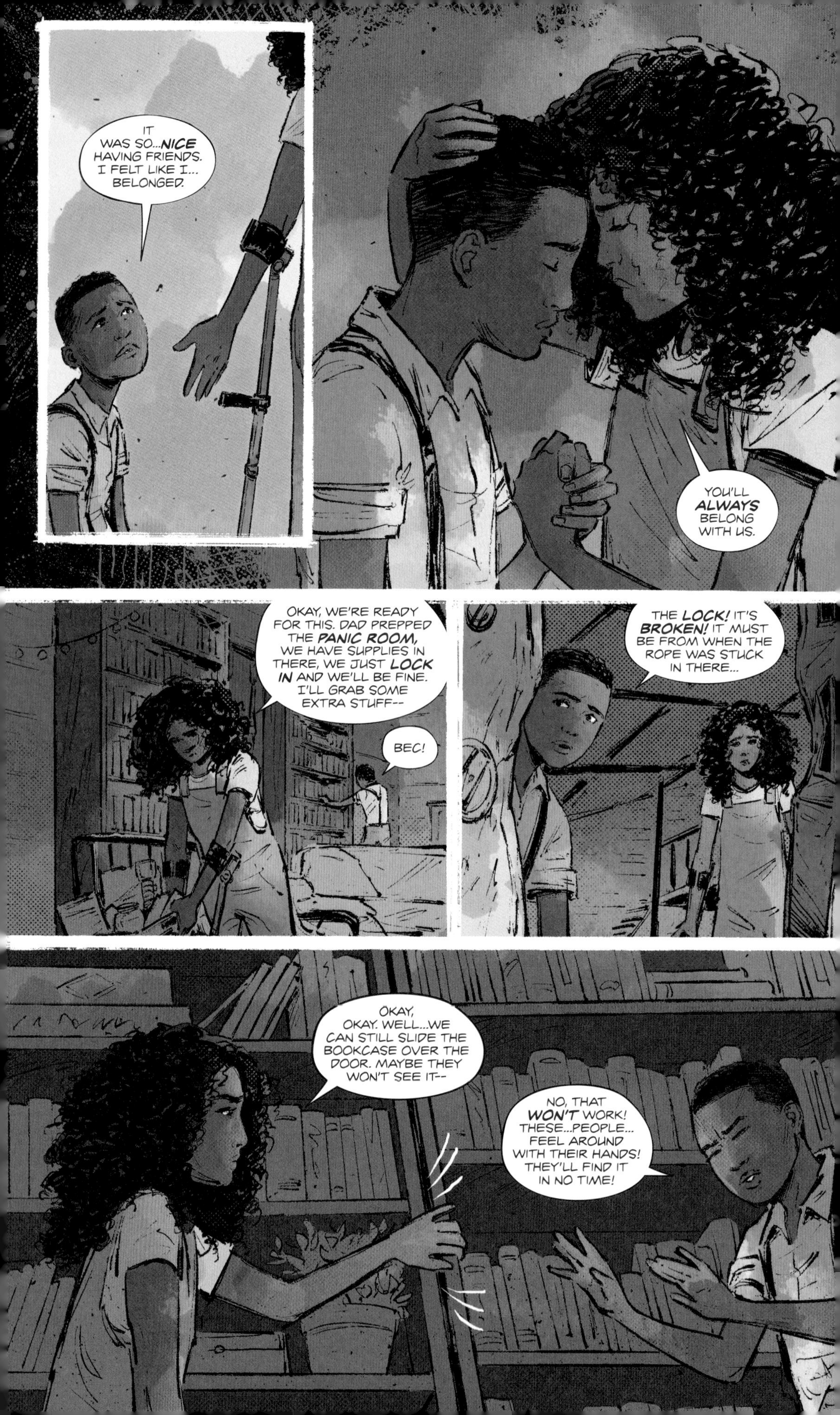
IT WAS SO...NICE HAVING FRIENDS. I FELT LIKE I... BELONGED.
YOU'LL ALWAYS BELONG WITH US.
OKAY, WE'RE READY FOR THIS. DAD PREPPED THE PANIC ROOM, WE HAVE SUPPLIES IN THERE, WE JUST LOCK IN AND WE'LL BE FINE. I'LL GRAB SOME EXTRA STUFF--
BEC!
THE LOCK! IT'S BROKEN! IT MUST BE FROM WHEN THE ROPE WAS STUCK IN THERE...
OKAY, OKAY. WELL...WE CAN STILL SLIDE THE BOOKCASE OVER THE DOOR. MAYBE THEY WON'T SEE IT--
NO, THAT WON'T WORK! THESE...PEOPLE... FEEL AROUND WITH THEIR HANDS! THEY'LL FIND IT IN NO TIME!

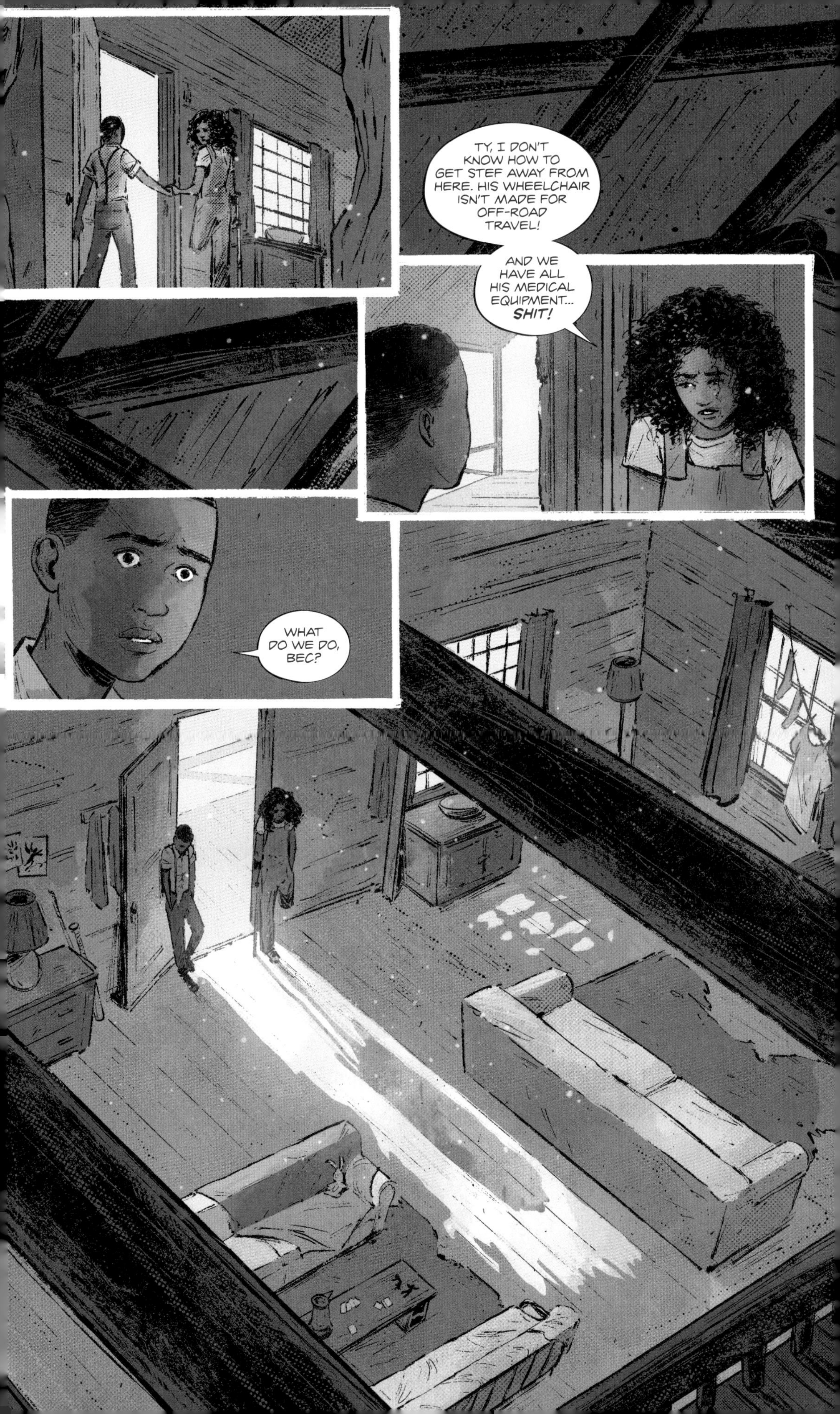
TY, I DON'T KNOW HOW TO GET STEF AWAY FROM HERE. HIS WHEELCHAIR ISN'T MADE FOR OFF-ROAD TRAVEL!
AND WE HAVE ALL HIS MEDICAL EQUIPMENT... SHIT!
WHAT DO WE DO, BEC?

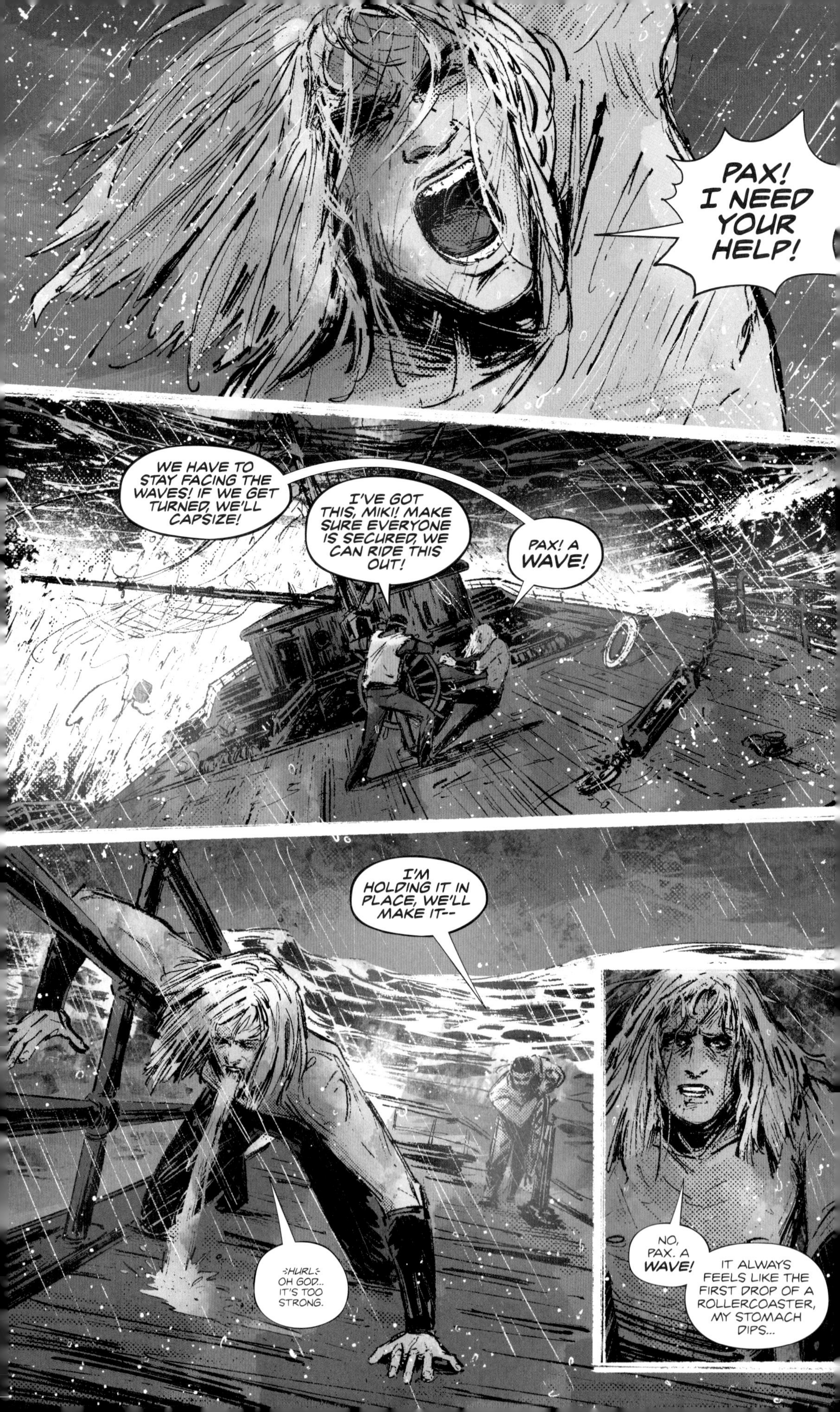
PAX! I NEED YOUR HELP!
WE HAVE TO STAY FACING THE WAVES! IF WE GET TURNED, WE'LL CAPSIZE!
I'VE GOT THIS, MIKI! MAKE SURE EVERYONE IS SECURED, WE CAN RIDE THIS OUT!
PAX! A WAVE!
I'M HOLDING IT IN PLACE, WE'LL MAKE IT--
HURL OH GOD... IT'S TOO STRONG.
NO, PAX. A WAVE!
IT ALWAYS FEELS LIKE THE FIRST DROP OF A ROLLERCOASTER, MY STOMACH DIPS...

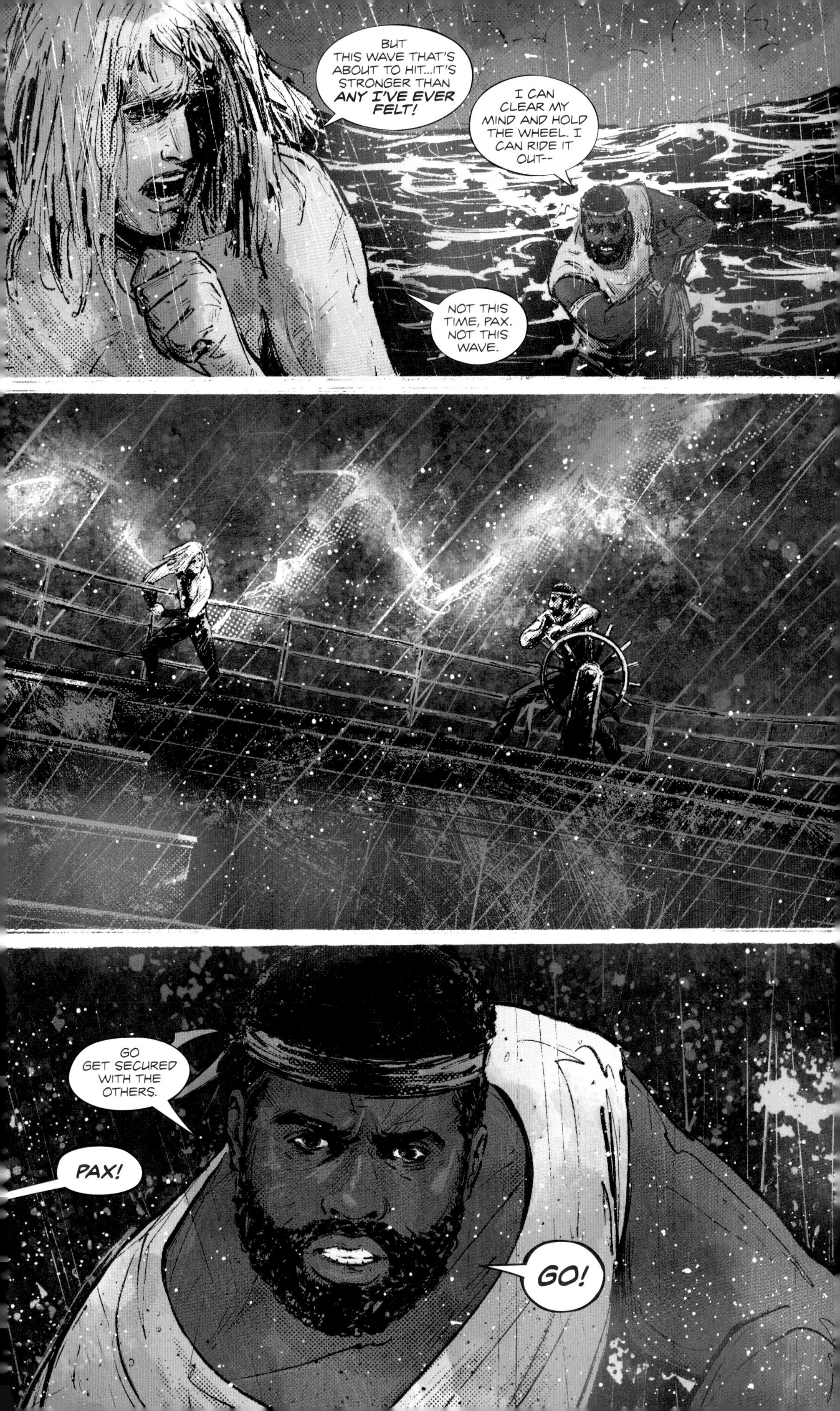
BUT THIS WAVE THAT'S ABOUT TO HIT...IT'S STRONGER THAN ANY I'VE EVER FELT!
I CAN CLEAR MY MIND AND HOLD THE WHEEL. I CAN RIDE IT OUT--
NOT THIS TIME, PAX. NOT THIS WAVE.
GO GET SECURED WITH THE OTHERS.
PAX!
GO!

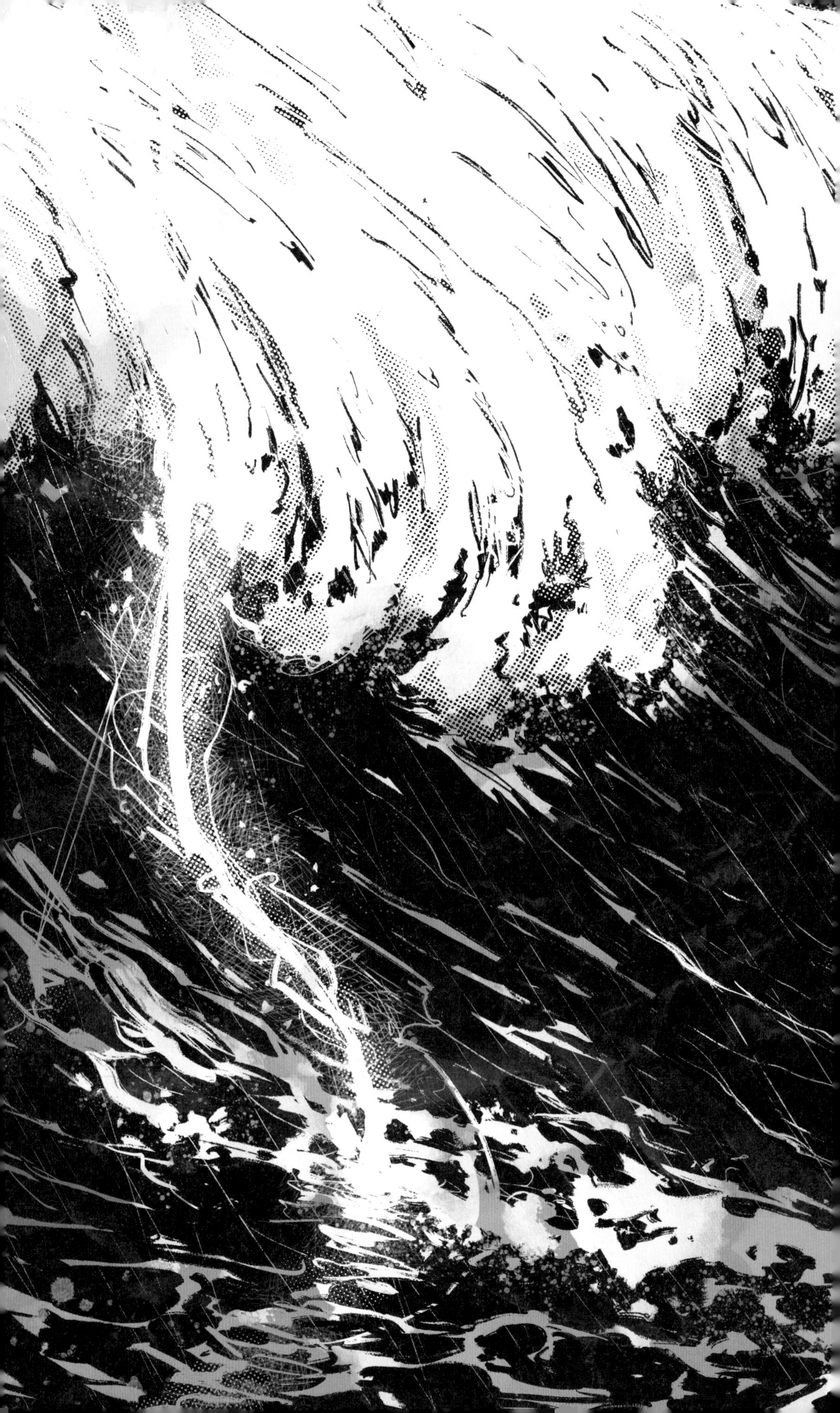

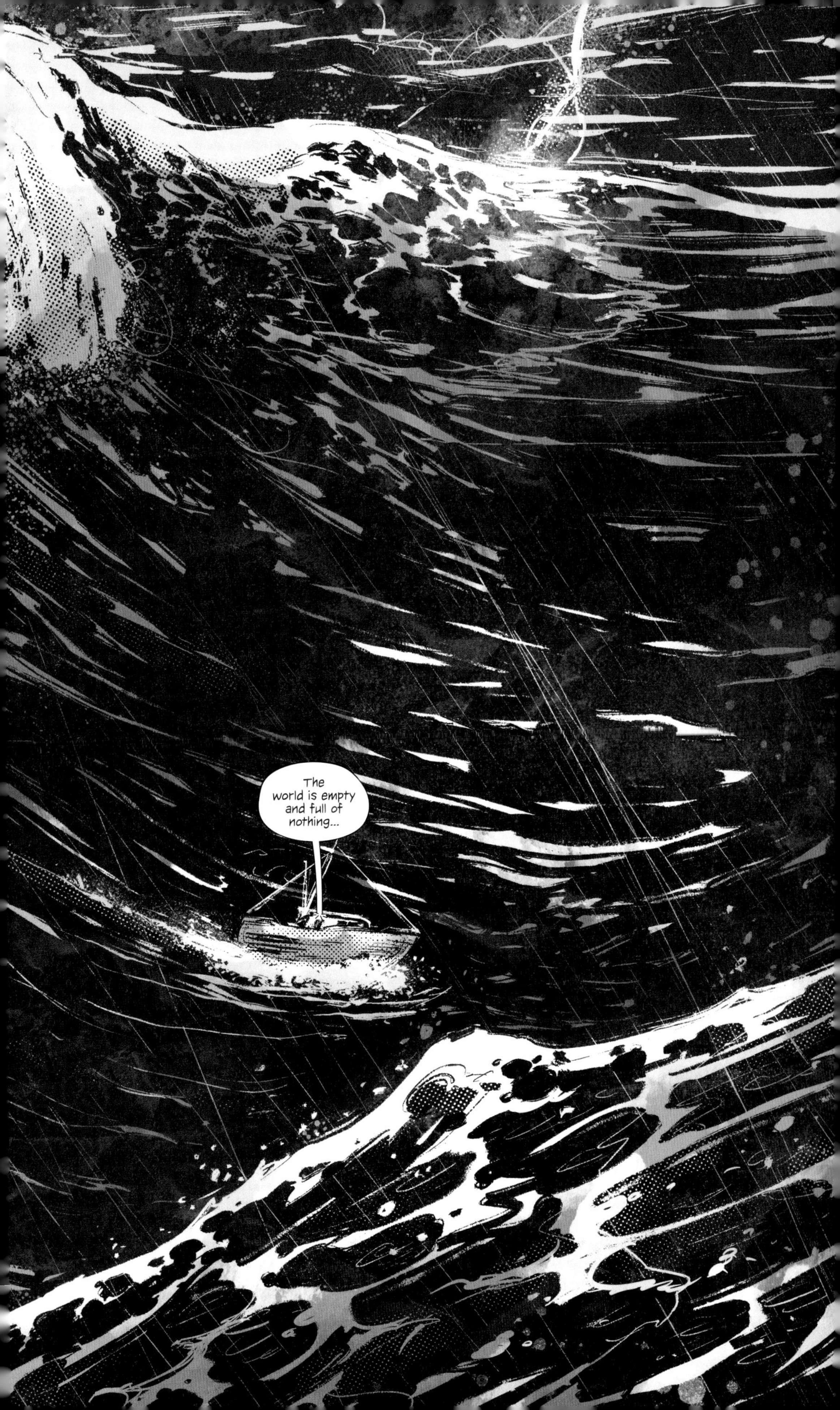
The world is empty and full of nothing...

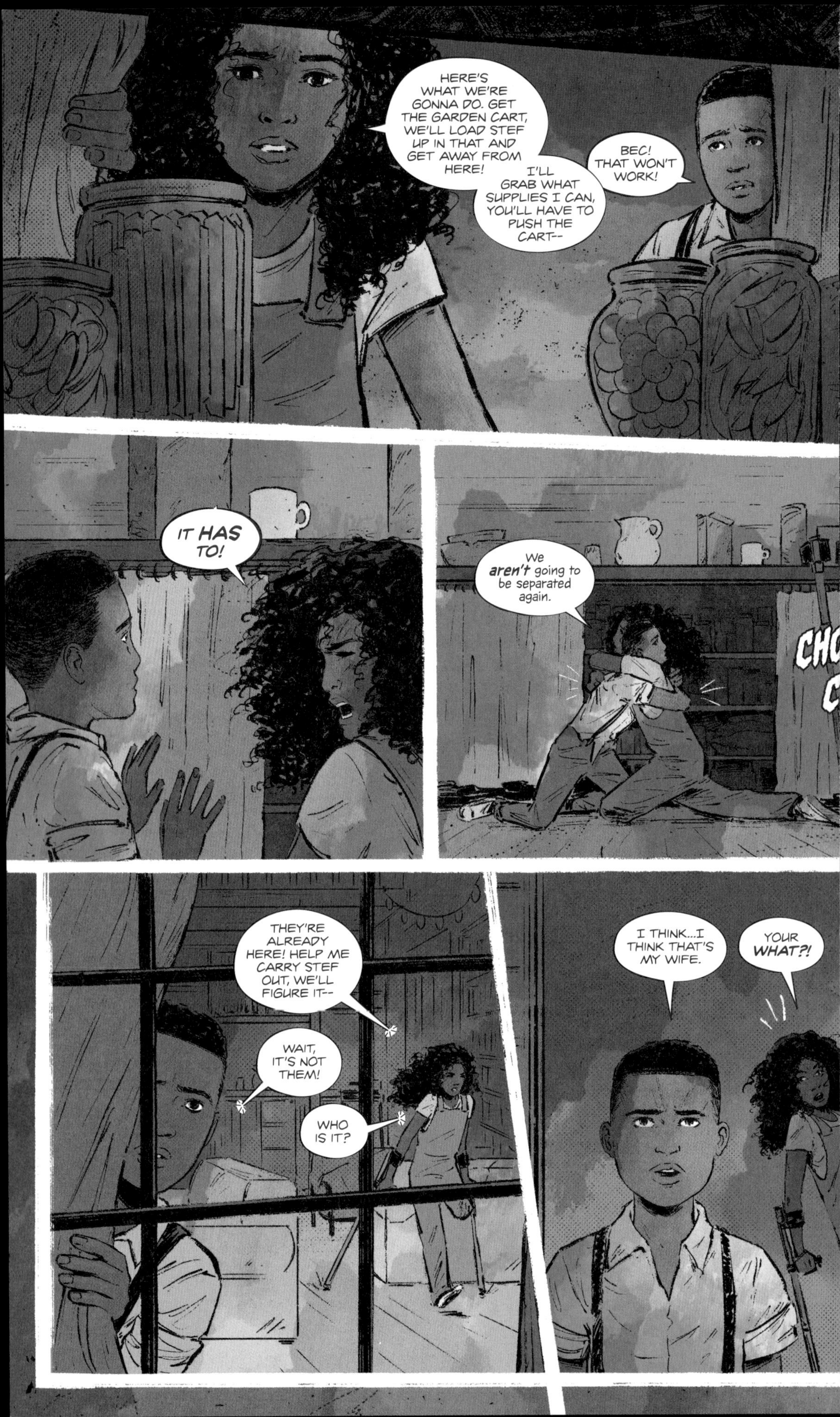
HERE'S WHAT WE'RE GONNA DO. GET THE GARDEN CART, WE'LL LOAD STEF UP IN THAT AND GET AWAY FROM HERE!
I'LL GRAB WHAT SUPPLIES I CAN, YOU'LL HAVE TO PUSH THE CART--
BEC! THAT WON'T WORK!
IT HAS TO!
We aren't going to be separated again.
THEY'RE ALREADY HERE! HELP ME CARRY STEF OUT, WE'LL FIGURE IT--
WAIT, IT'S NOT THEM!
WHO IS IT?
I THINK...I THINK THAT'S MY WIFE.
YOUR WHAT?!

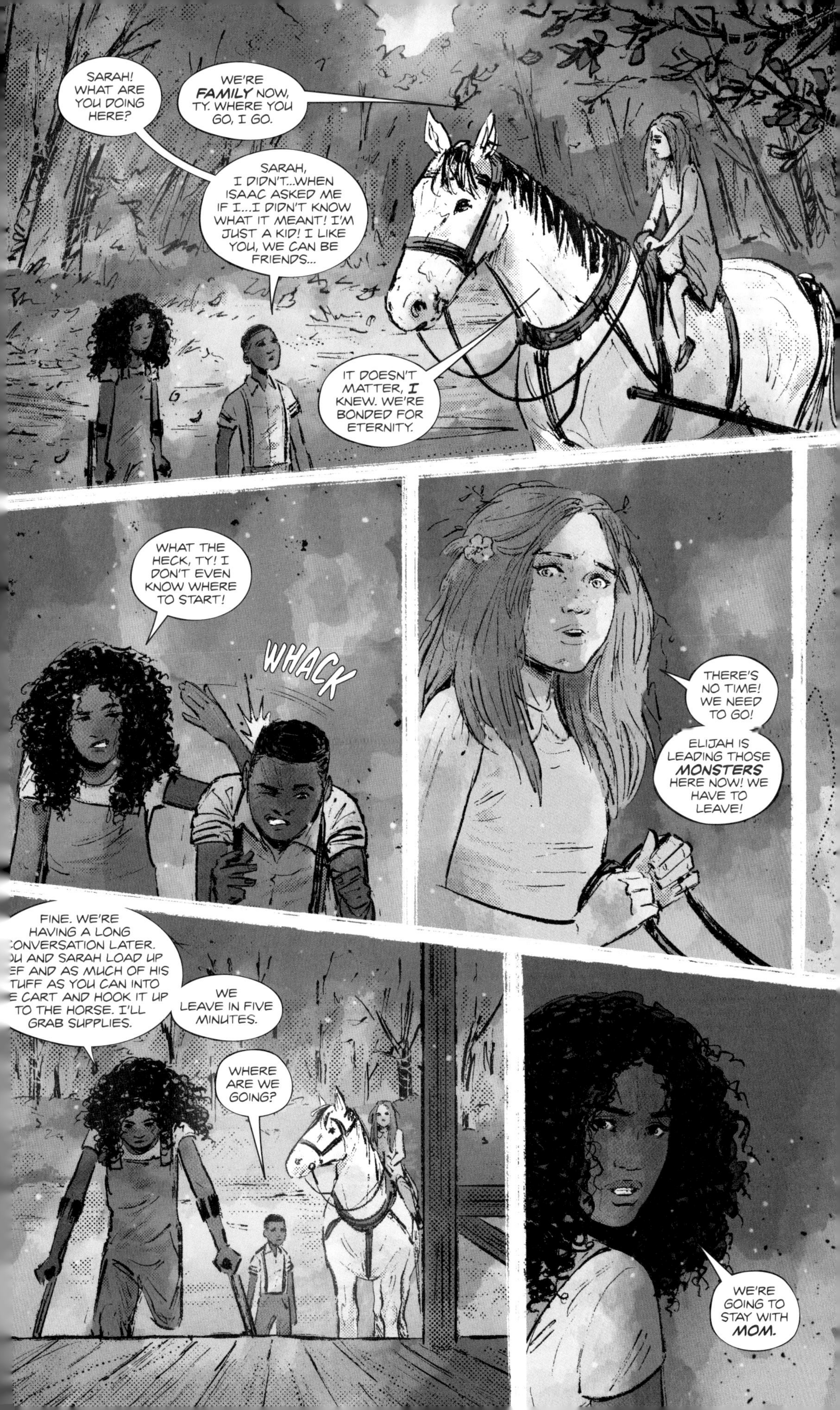
SARAH! WHAT ARE YOU DOING HERE?
WE'RE FAMILY NOW, TY. WHERE YOU GO, I GO.
SARAH, I DIDN'T...WHEN ISAAC ASKED ME IF I...I DIDN'T KNOW WHAT IT MEANT! I'M JUST A KID! I LIKE YOU, WE CAN BE FRIENDS...
IT DOESN'T MATTER, I KNEW. WE'RE BONDED FOR ETERNITY.
WHAT THE HECK, TY! I DON'T EVEN KNOW WHERE TO START!
WHACK
THERE'S NO TIME! WE NEED TO GO!
ELIJAH IS LEADING THOSE MONSTERS HERE NOW! WE HAVE TO LEAVE!
FINE. WE'RE HAVING A LONG ONVERSATION LATER. OU AND SARAH LOAD UP EF AND AS MUCH OF HIS TUFF AS YOU CAN INTO E CART AND HOOK IT UP TO THE HORSE. I'LL GRAB SUPPLIES.
WE LEAVE IN FIVE MINUTES.
WHERE ARE WE GOING?
WE'RE GOING TO STAY WITH MOM.

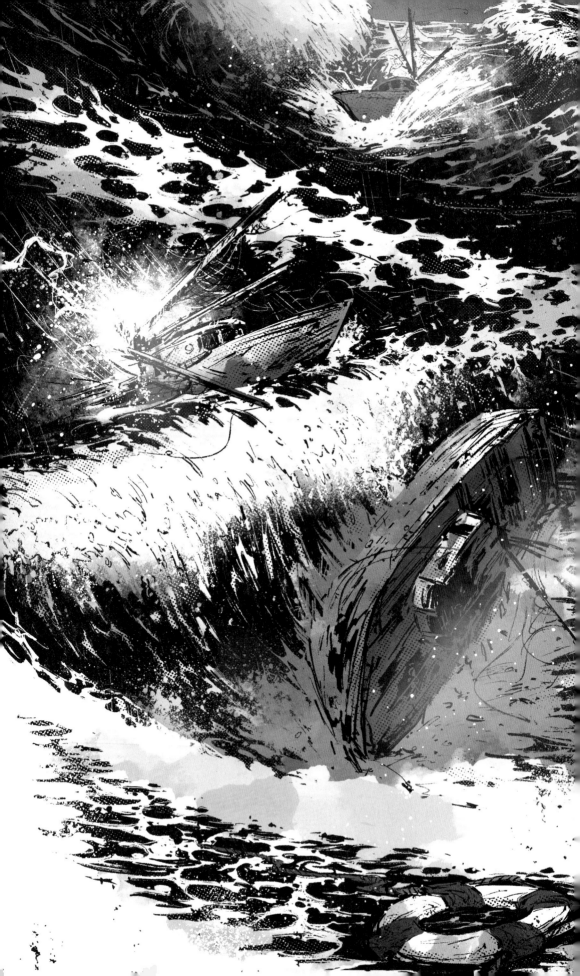

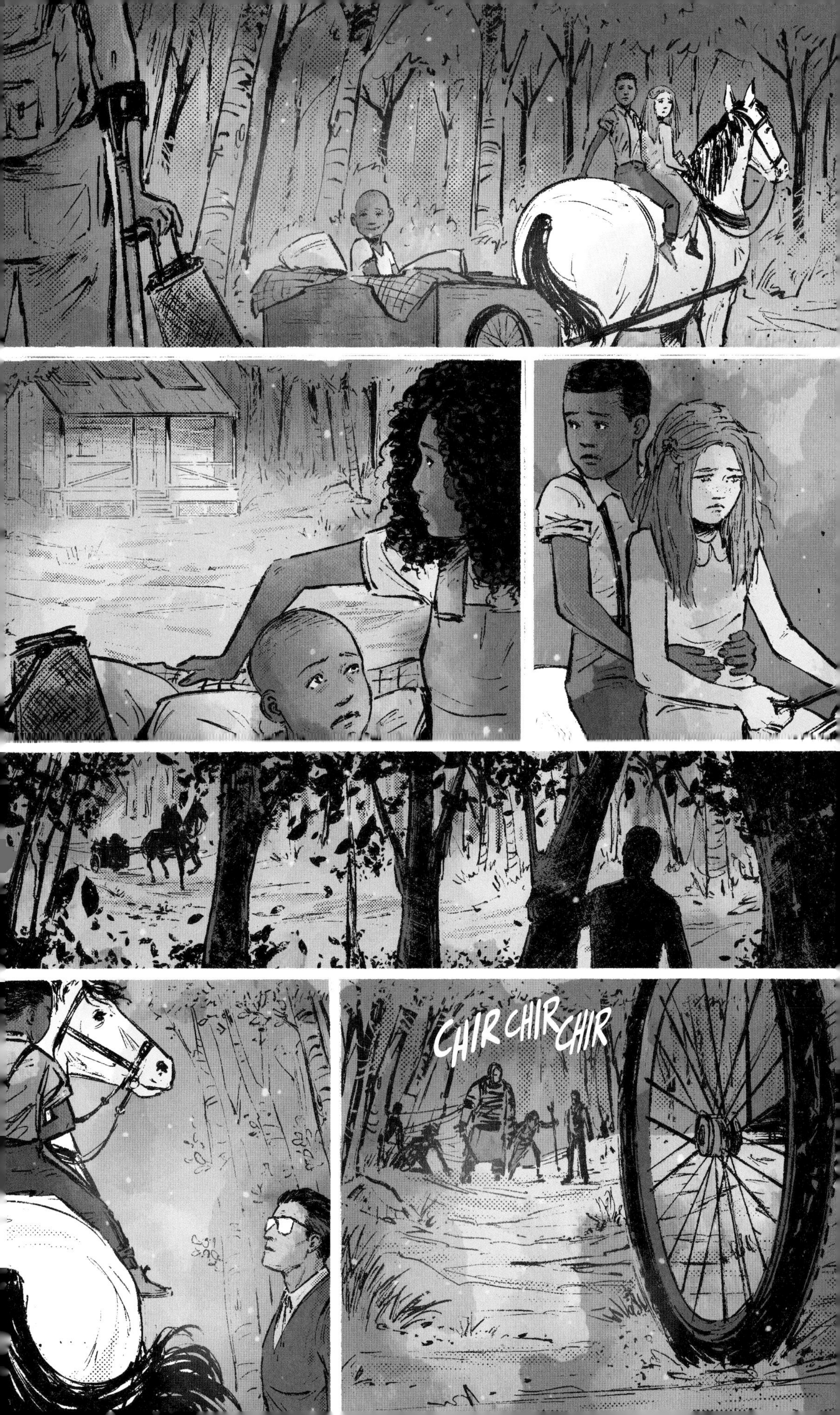
CHIR CHIR CHIR

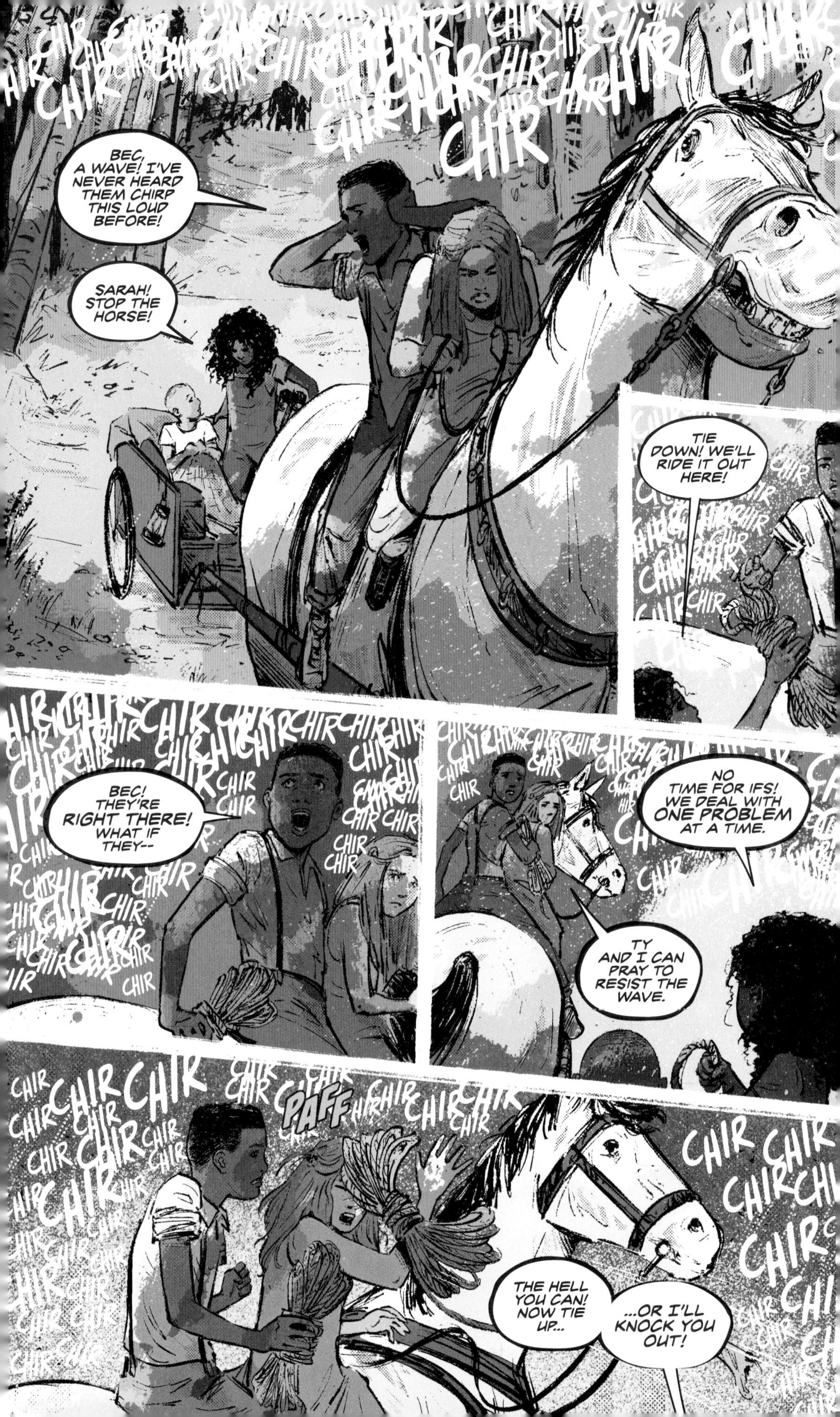
CHIR CHIR CHIR
BEC, A WAVE! I'VE NEVER HEARD THEM CHIRP THIS LOUD BEFORE!
SARAH! STOP THE HORSE!
CHIR CHIR
TIE DOWN! WE'LL RIDE IT OUT HERE!
CHIR CHIR CHIR
BEC! THEY'RE RIGHT THERE! WHAT IF THEY--
CHIR CHIR
NO TIME FOR IFS! WE DEAL WITH ONE PROBLEM AT A TIME.
TY AND I CAN PRAY TO RESIST THE WAVE.
CHIR CHIR CHIR
PAFF
THE HELL YOU CAN! NOW TIE UP...
...OR I'LL KNOCK YOU OUT!

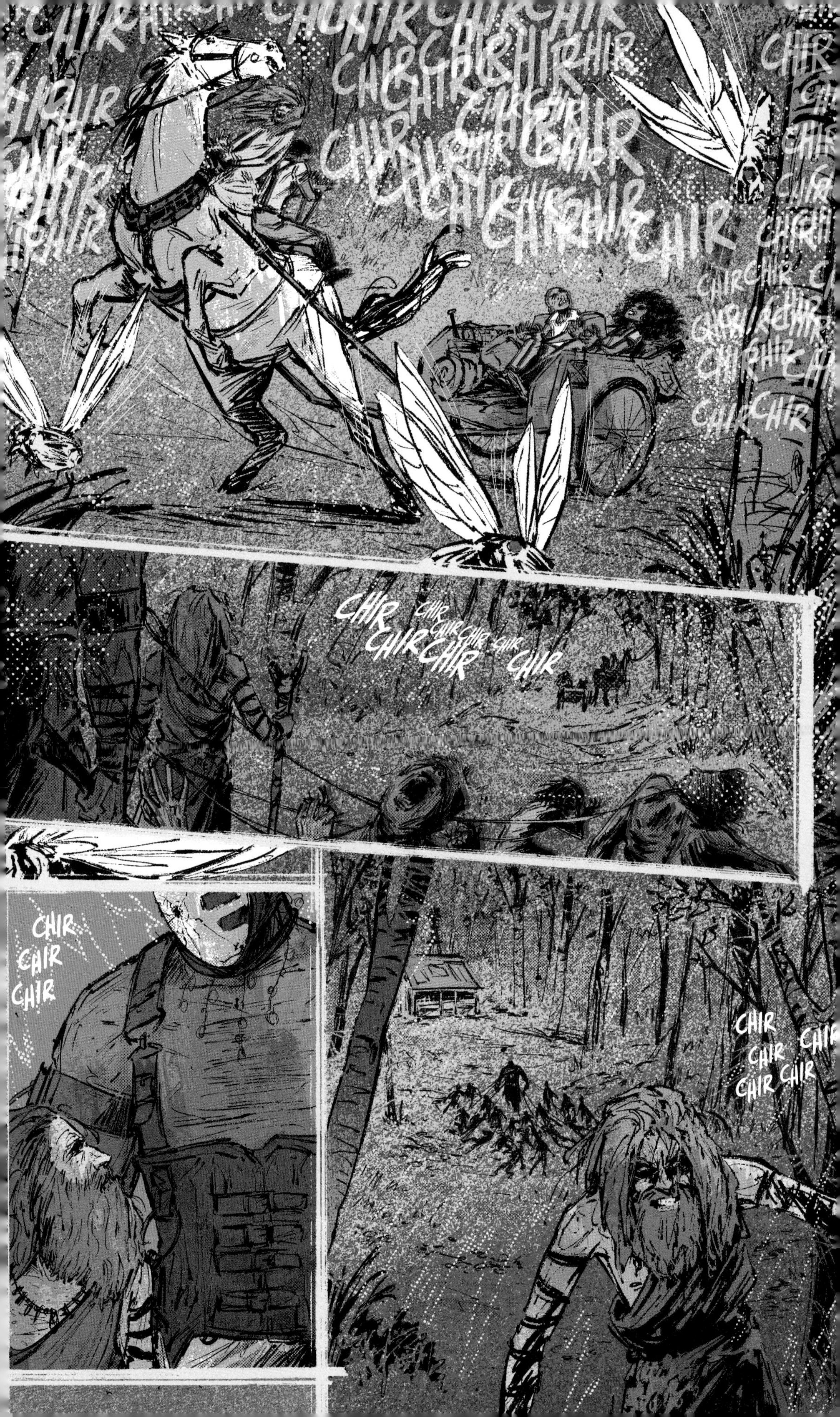
CHIR CHIR CHIR CHIR CHIR CHIR CHIR CHIR
CHIR CHIR CHIR CHIR CHIR
CHIR CHIR CHIR CHIR CHIR CHIR CHIR
CHIR CHIR CHIR CHIR CHIR CHIR CHIR
CHIR CHIR CHIR
CHIR CHIR CHIR CHIR CHIR

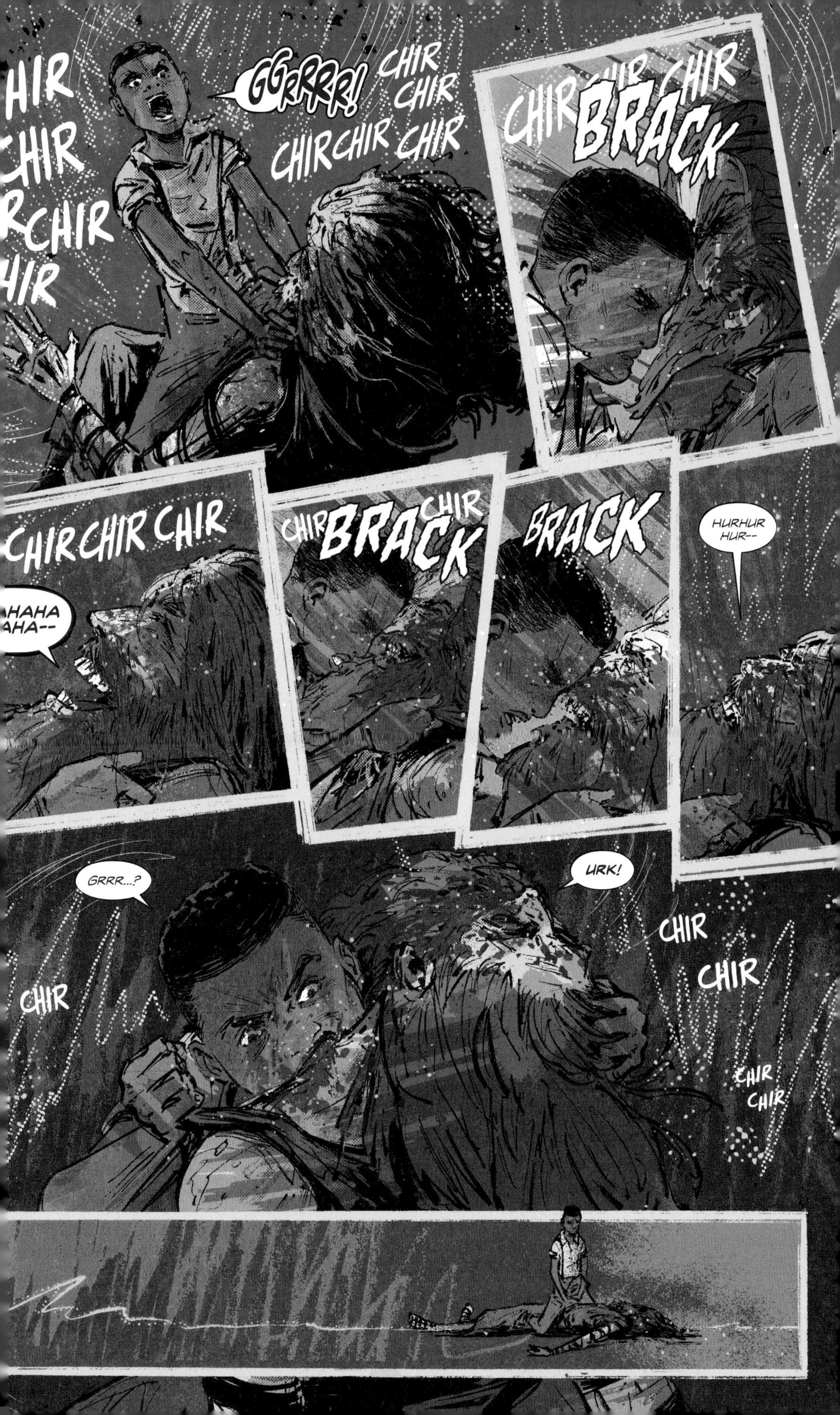
CHIR CHIR CHIR CHIR
GGRRRR!
CHIR CHIR CHIRCHIR CHIR
CHIR CHIR CHIR
BRACK
CHIRCHIR CHIR
AHAHA AHA--
CHIR CHIR
BRACK
BRACK
HURHUR HUR--
GRRR...?
URK!
CHIR
CHIR
CHIR
CHIR CHIR

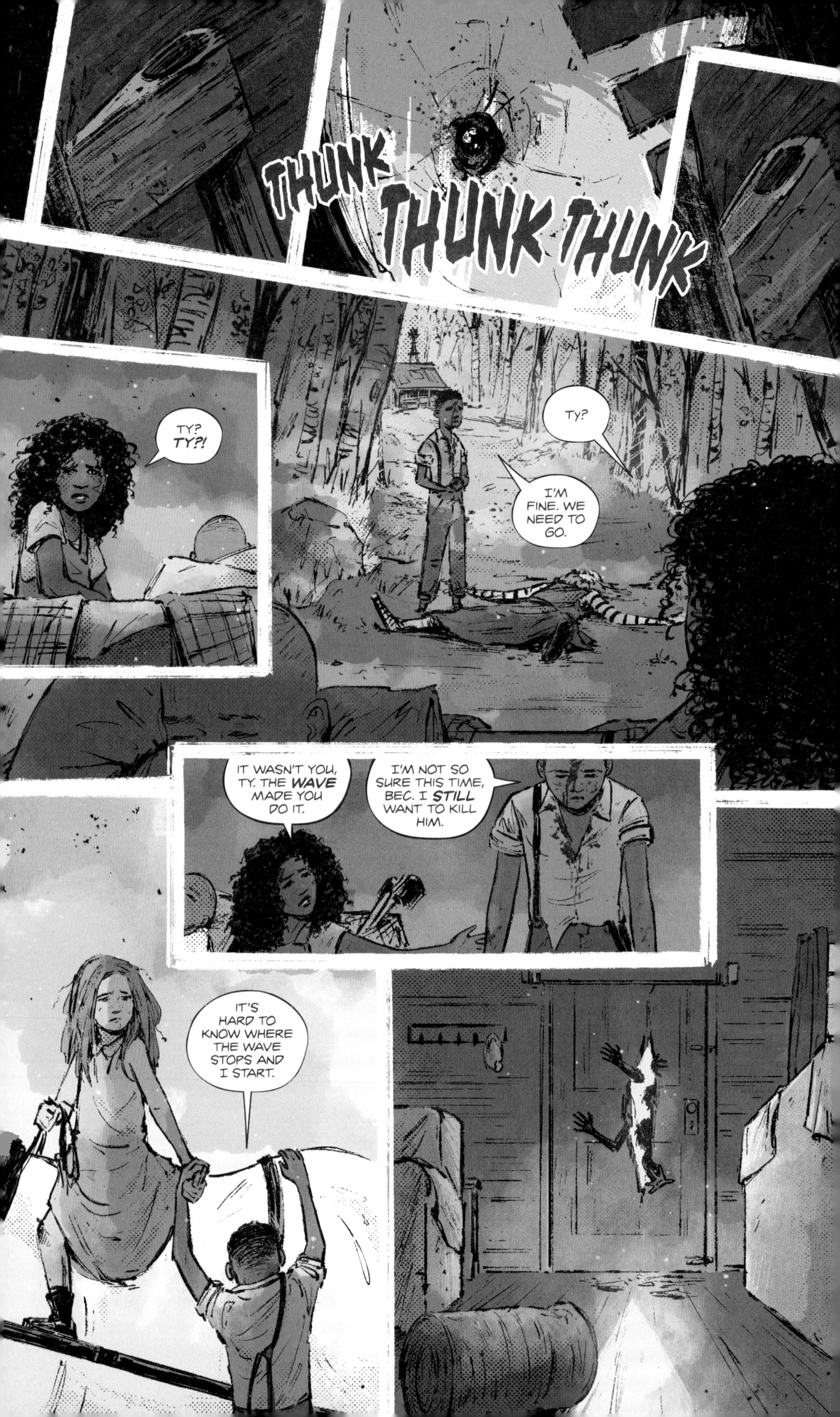
THUNK
THUNK THUNK
TY? TY?!
TY?
I'M FINE. WE NEED TO GO.
IT WASN'T YOU, TY. THE WAVE MADE YOU DO IT.
I'M NOT SO SURE THIS TIME, BEC. I STILL WANT TO KILL HIM.
IT'S HARD TO KNOW WHERE THE WAVE STOPS AND I START.

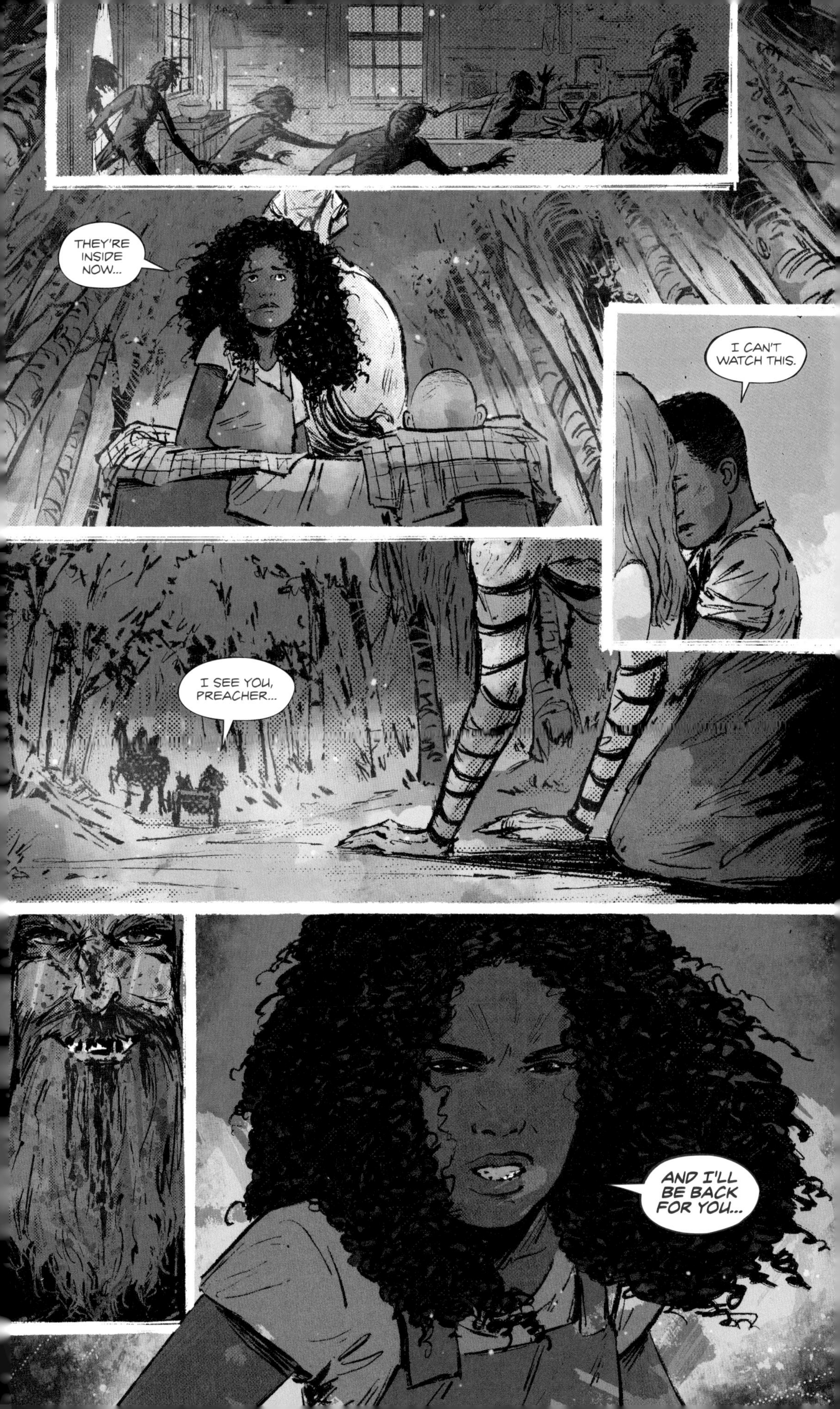
THEY'RE INSIDE NOW...
I CAN'T WATCH THIS.
I SEE YOU, PREACHER...
AND I'LL BE BACK FOR YOU...

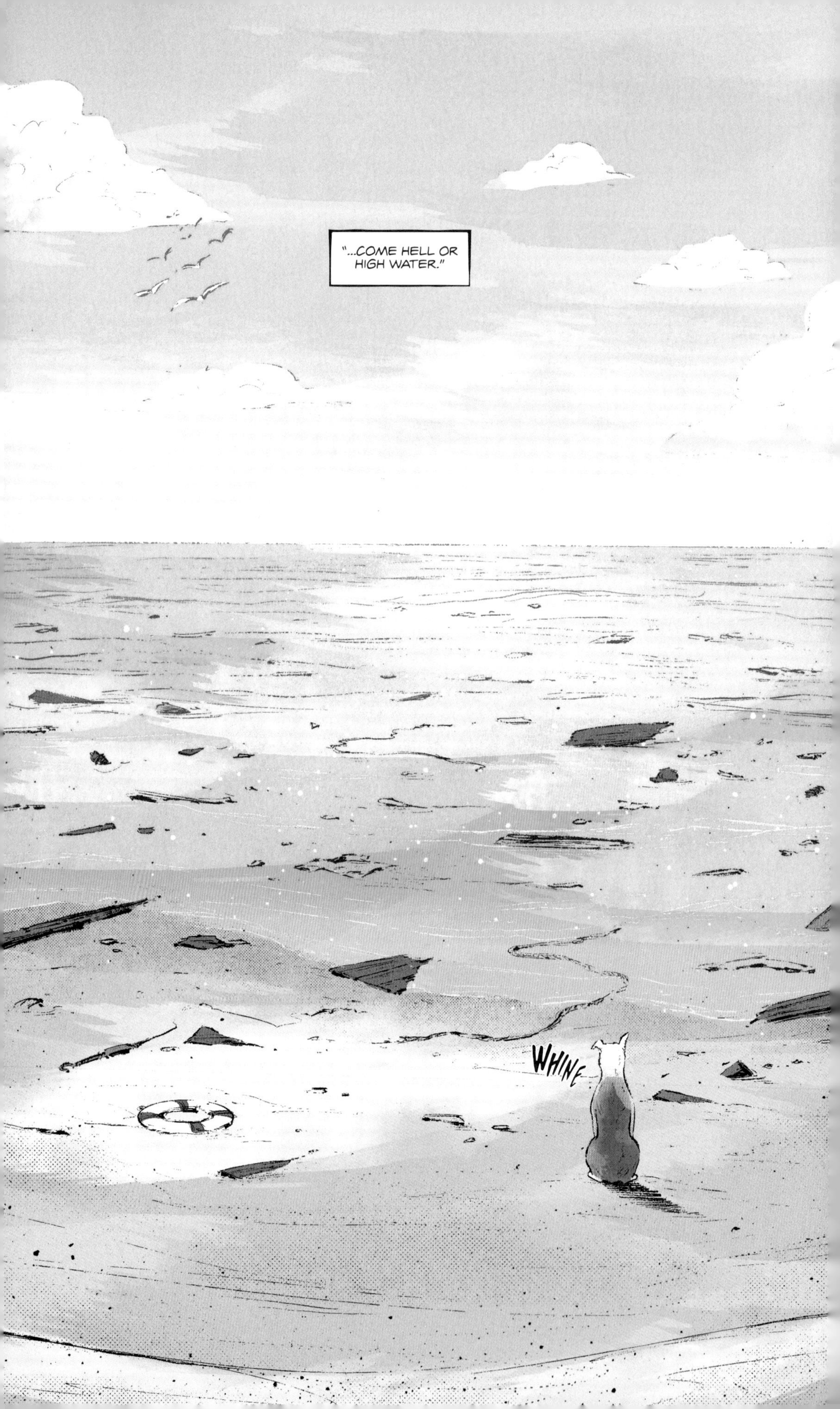
"...COME HELL OR HIGH WATER."
WHINE

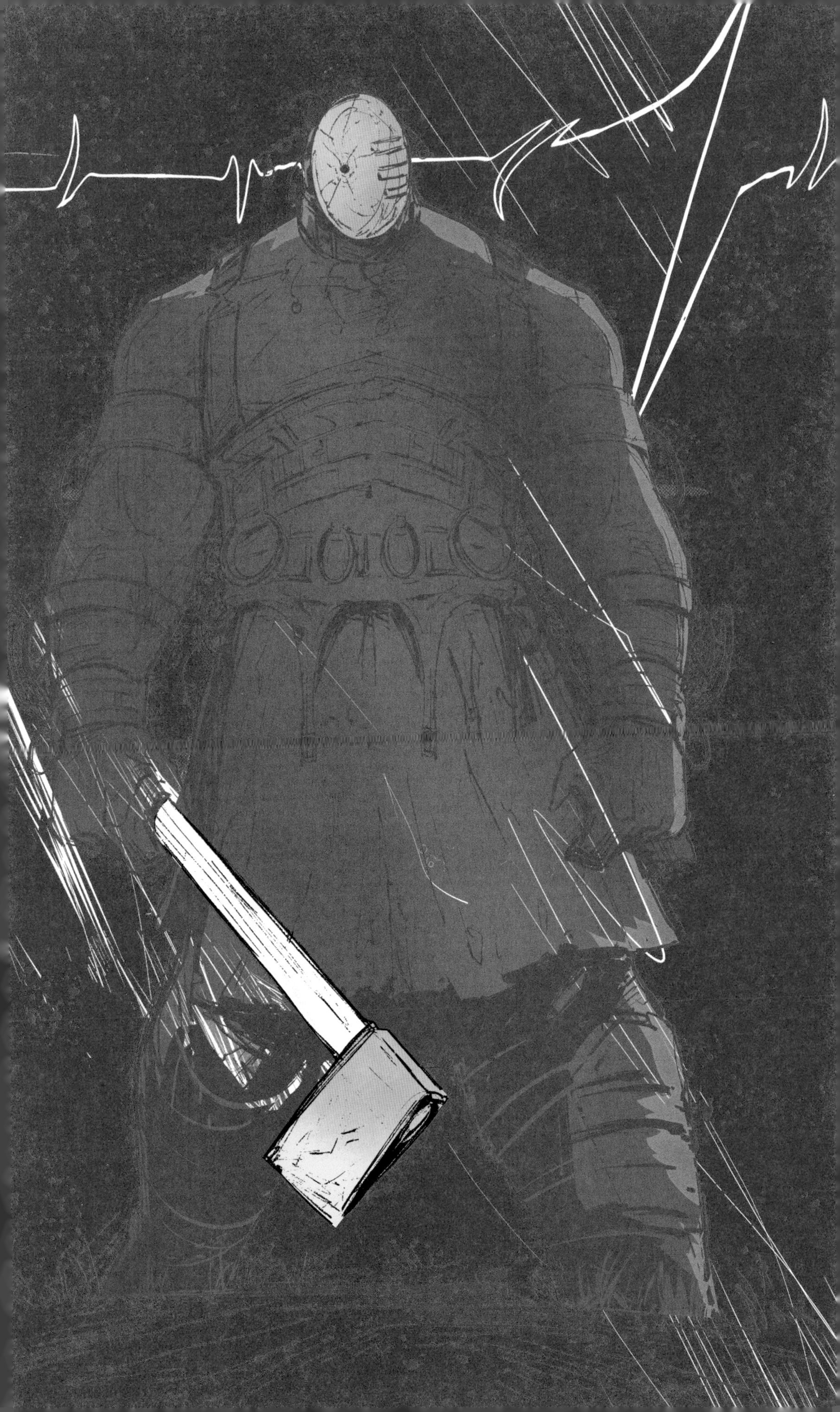

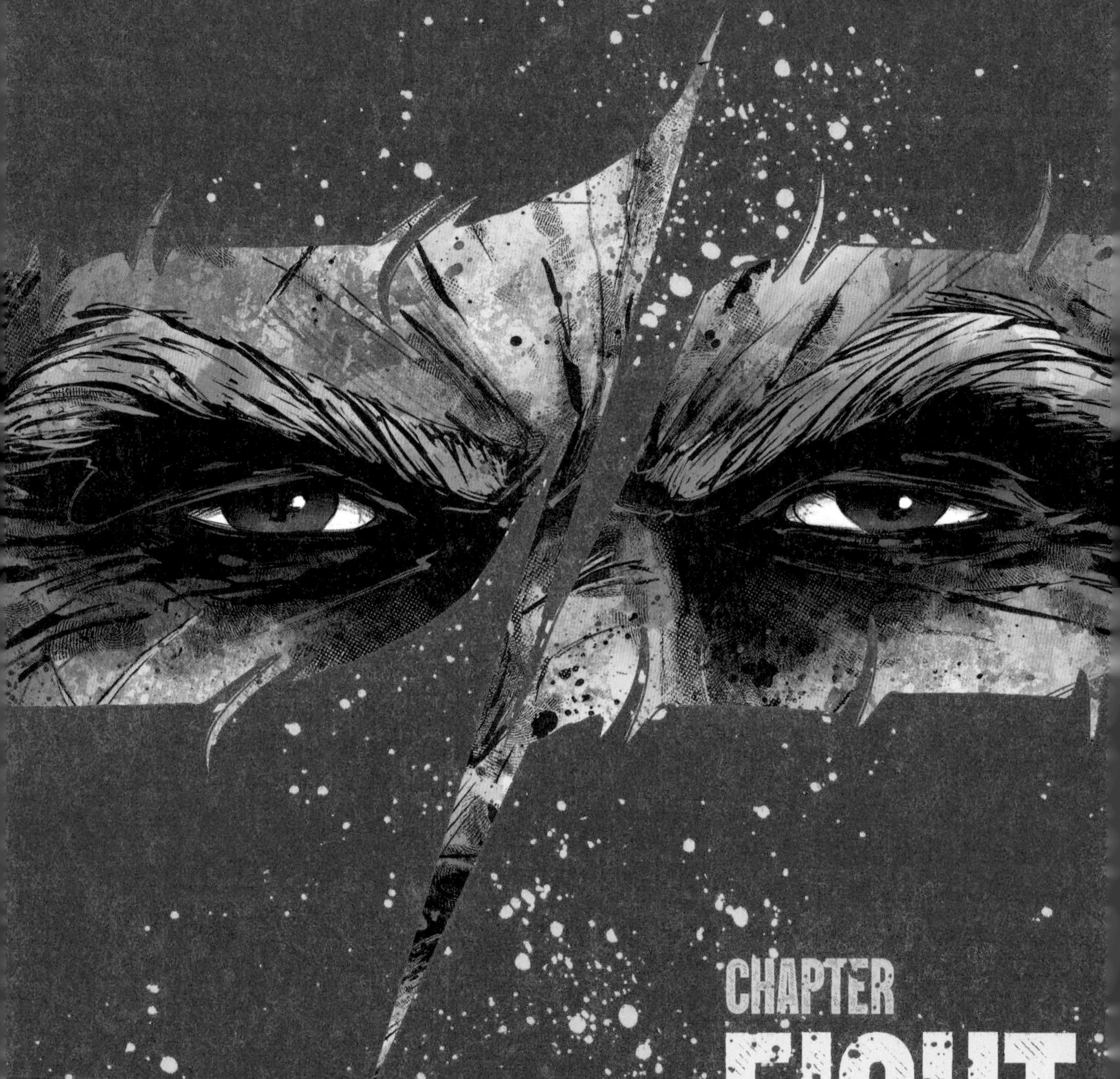

CHAPTER EIGHT

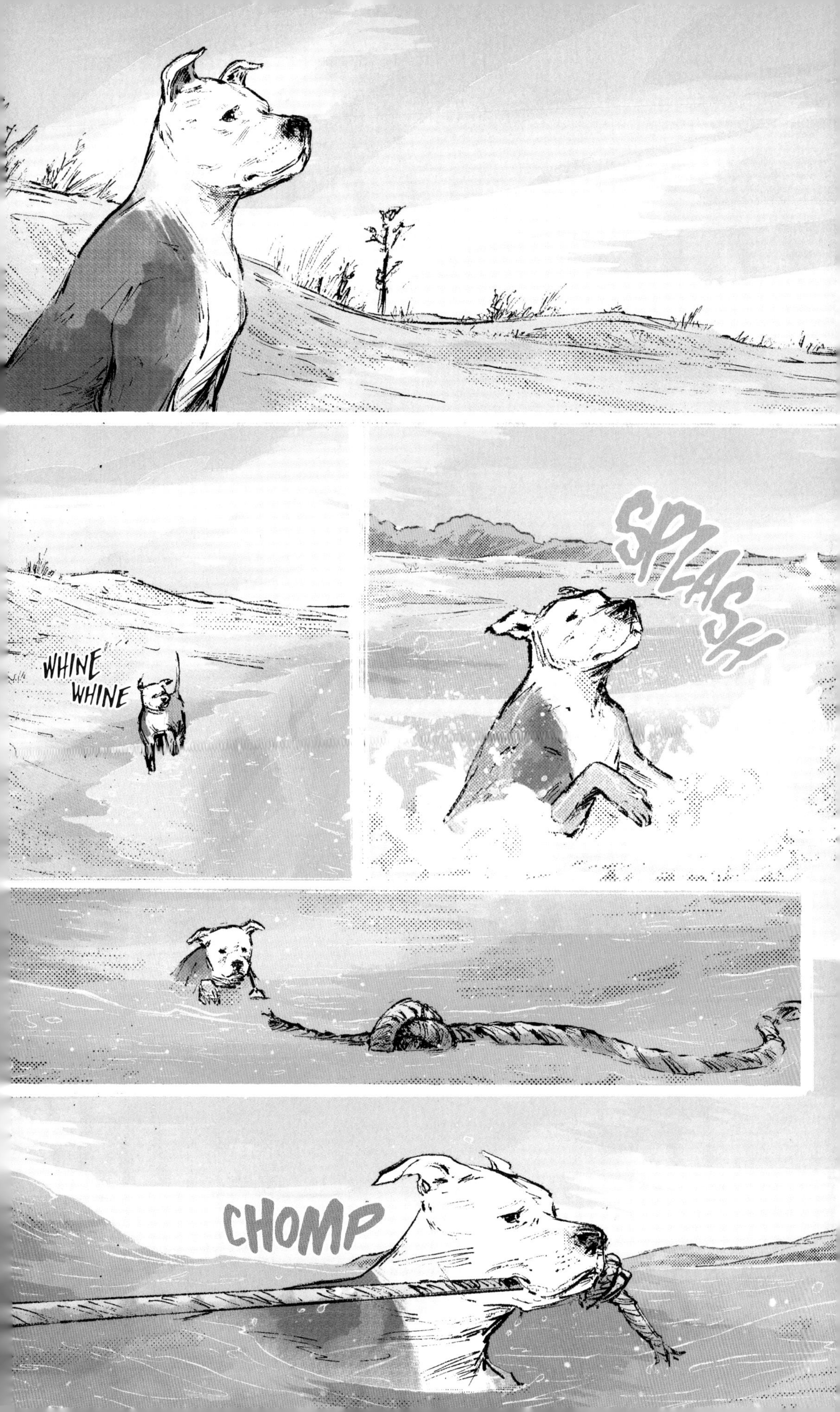
WHINE
WHINE
SPLASH
CHOMP

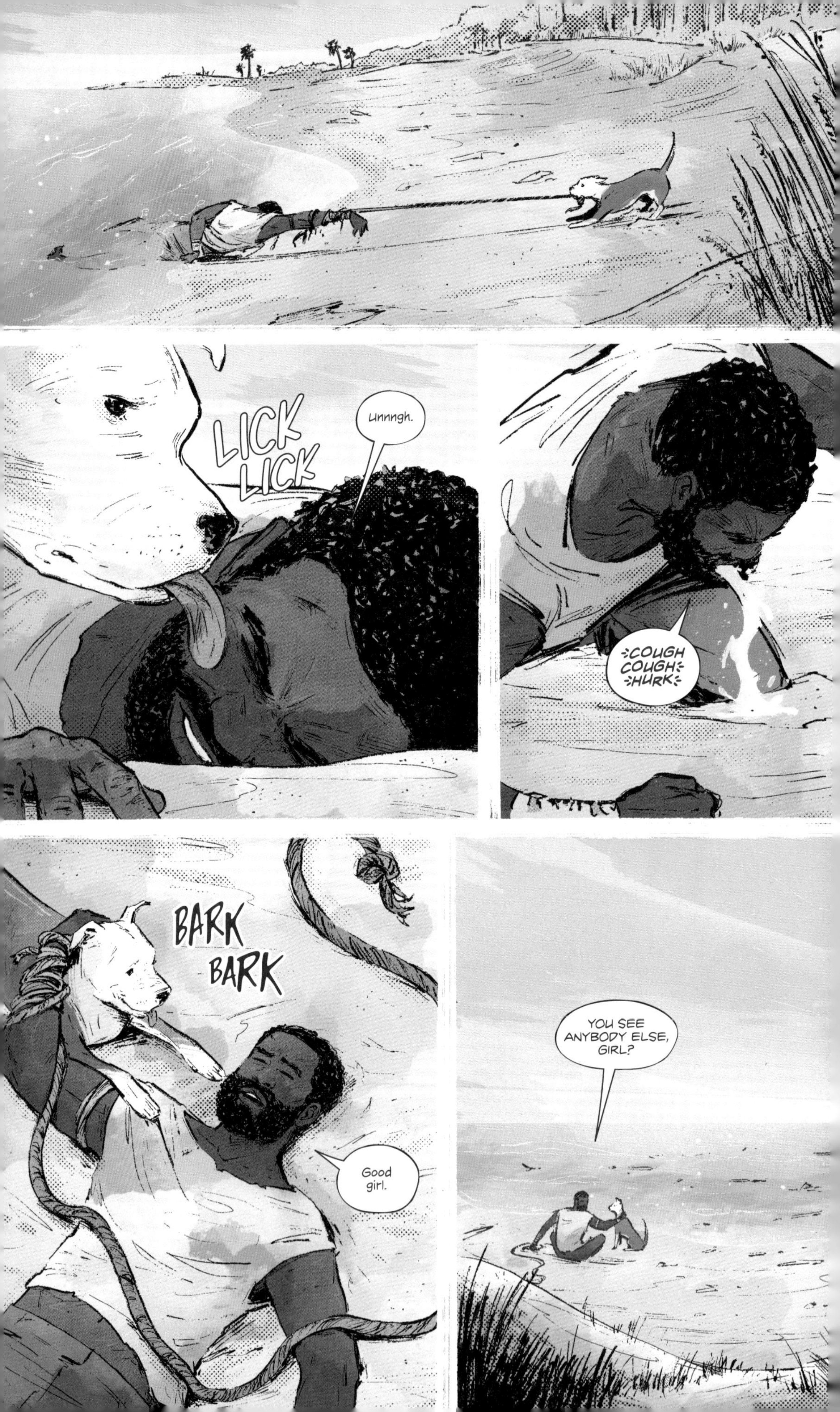
LICK LICK
Unnngh.
COUGH COUGH HURK
BARK BARK
Good girl.
YOU SEE ANYBODY ELSE, GIRL?

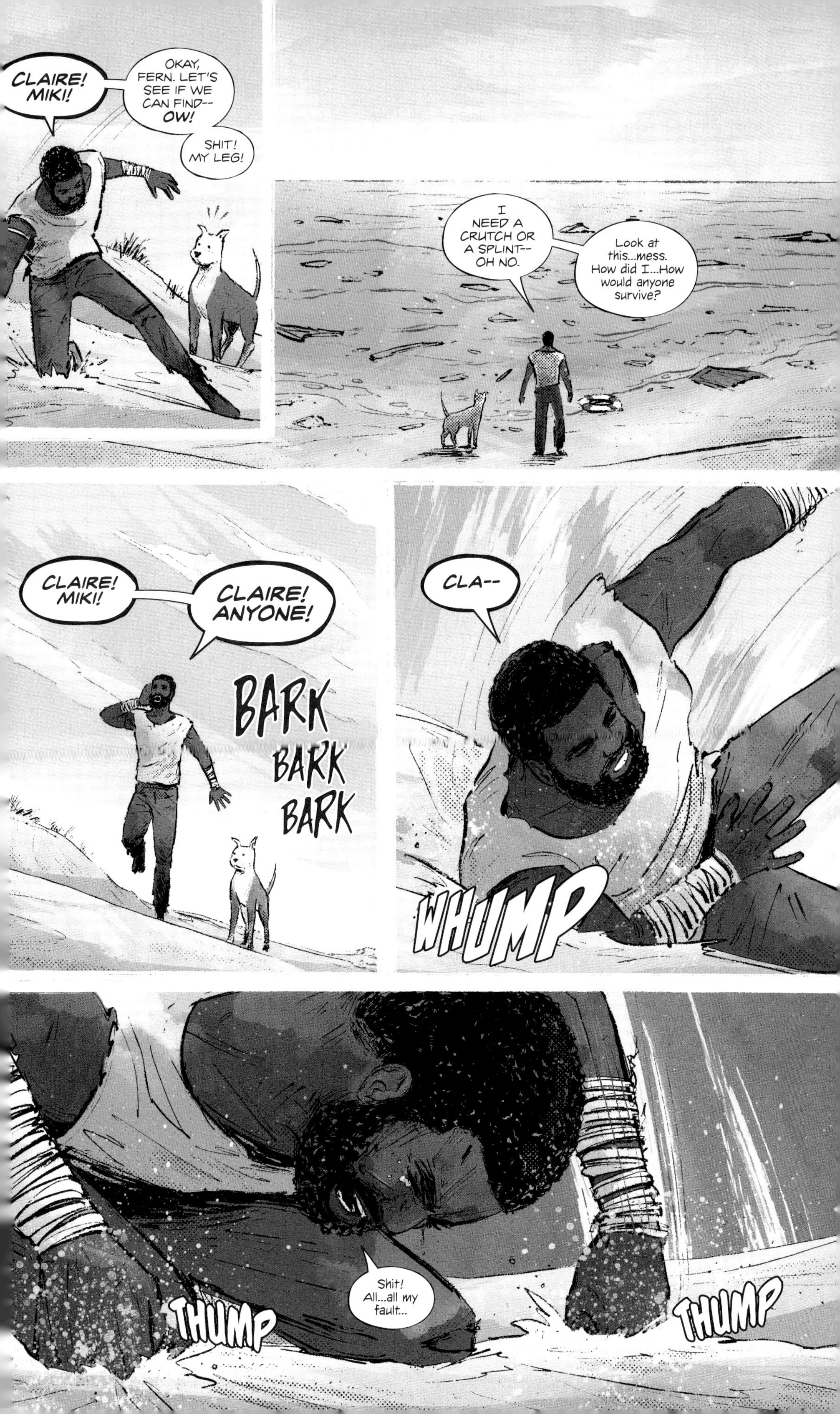
CLAIRE! MIKI!
OKAY, FERN. LET'S SEE IF WE CAN FIND-- OW!
SHIT! MY LEG!
I NEED A CRUTCH OR A SPLINT-- OH NO.
Look at this...mess. How did I...How would anyone survive?
CLAIRE! MIKI!
CLAIRE! ANYONE!
BARK
BARK
BARK
CLA--
WHUMP
THUMP
Shit! All...all my fault...
THUMP

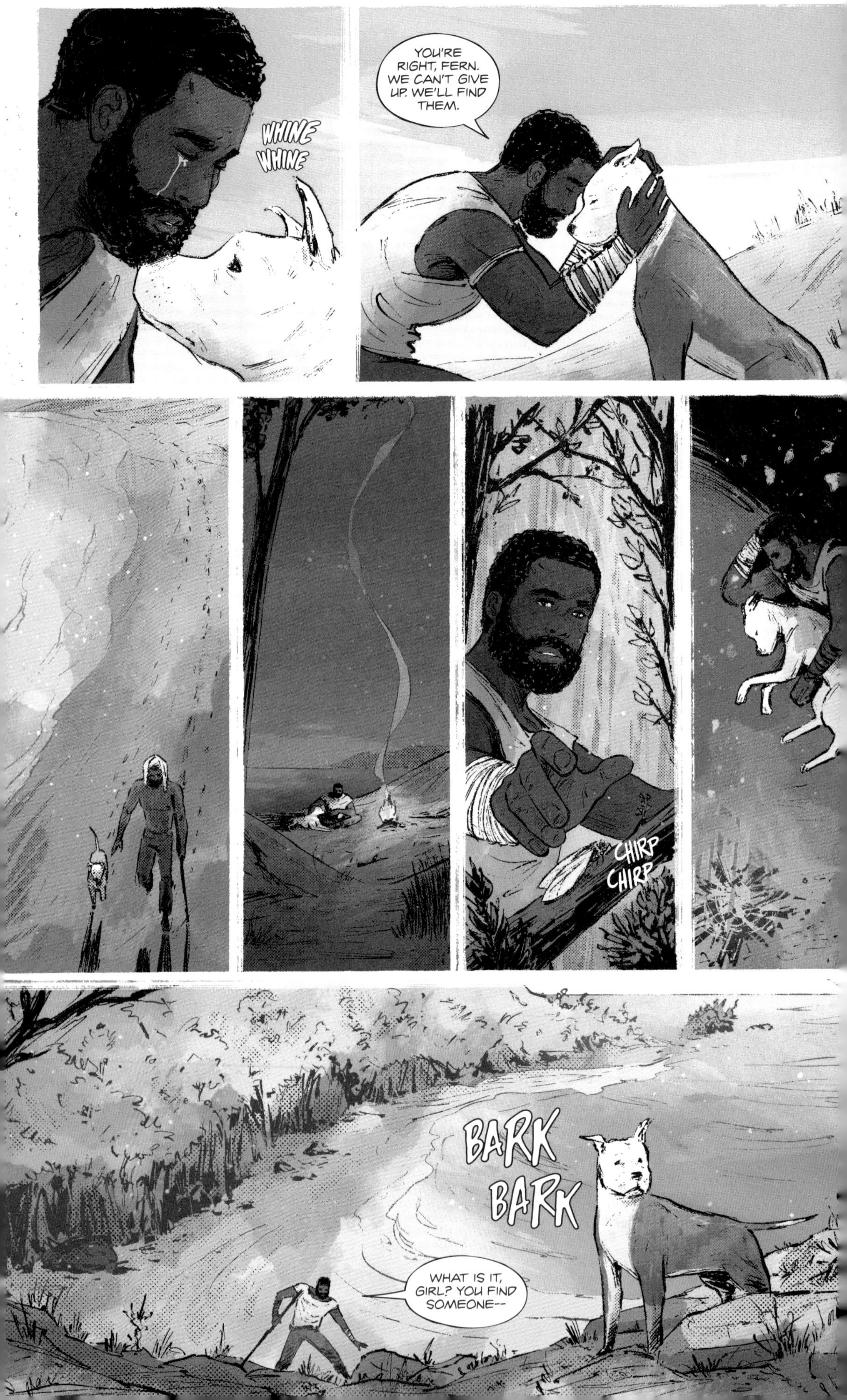
WHINE
WHINE
YOU'RE RIGHT, FERN. WE CAN'T GIVE UP. WE'LL FIND THEM.
CHIRP
CHIRP
BARK
BARK
WHAT IS IT, GIRL? YOU FIND SOMEONE--

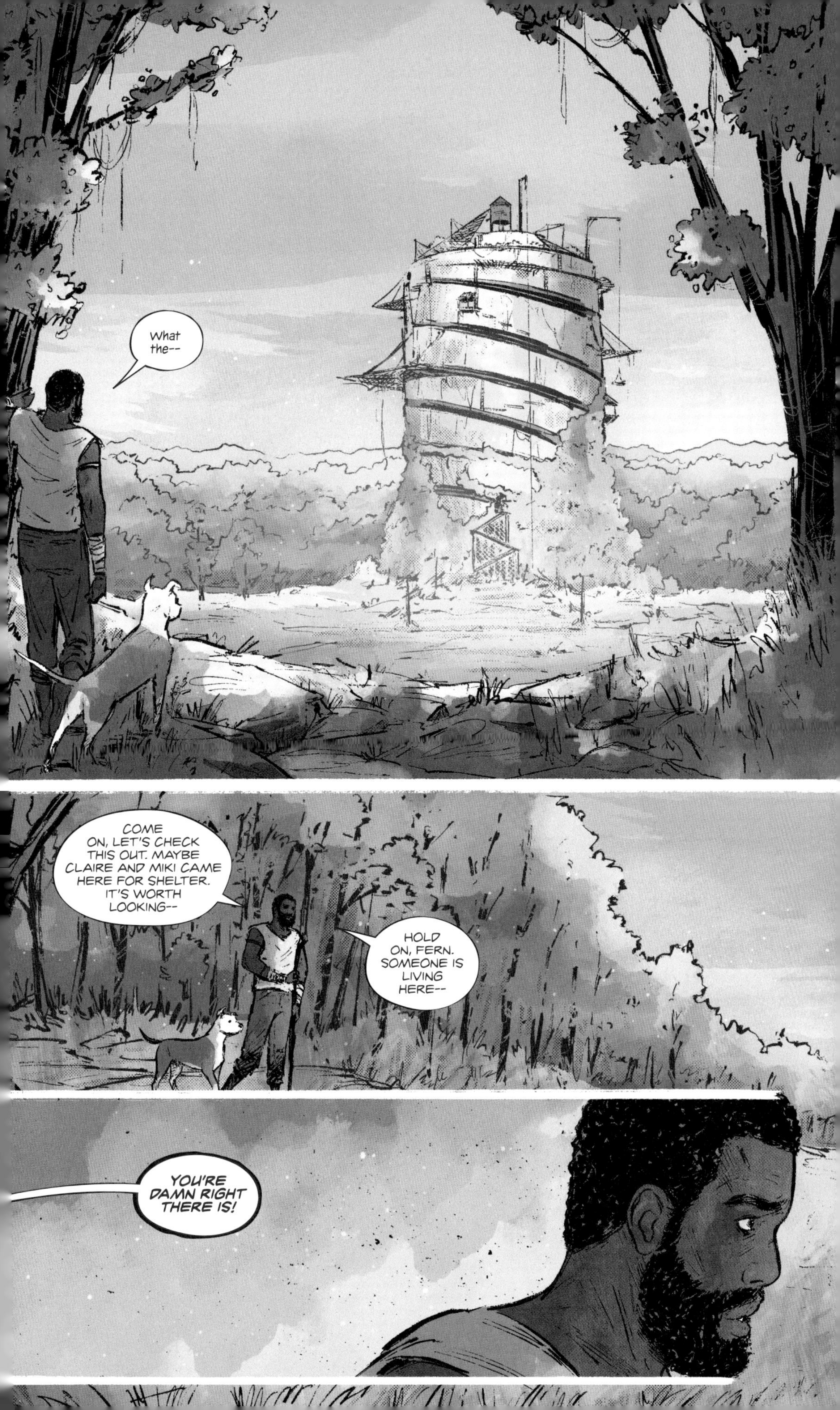
What the--
COME ON, LET'S CHECK THIS OUT. MAYBE CLAIRE AND MIKI CAME HERE FOR SHELTER. IT'S WORTH LOOKING--
HOLD ON, FERN. SOMEONE IS LIVING HERE--
YOU'RE DAMN RIGHT THERE IS!

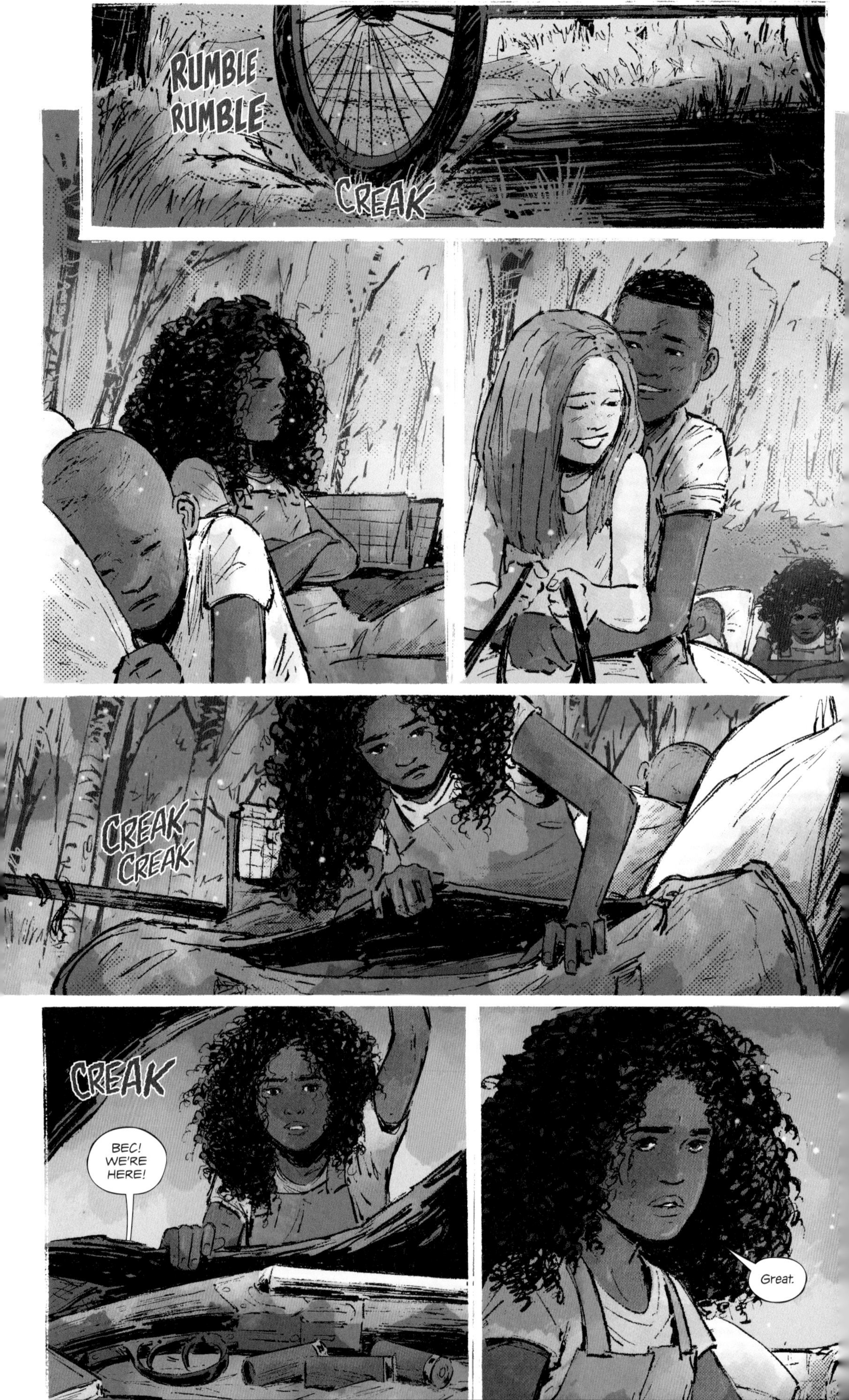
RUMBLE
RUMBLE
CREAK
CREAK
CREAK
CREAK
BEC! WE'RE HERE!
Great.

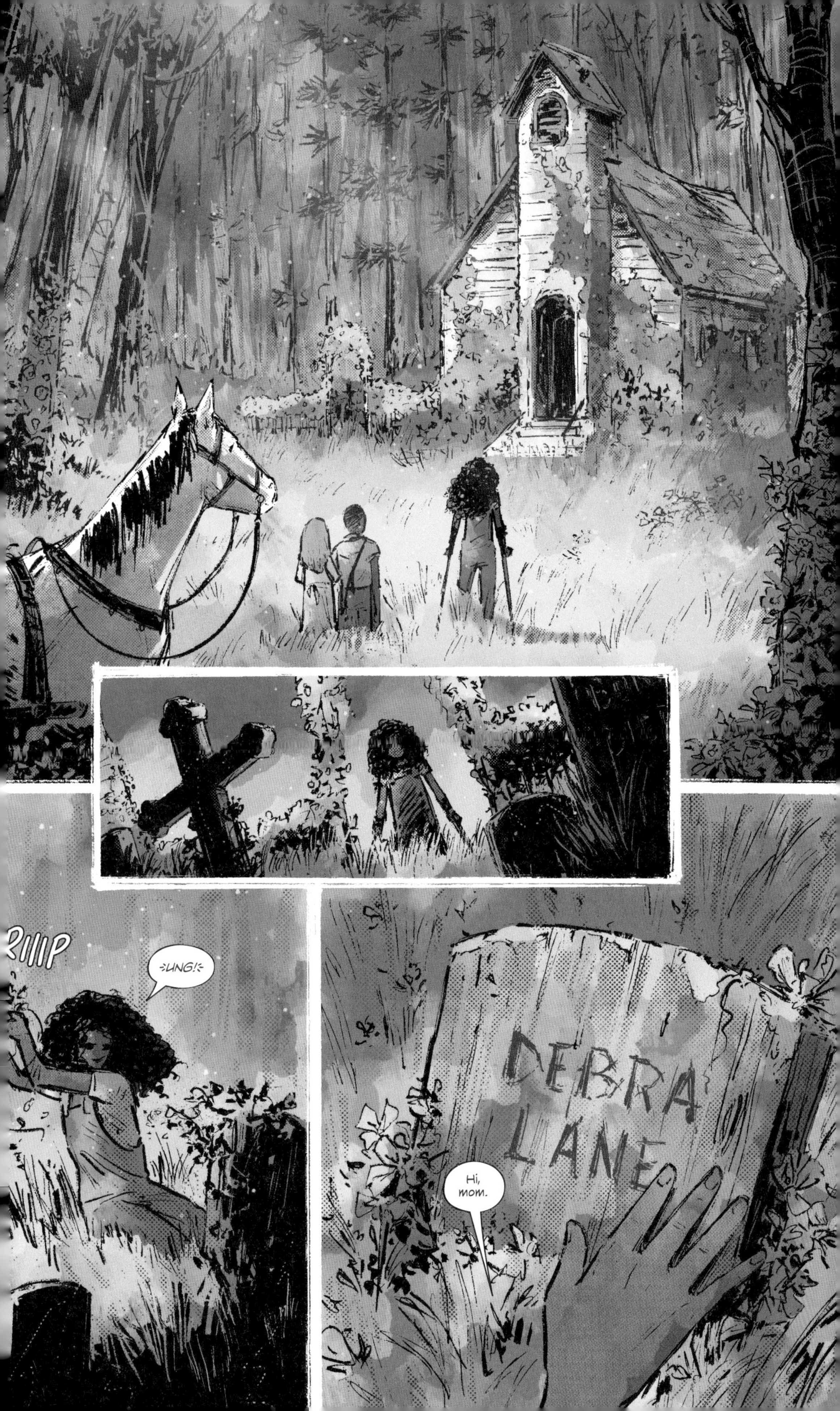
RIIIP
UNG!
DEBRA LANE
Hi, mom.

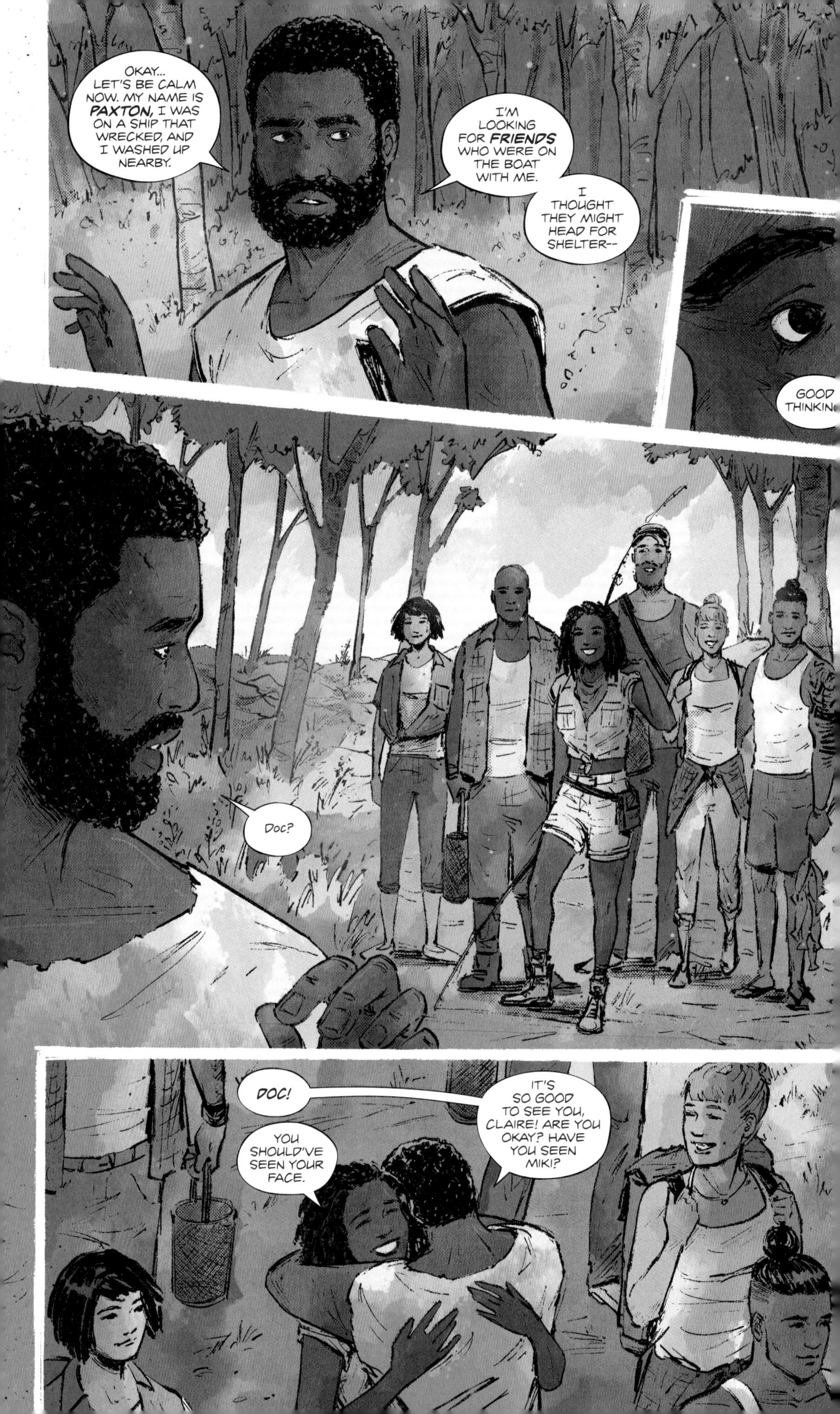
OKAY... LET'S BE CALM NOW. MY NAME IS **PAXTON,** I WAS ON A SHIP THAT WRECKED, AND I WASHED UP NEARBY.
I'M LOOKING FOR **FRIENDS** WHO WERE ON THE BOAT WITH ME.
I THOUGHT THEY MIGHT HEAD FOR SHELTER--
GOOD THINKIN
Doc?
DOC!
IT'S SO GOOD TO SEE YOU, CLAIRE! ARE YOU OKAY? HAVE YOU SEEN MIKI?
YOU SHOULD'VE SEEN YOUR FACE.

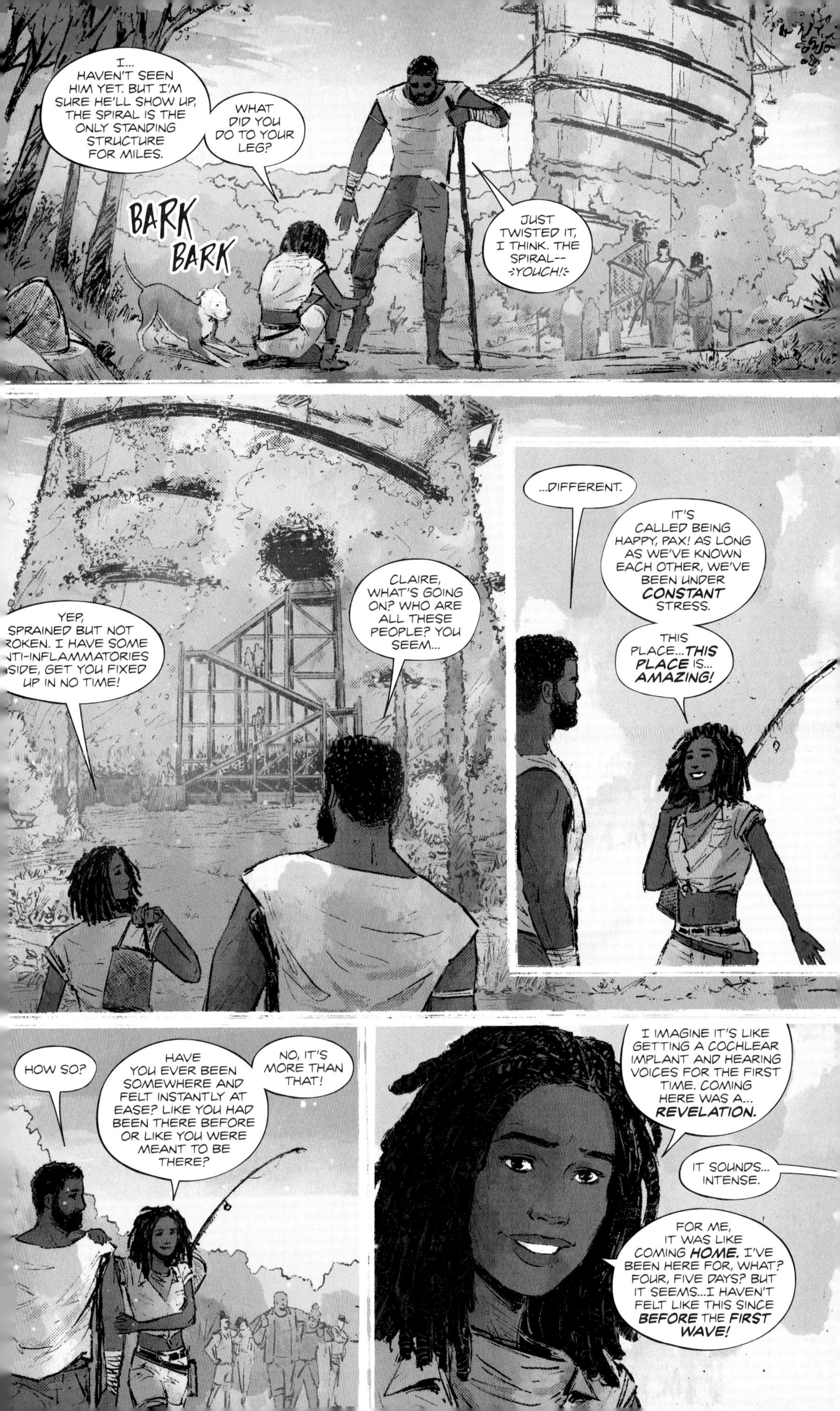
I... HAVEN'T SEEN HIM YET. BUT I'M SURE HE'LL SHOW UP, THE SPIRAL IS THE ONLY STANDING STRUCTURE FOR MILES.
WHAT DID YOU DO TO YOUR LEG?
BARK BARK
JUST TWISTED IT, I THINK. THE SPIRAL-- YOUCH!
YEP, SPRAINED BUT NOT ROKEN. I HAVE SOME NTI-INFLAMMATORIES ISIDE, GET YOU FIXED UP IN NO TIME!
CLAIRE, WHAT'S GOING ON? WHO ARE ALL THESE PEOPLE? YOU SEEM...
...DIFFERENT.
IT'S CALLED BEING HAPPY, PAX! AS LONG AS WE'VE KNOWN EACH OTHER, WE'VE BEEN UNDER CONSTANT STRESS.
THIS PLACE...THIS PLACE IS... AMAZING!
HOW SO?
NO, IT'S MORE THAN THAT!
HAVE YOU EVER BEEN SOMEWHERE AND FELT INSTANTLY AT EASE? LIKE YOU HAD BEEN THERE BEFORE OR LIKE YOU WERE MEANT TO BE THERE?
I IMAGINE IT'S LIKE GETTING A COCHLEAR IMPLANT AND HEARING VOICES FOR THE FIRST TIME. COMING HERE WAS A... REVELATION.
IT SOUNDS... INTENSE.
FOR ME, IT WAS LIKE COMING HOME. I'VE BEEN HERE FOR, WHAT? FOUR, FIVE DAYS? BUT IT SEEMS...I HAVEN'T FELT LIKE THIS SINCE BEFORE THE FIRST WAVE!

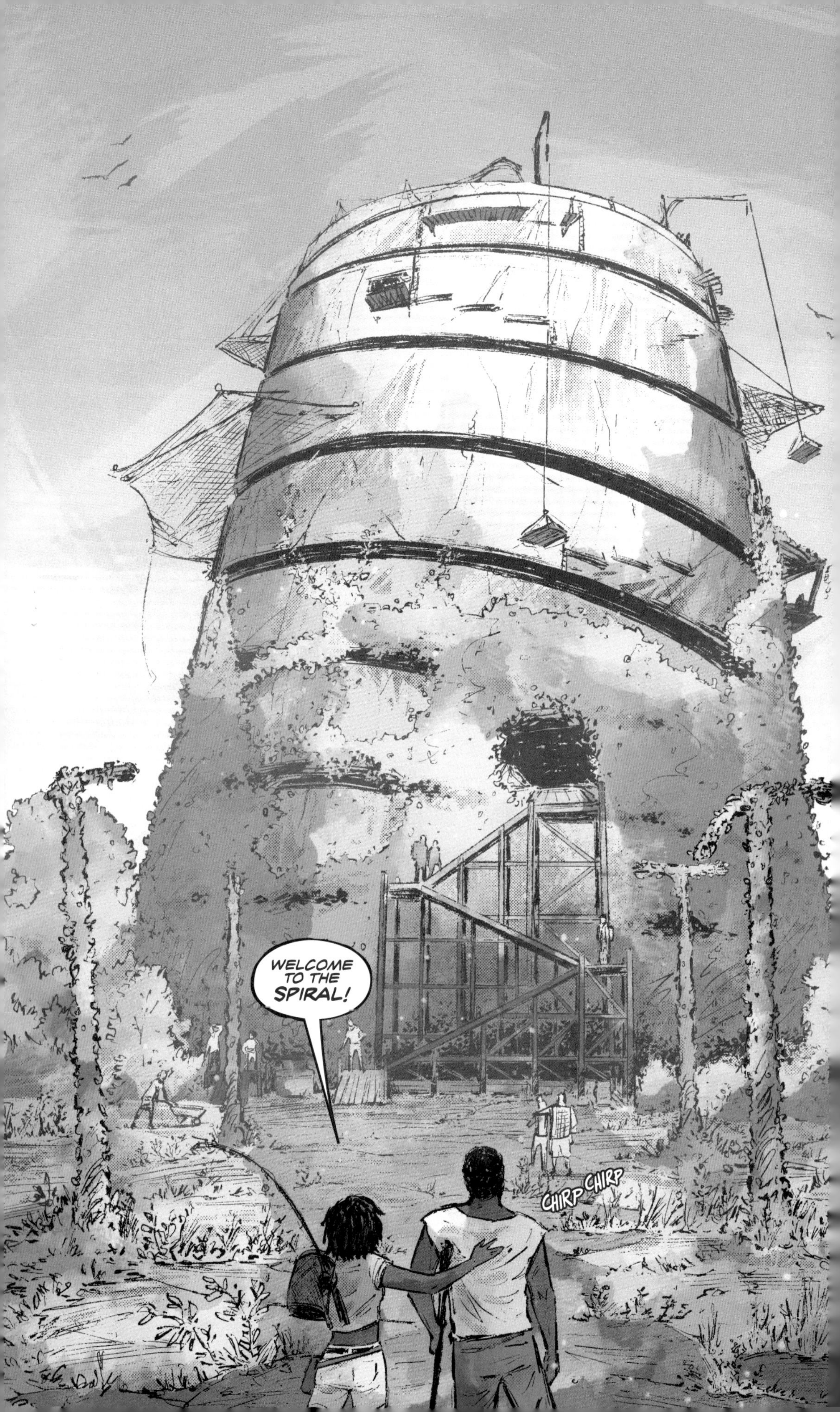
WELCOME TO THE SPIRAL!
CHIRP CHIRP

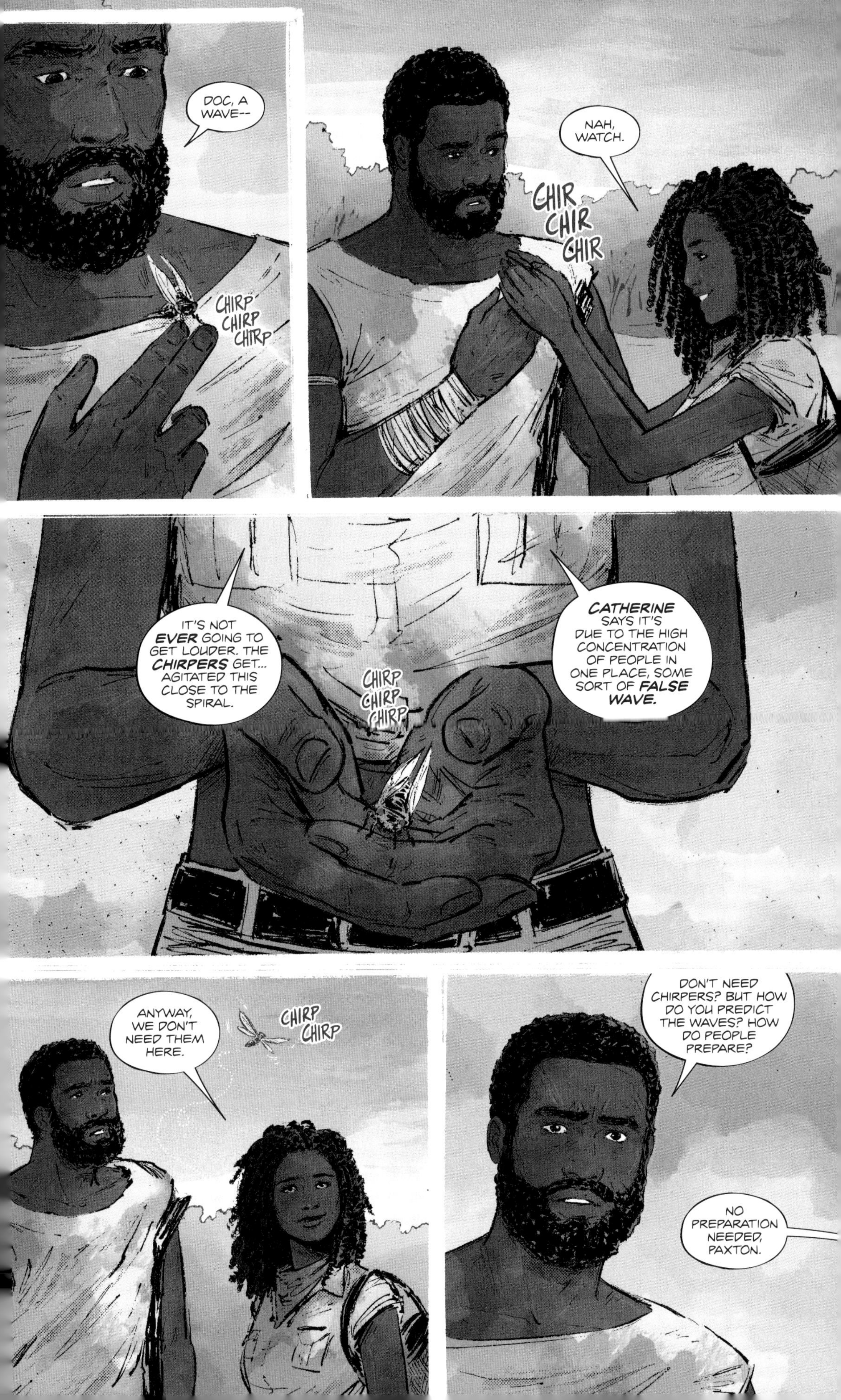
DOC, A WAVE--
CHIRP CHIRP CHIRP
NAH, WATCH.
CHIR CHIR CHIR
IT'S NOT **EVER** GOING TO GET LOUDER. THE **CHIRPERS** GET... AGITATED THIS CLOSE TO THE SPIRAL.
CHIRP CHIRP CHIRP
CATHERINE SAYS IT'S DUE TO THE HIGH CONCENTRATION OF PEOPLE IN ONE PLACE, SOME SORT OF **FALSE WAVE.**
ANYWAY, WE DON'T NEED THEM HERE.
CHIRP CHIRP
DON'T NEED CHIRPERS? BUT HOW DO YOU PREDICT THE WAVES? HOW DO PEOPLE PREPARE?
NO PREPARATION NEEDED, PAXTON.

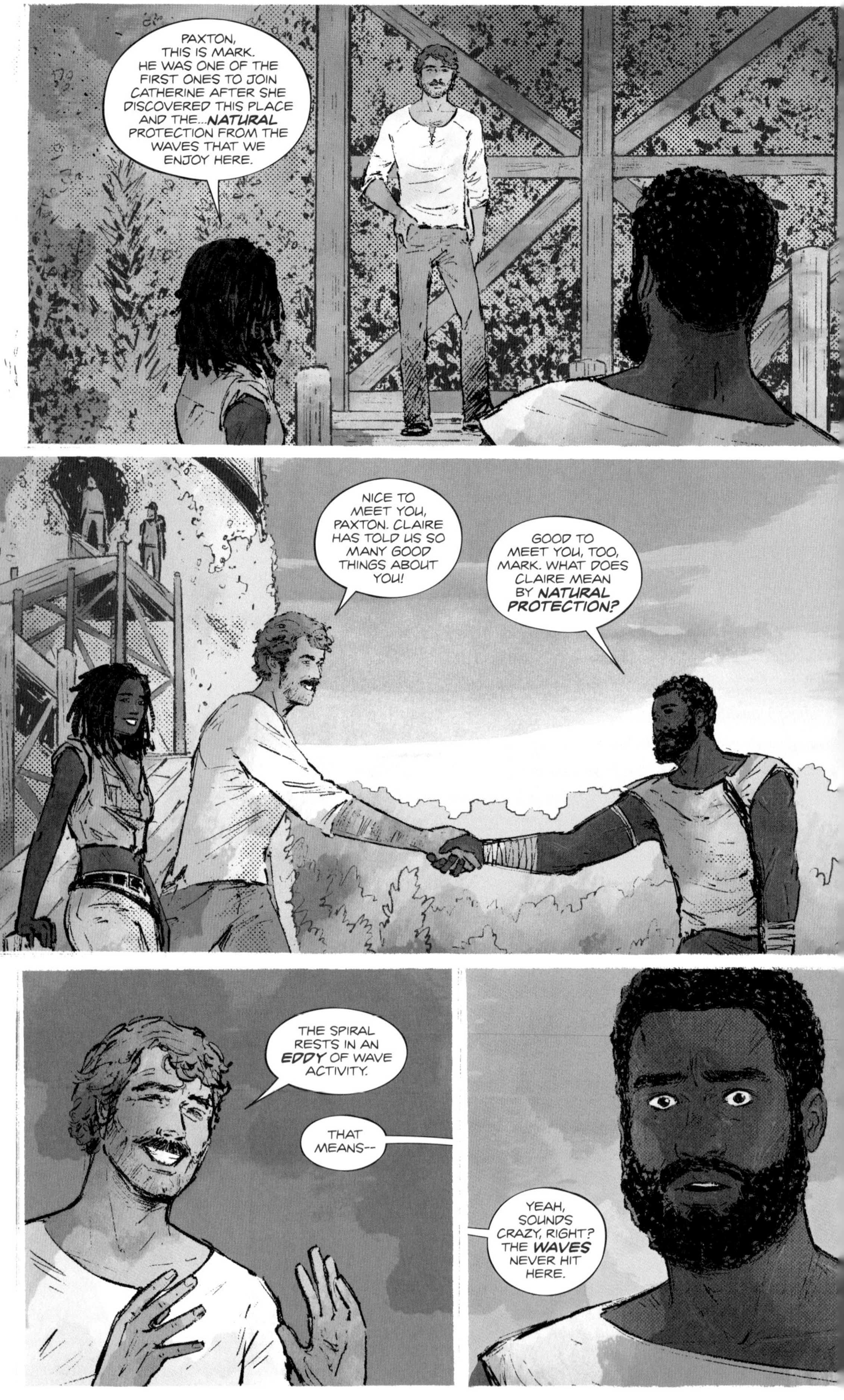
PAXTON, THIS IS MARK. HE WAS ONE OF THE FIRST ONES TO JOIN CATHERINE AFTER SHE DISCOVERED THIS PLACE AND THE...**NATURAL** PROTECTION FROM THE WAVES THAT WE ENJOY HERE.
NICE TO MEET YOU, PAXTON. CLAIRE HAS TOLD US SO MANY GOOD THINGS ABOUT YOU!
GOOD TO MEET YOU, TOO, MARK. WHAT DOES CLAIRE MEAN BY **NATURAL PROTECTION?**
THE SPIRAL RESTS IN AN **EDDY** OF WAVE ACTIVITY.
THAT MEANS--
YEAH, SOUNDS CRAZY, RIGHT? THE **WAVES** NEVER HIT HERE.

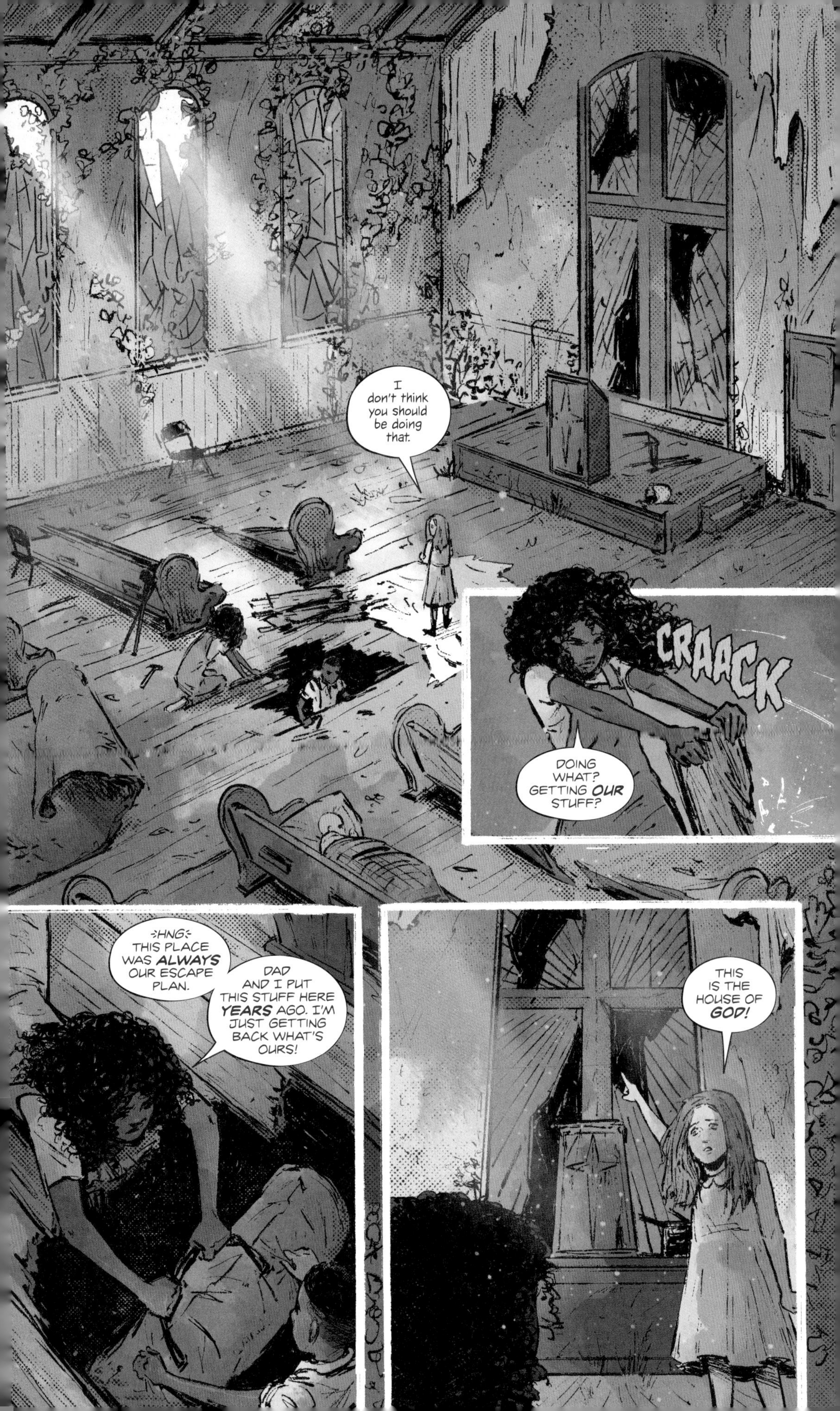
I don't think you should be doing that.
CRAACK
DOING WHAT? GETTING OUR STUFF?
HNG
THIS PLACE WAS ALWAYS OUR ESCAPE PLAN.
DAD AND I PUT THIS STUFF HERE YEARS AGO. I'M JUST GETTING BACK WHAT'S OURS!
THIS IS THE HOUSE OF GOD!

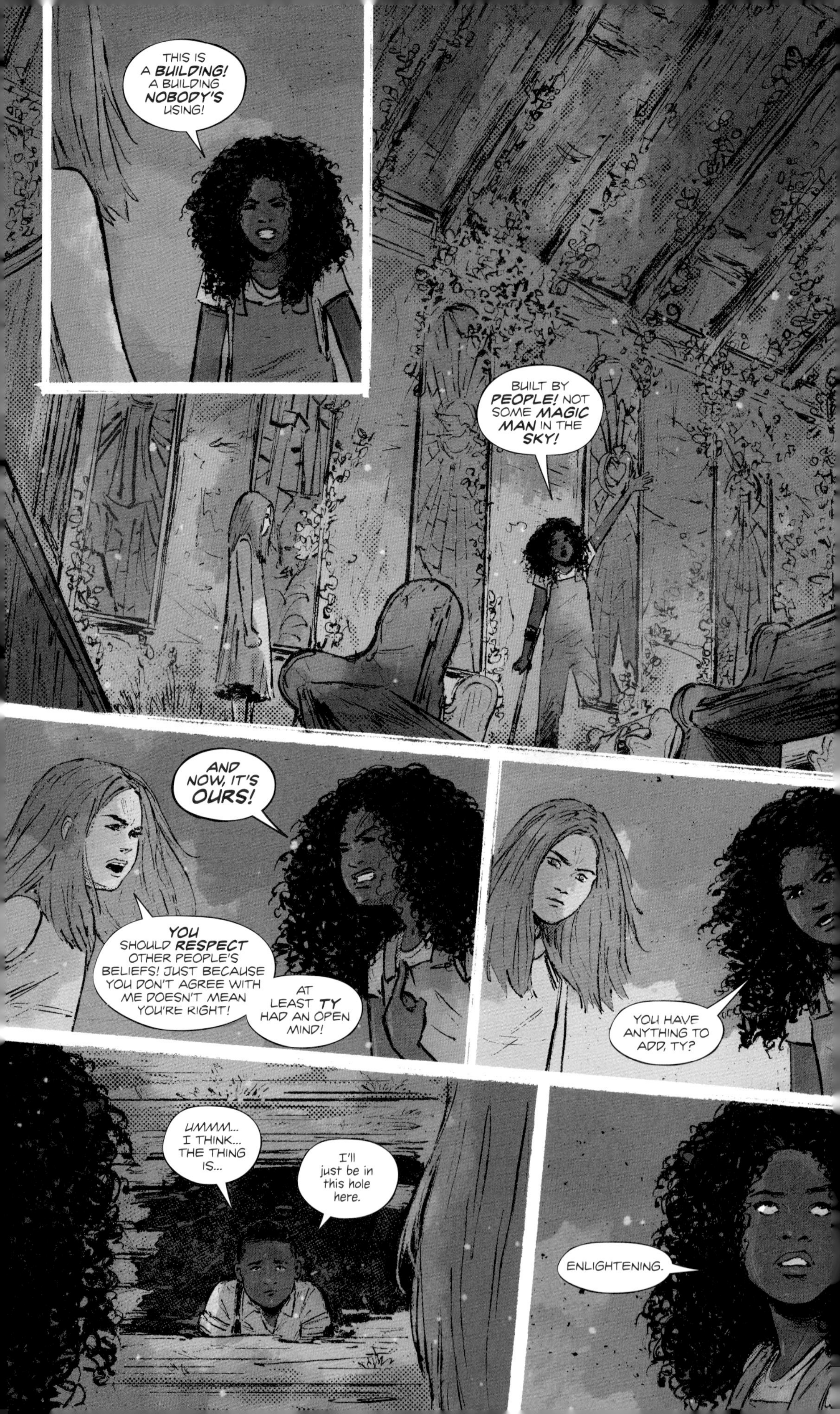
THIS IS A BUILDING! A BUILDING NOBODY'S USING!
BUILT BY PEOPLE! NOT SOME MAGIC MAN IN THE SKY!
AND NOW, IT'S OURS!
YOU SHOULD RESPECT OTHER PEOPLE'S BELIEFS! JUST BECAUSE YOU DON'T AGREE WITH ME DOESN'T MEAN YOU'RE RIGHT!
AT LEAST TY HAD AN OPEN MIND!
YOU HAVE ANYTHING TO ADD, TY?
UMMM... I THINK... THE THING IS...
I'll just be in this hole here.
ENLIGHTENING.

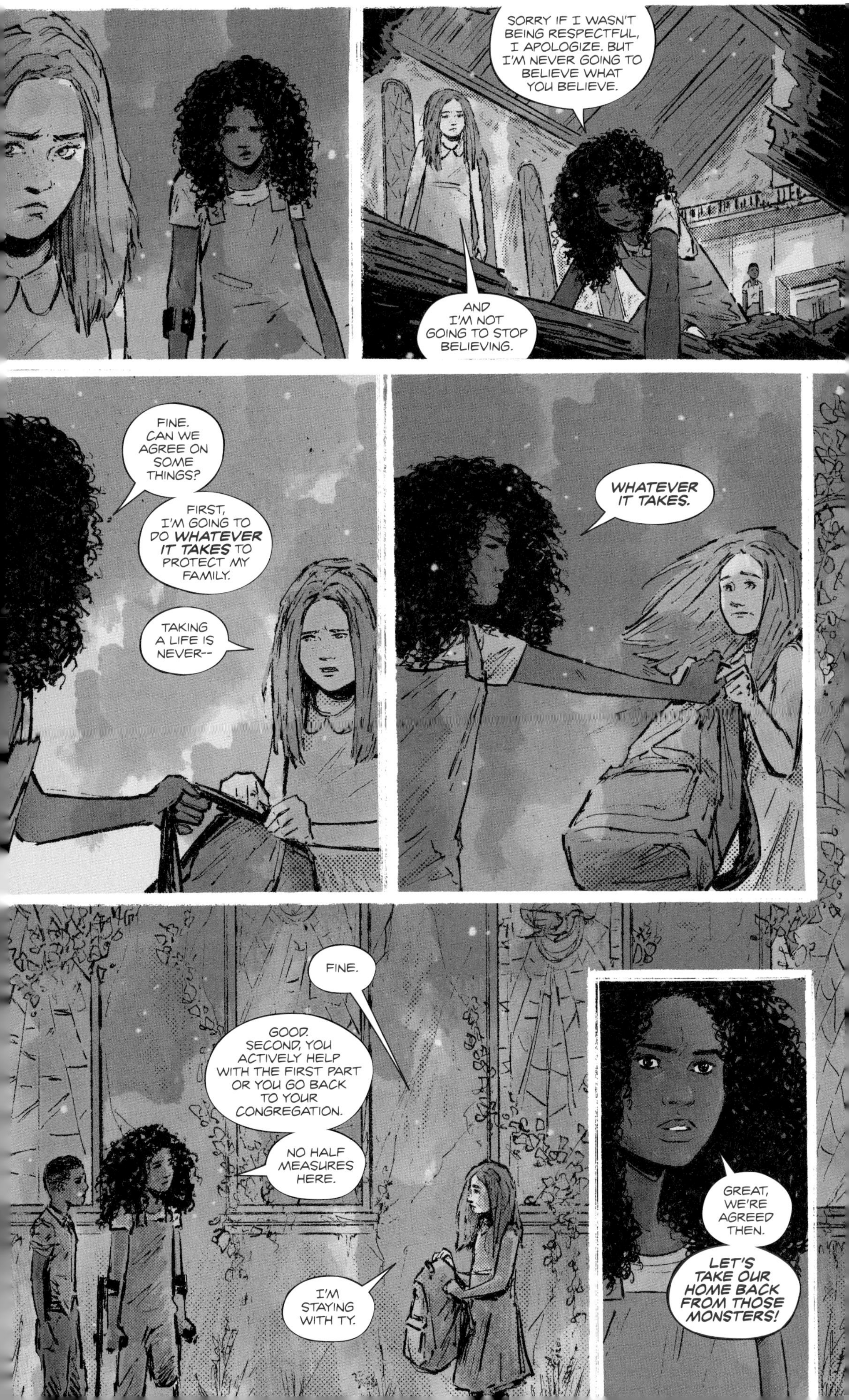
SORRY IF I WASN'T BEING RESPECTFUL, I APOLOGIZE. BUT I'M NEVER GOING TO BELIEVE WHAT YOU BELIEVE.
AND I'M NOT GOING TO STOP BELIEVING.
FINE. CAN WE AGREE ON SOME THINGS?
FIRST, I'M GOING TO DO **WHATEVER IT TAKES** TO PROTECT MY FAMILY.
TAKING A LIFE IS NEVER--
WHATEVER IT TAKES.
FINE.
GOOD. SECOND, YOU ACTIVELY HELP WITH THE FIRST PART OR YOU GO BACK TO YOUR CONGREGATION.
NO HALF MEASURES HERE.
I'M STAYING WITH TY.
GREAT, WE'RE AGREED THEN.
LET'S TAKE OUR HOME BACK FROM THOSE MONSTERS!

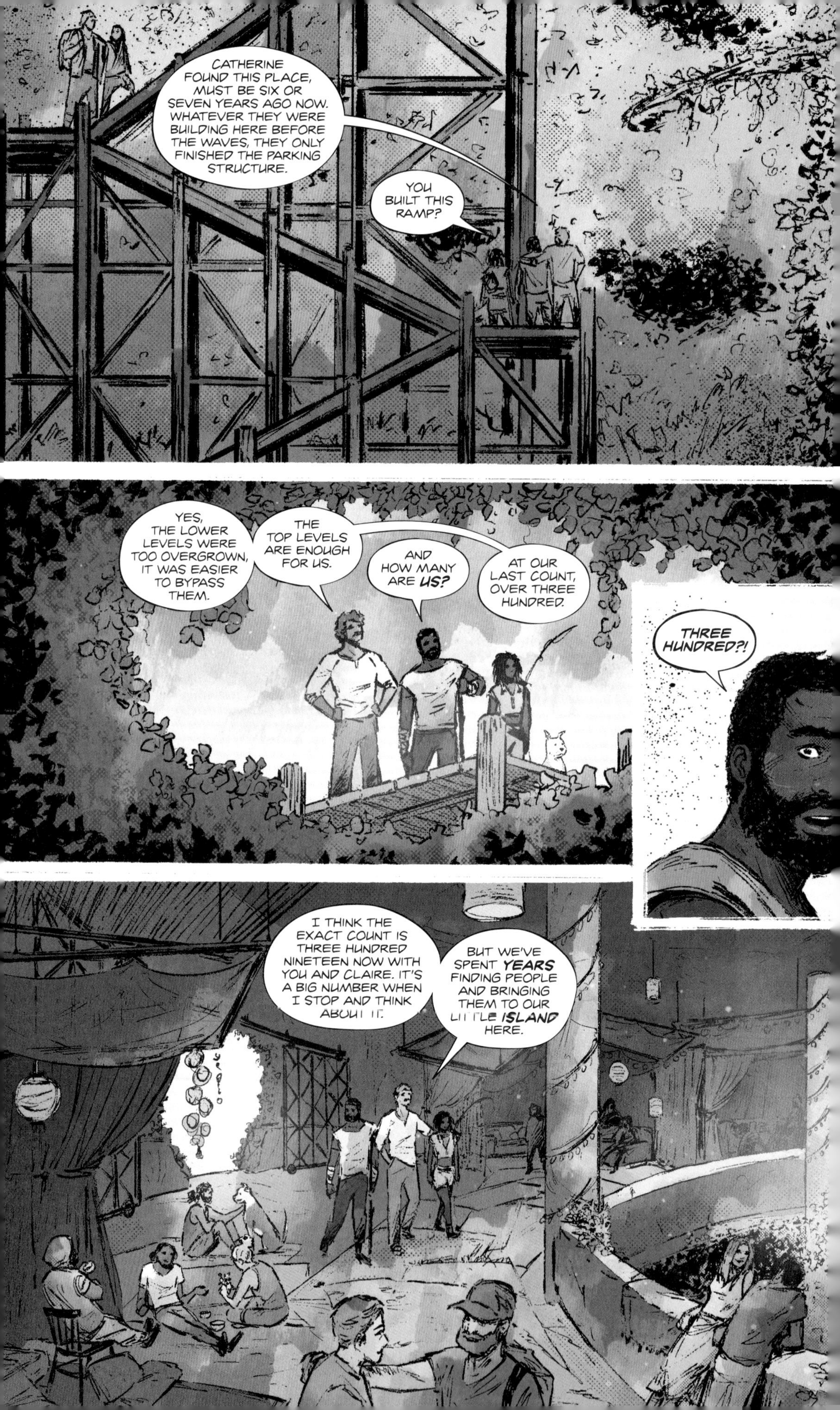
CATHERINE FOUND THIS PLACE, MUST BE SIX OR SEVEN YEARS AGO NOW. WHATEVER THEY WERE BUILDING HERE BEFORE THE WAVES, THEY ONLY FINISHED THE PARKING STRUCTURE.
YOU BUILT THIS RAMP?
YES, THE LOWER LEVELS WERE TOO OVERGROWN, IT WAS EASIER TO BYPASS THEM.
THE TOP LEVELS ARE ENOUGH FOR US.
AND HOW MANY ARE *US?*
AT OUR LAST COUNT, OVER THREE HUNDRED.
THREE HUNDRED?!
I THINK THE EXACT COUNT IS THREE HUNDRED NINETEEN NOW WITH YOU AND CLAIRE. IT'S A BIG NUMBER WHEN I STOP AND THINK ABOUT IT.
BUT WE'VE SPENT **YEARS** FINDING PEOPLE AND BRINGING THEM TO OUR LITTLE ***ISLAND*** HERE.

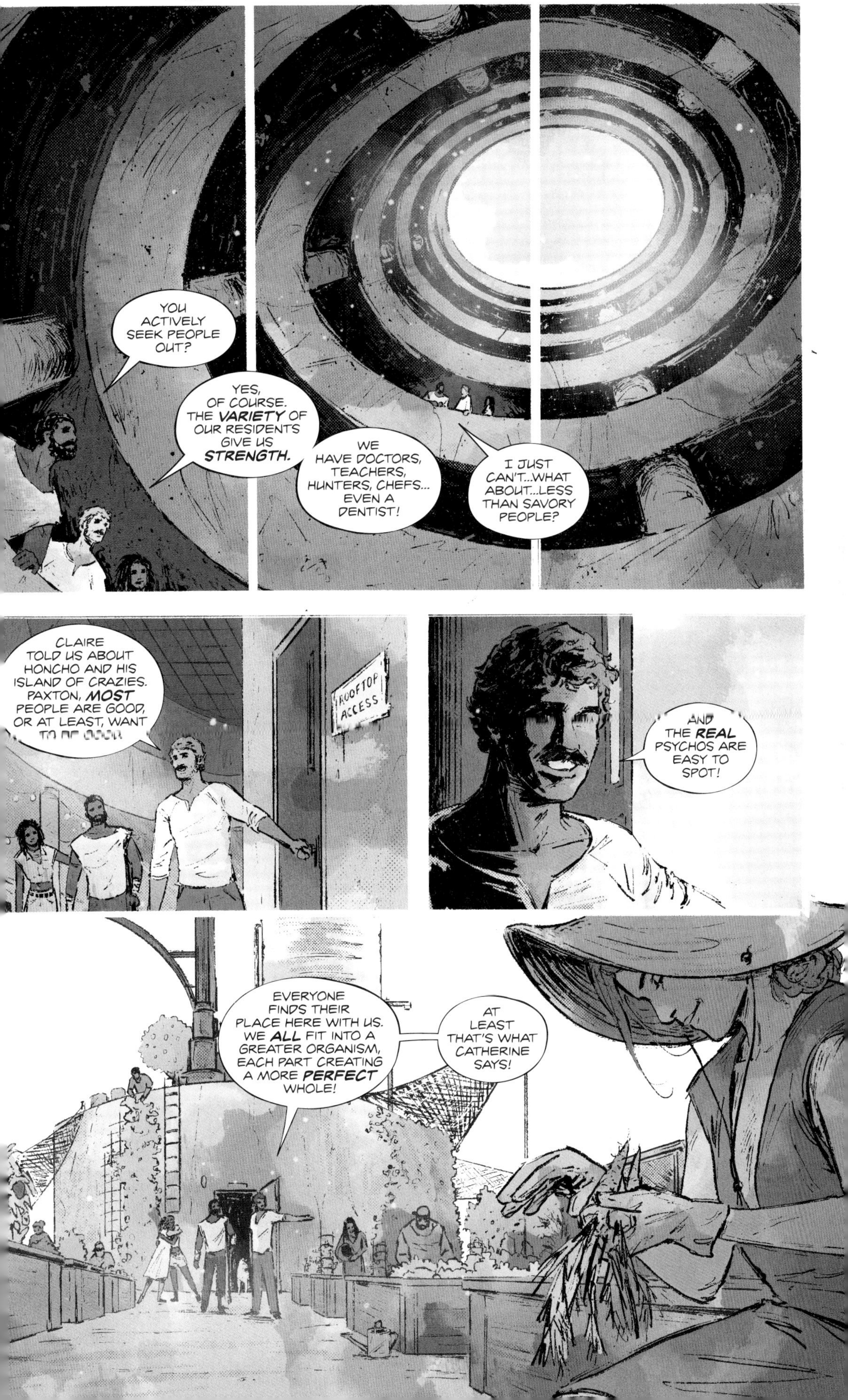
YOU ACTIVELY SEEK PEOPLE OUT?
YES, OF COURSE. THE **VARIETY** OF OUR RESIDENTS GIVE US **STRENGTH.**
WE HAVE DOCTORS, TEACHERS, HUNTERS, CHEFS... EVEN A DENTIST!
I JUST CAN'T...WHAT ABOUT...LESS THAN SAVORY PEOPLE?
CLAIRE TOLD US ABOUT HONCHO AND HIS ISLAND OF CRAZIES. PAXTON, **MOST** PEOPLE ARE GOOD, OR AT LEAST, WANT
ROOFTOP ACCESS
AND THE **REAL** PSYCHOS ARE EASY TO SPOT!
EVERYONE FINDS THEIR PLACE HERE WITH US. WE **ALL** FIT INTO A GREATER ORGANISM, EACH PART CREATING A MORE **PERFECT** WHOLE!
AT LEAST THAT'S WHAT CATHERINE SAYS!

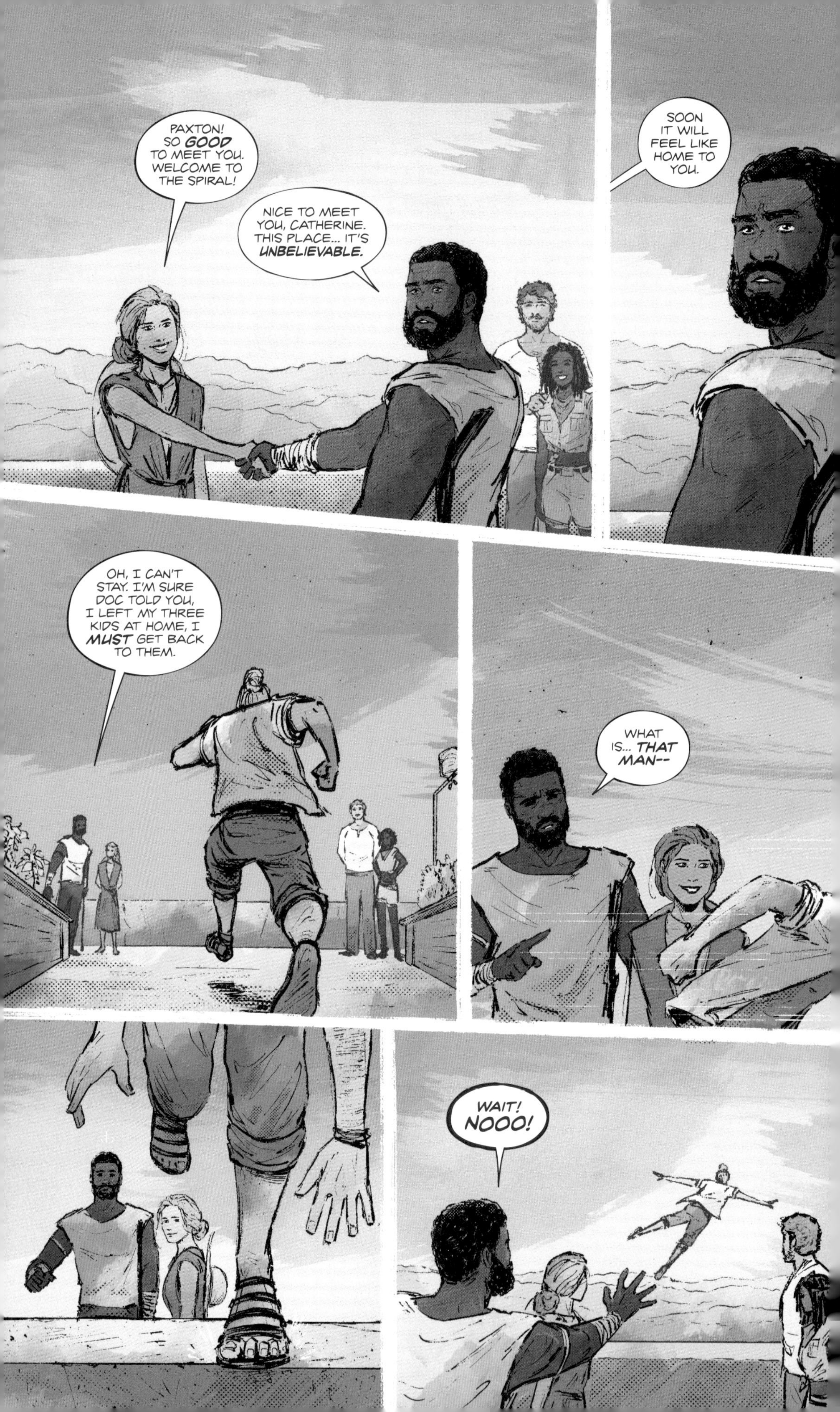
PAXTON! SO GOOD TO MEET YOU. WELCOME TO THE SPIRAL!
NICE TO MEET YOU, CATHERINE. THIS PLACE... IT'S UNBELIEVABLE.
SOON IT WILL FEEL LIKE HOME TO YOU.
OH, I CAN'T STAY. I'M SURE DOC TOLD YOU, I LEFT MY THREE KIDS AT HOME, I MUST GET BACK TO THEM.
WHAT IS... THAT MAN--
WAIT! NOOO!

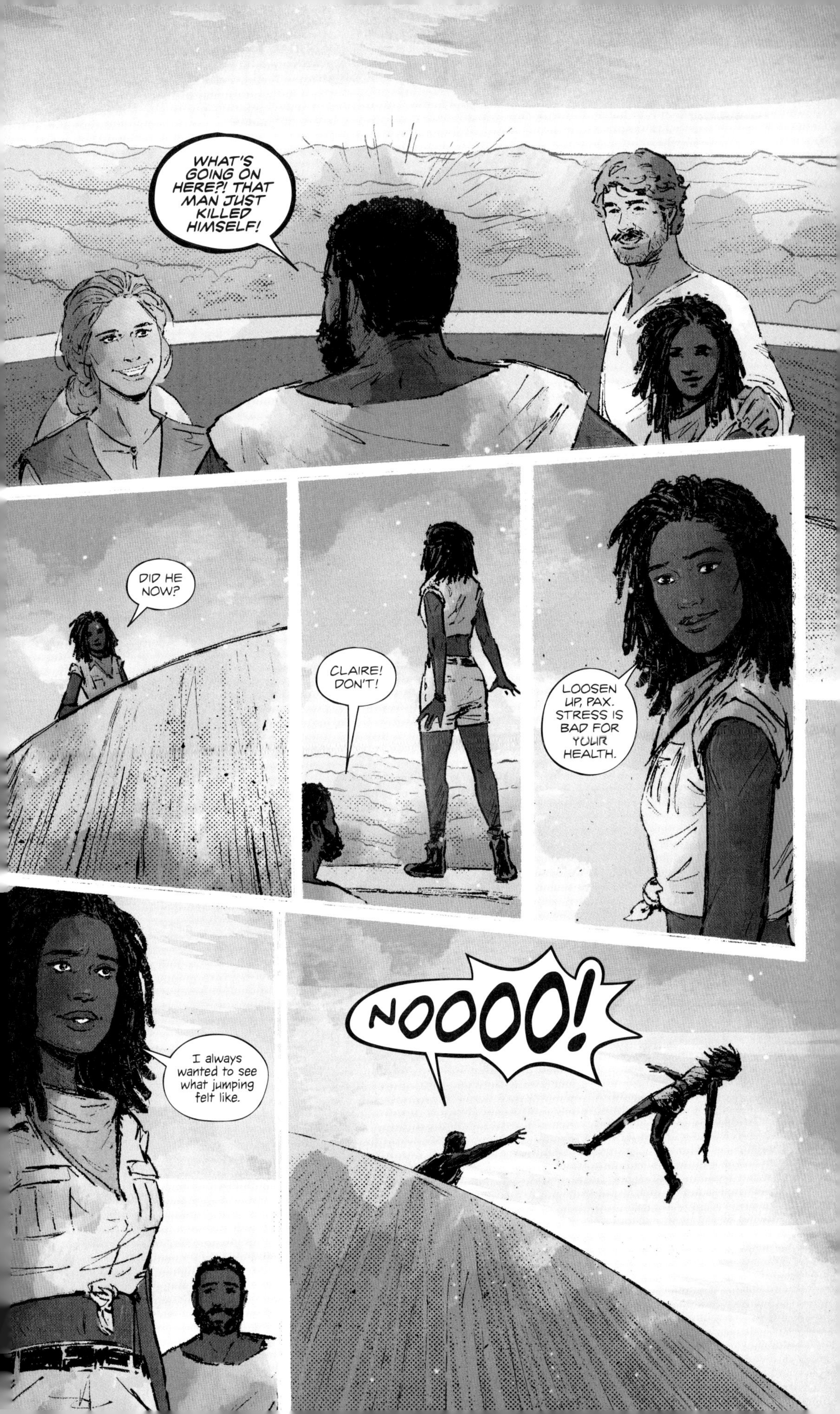
WHAT'S GOING ON HERE?! THAT MAN JUST KILLED HIMSELF!
DID HE NOW?
CLAIRE! DON'T!
LOOSEN UP, PAX. STRESS IS BAD FOR YOUR HEALTH.
I always wanted to see what jumping felt like.
NOOOO!

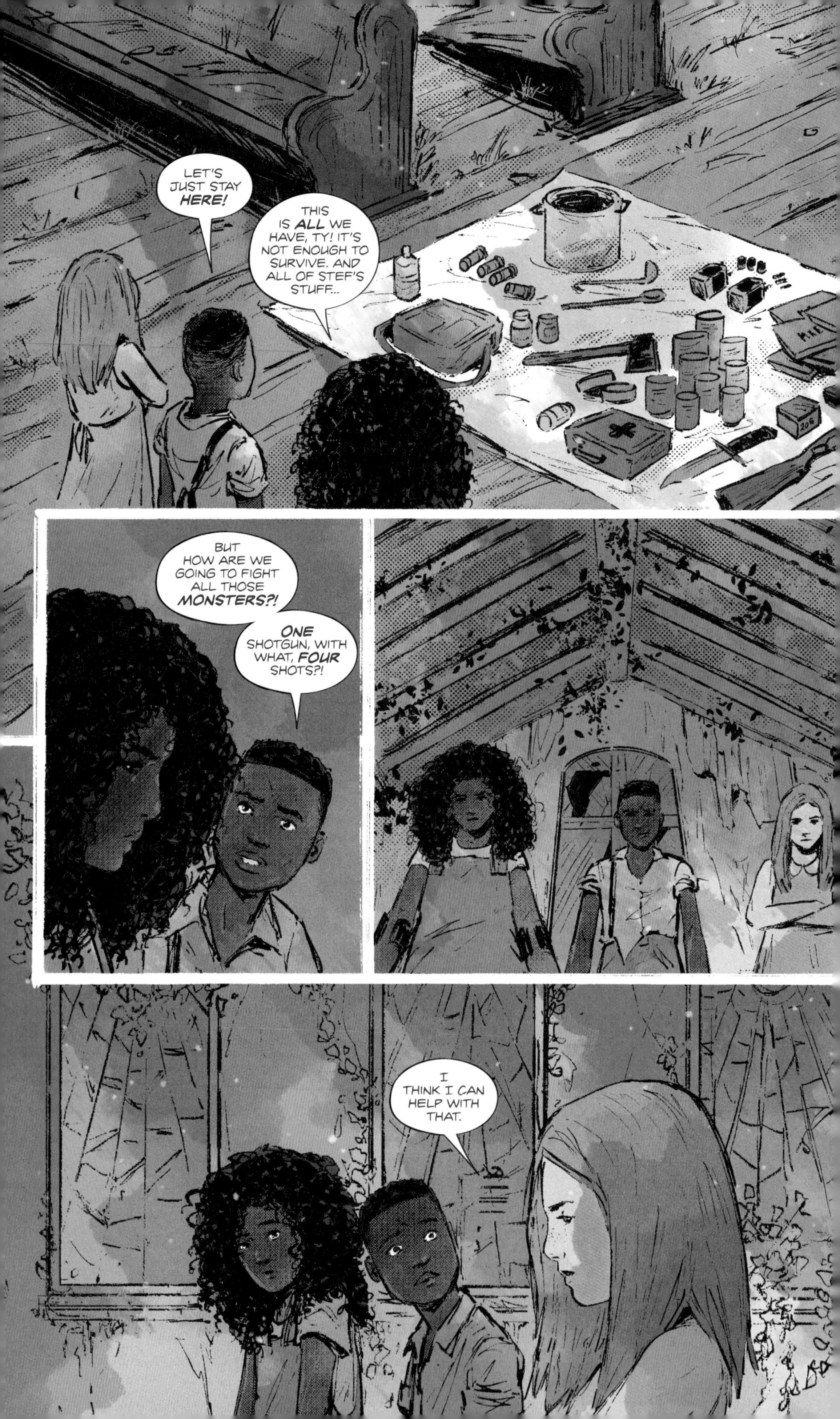
LET'S JUST STAY HERE!
THIS IS ALL WE HAVE, TY! IT'S NOT ENOUGH TO SURVIVE. AND ALL OF STEF'S STUFF...
BUT HOW ARE WE GOING TO FIGHT ALL THOSE MONSTERS?!
ONE SHOTGUN, WITH WHAT, FOUR SHOTS?!
I THINK I CAN HELP WITH THAT.

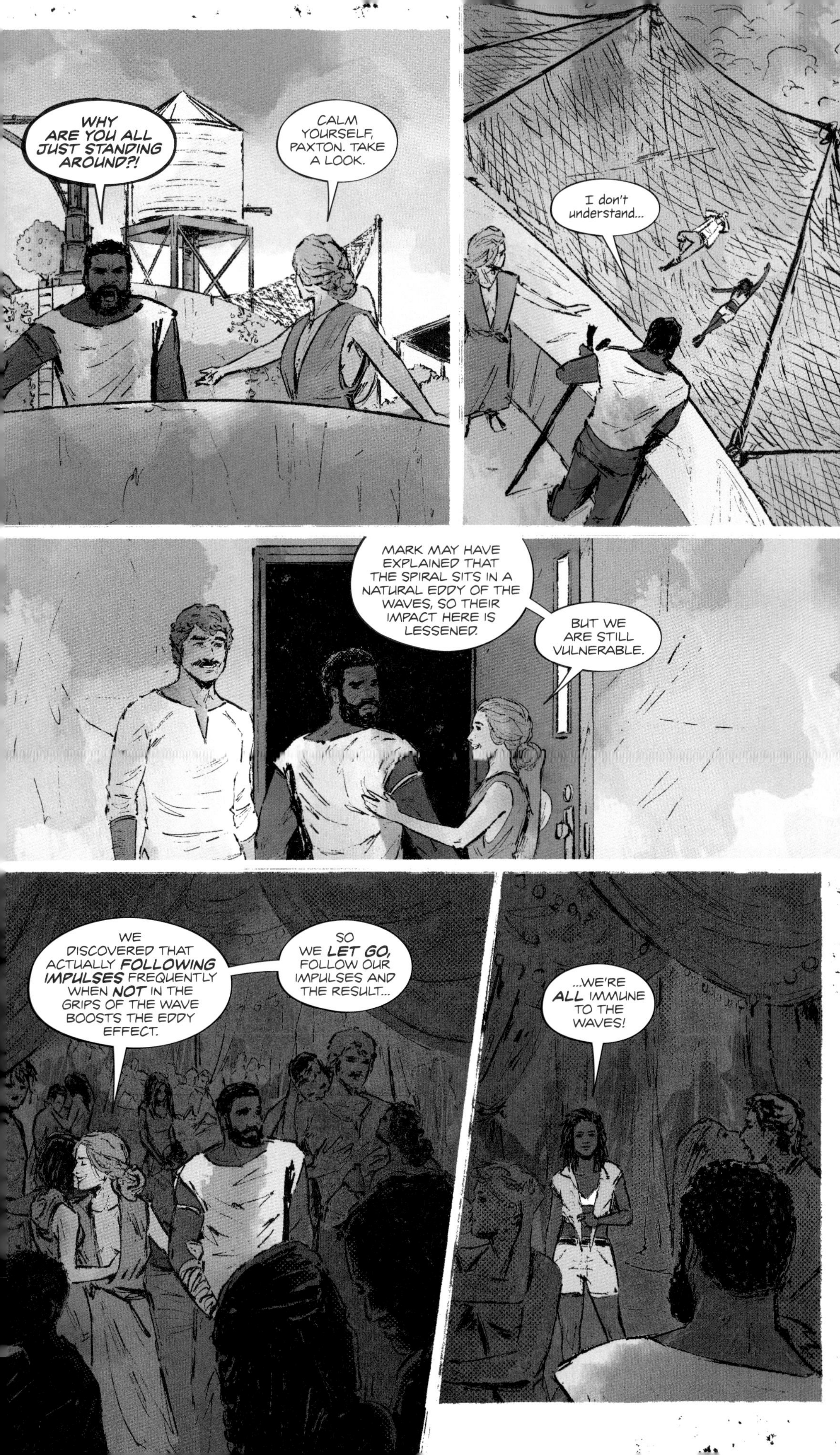
WHY ARE YOU ALL JUST STANDING AROUND?!
CALM YOURSELF, PAXTON. TAKE A LOOK.
I don't understand...
MARK MAY HAVE EXPLAINED THAT THE SPIRAL SITS IN A NATURAL EDDY OF THE WAVES, SO THEIR IMPACT HERE IS LESSENED.
BUT WE ARE STILL VULNERABLE.
WE DISCOVERED THAT ACTUALLY FOLLOWING IMPULSES FREQUENTLY WHEN NOT IN THE GRIPS OF THE WAVE BOOSTS THE EDDY EFFECT.
SO WE LET GO, FOLLOW OUR IMPULSES AND THE RESULT...
...WE'RE ALL IMMUNE TO THE WAVES!

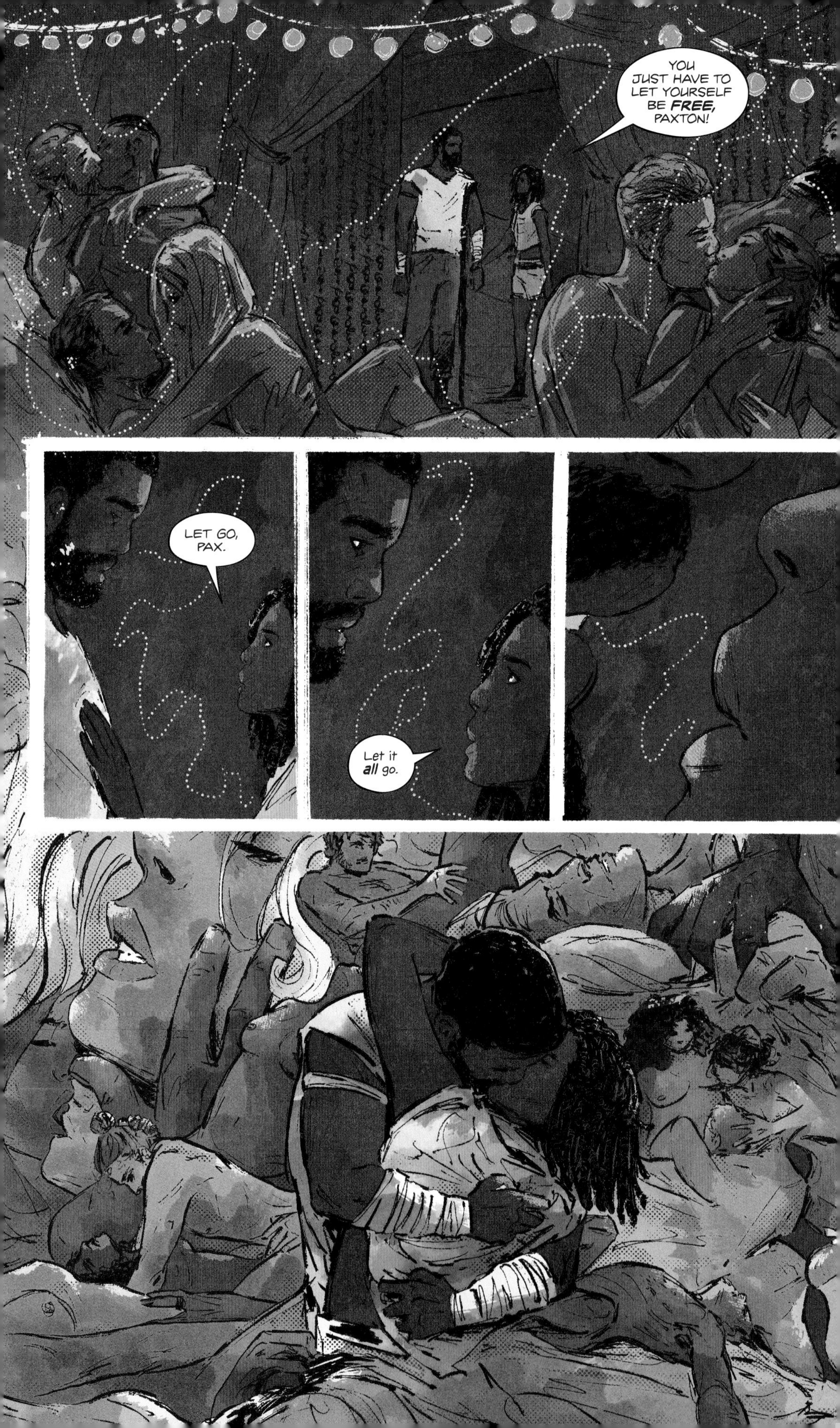
YOU JUST HAVE TO LET YOURSELF BE ***FREE,*** PAXTON!
LET GO, PAX.
Let it ***all*** go.

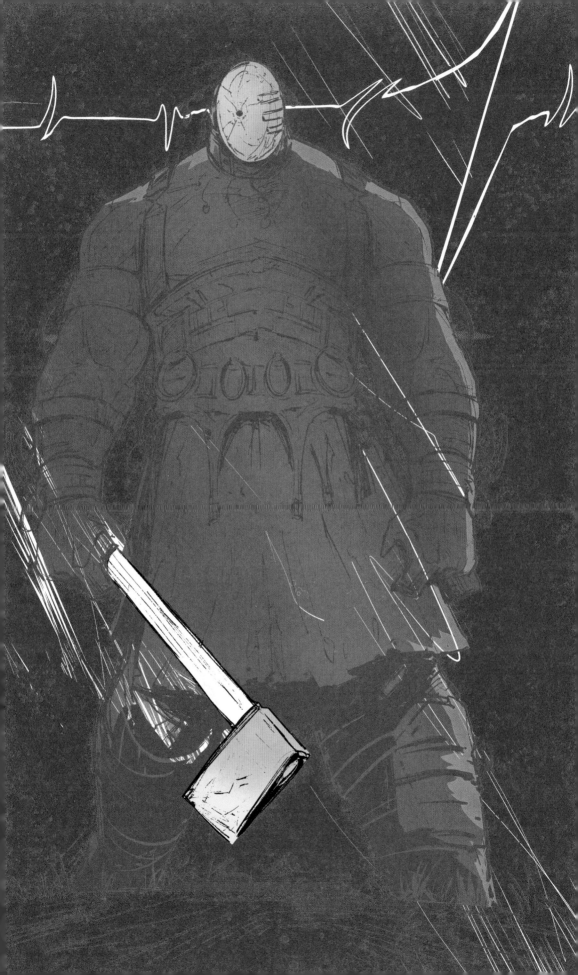

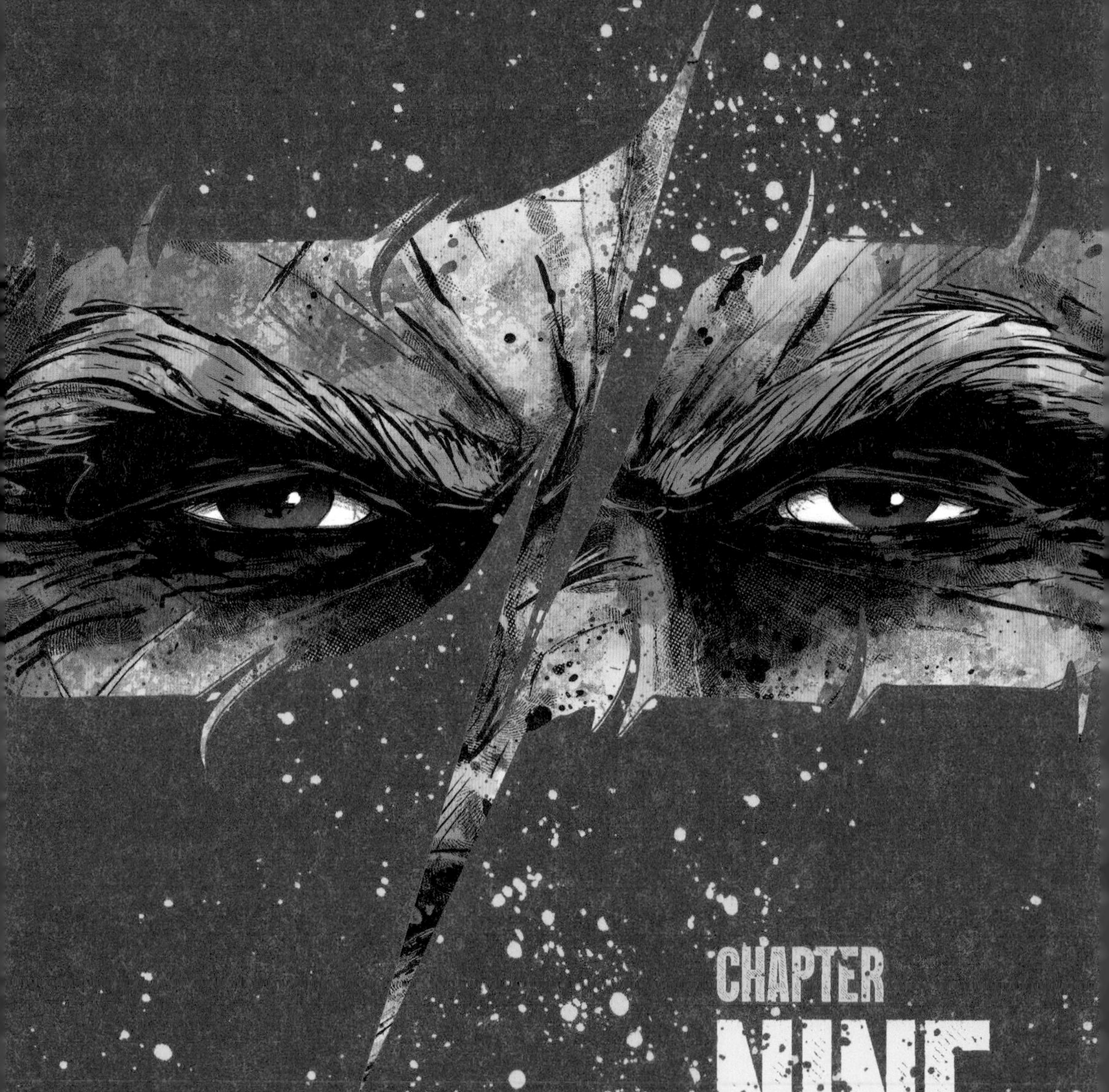

CHAPTER NINE

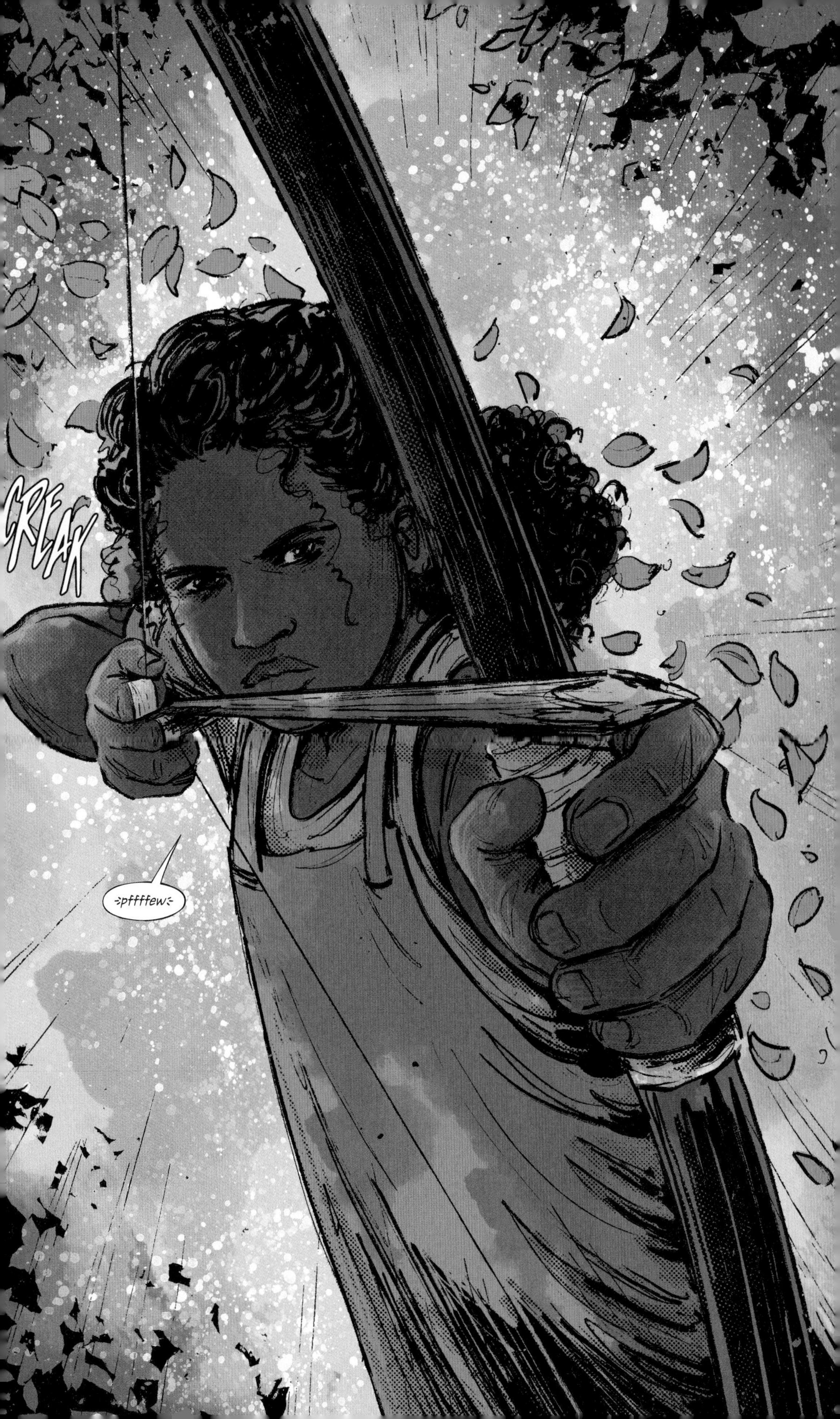
CREAK
pffffew

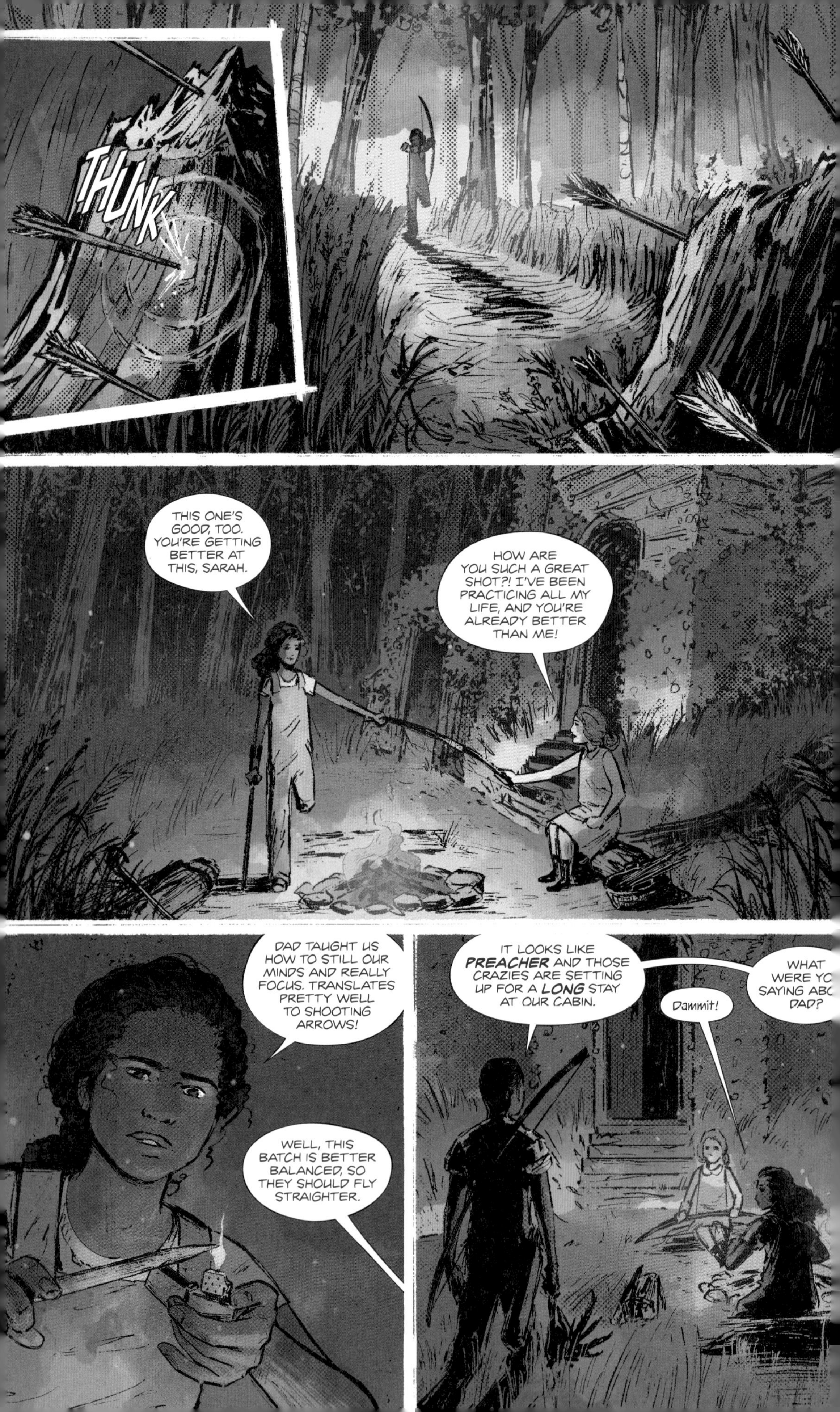
THUNK
THIS ONE'S GOOD, TOO. YOU'RE GETTING BETTER AT THIS, SARAH.
HOW ARE YOU SUCH A GREAT SHOT?! I'VE BEEN PRACTICING ALL MY LIFE, AND YOU'RE ALREADY BETTER THAN ME!
DAD TAUGHT US HOW TO STILL OUR MINDS AND REALLY FOCUS. TRANSLATES PRETTY WELL TO SHOOTING ARROWS!
WELL, THIS BATCH IS BETTER BALANCED, SO THEY SHOULD FLY STRAIGHTER.
IT LOOKS LIKE **PREACHER** AND THOSE CRAZIES ARE SETTING UP FOR A **LONG** STAY AT OUR CABIN.
Dammit!

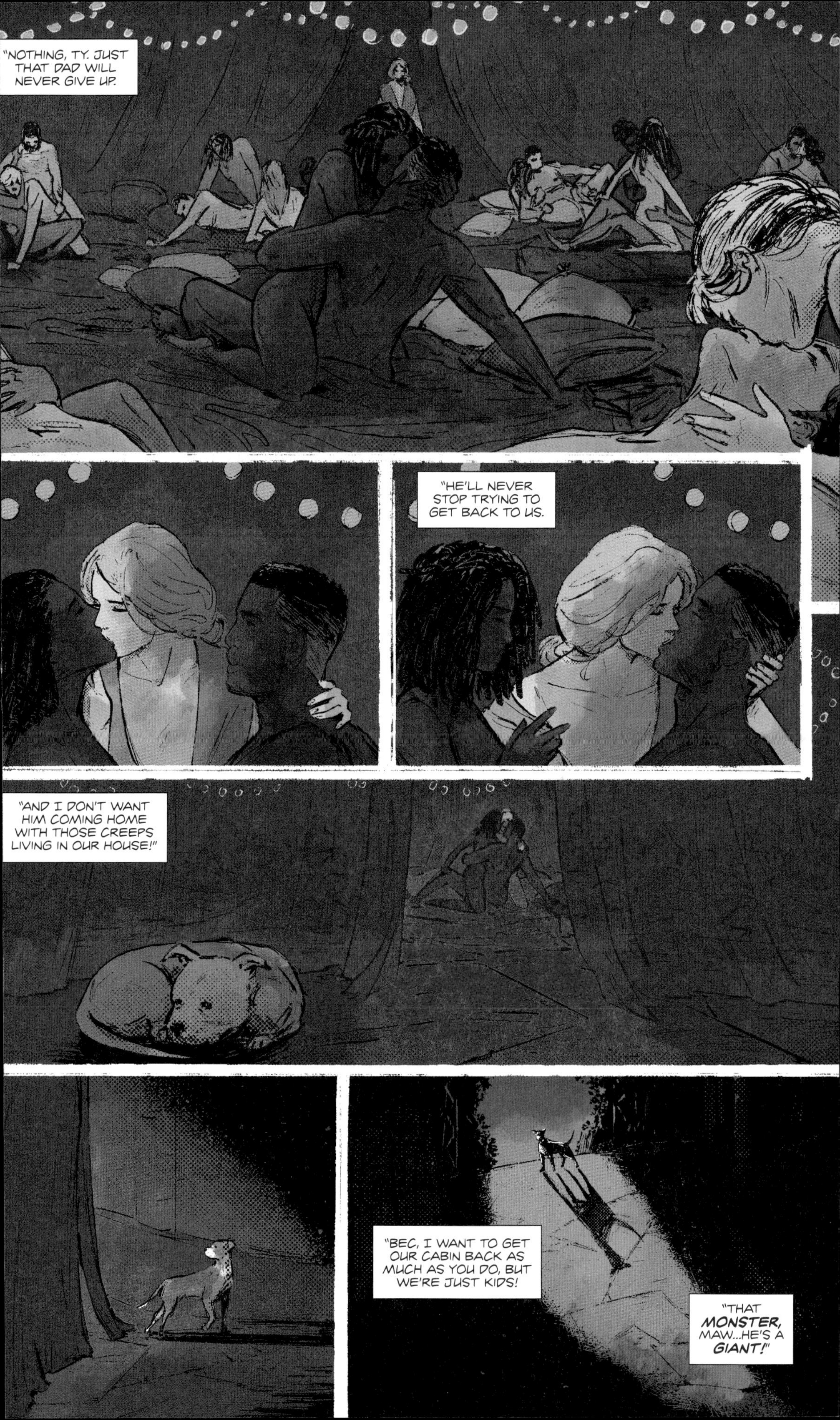
"NOTHING, TY. JUST THAT DAD WILL NEVER GIVE UP.
"HE'LL NEVER STOP TRYING TO GET BACK TO US.
"AND I DON'T WANT HIM COMING HOME WITH THOSE CREEPS LIVING IN OUR HOUSE!"
"BEC, I WANT TO GET OUR CABIN BACK AS MUCH AS YOU DO, BUT WE'RE JUST KIDS!
"THAT MONSTER, MAW...HE'S A GIANT!"

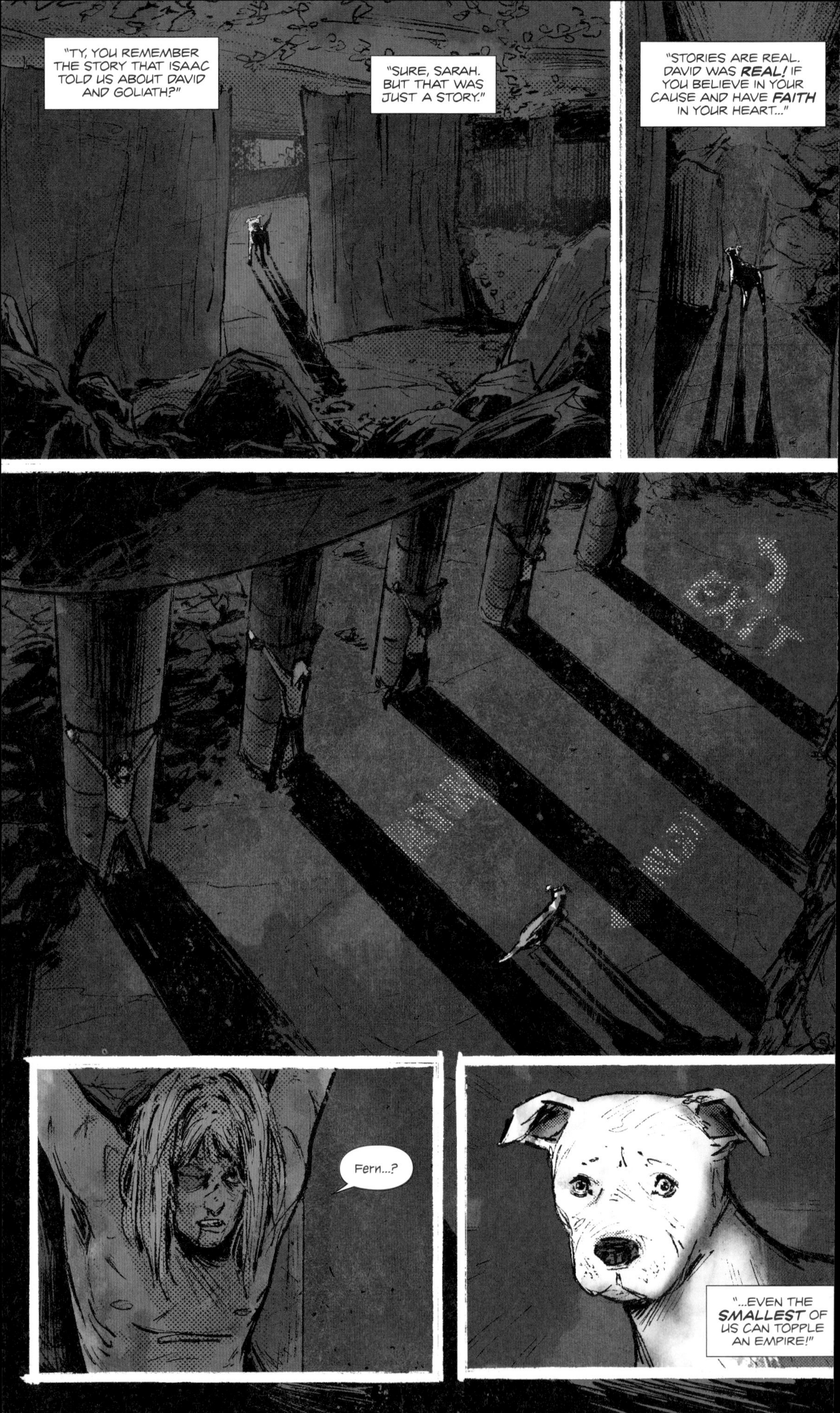
"TY, YOU REMEMBER THE STORY THAT ISAAC TOLD US ABOUT DAVID AND GOLIATH?"
"SURE, SARAH. BUT THAT WAS JUST A STORY."
"STORIES ARE REAL. DAVID WAS **REAL!** IF YOU BELIEVE IN YOUR CAUSE AND HAVE **FAITH** IN YOUR HEART..."
Fern...?
"...EVEN THE **SMALLEST** OF US CAN TOPPLE AN EMPIRE!"

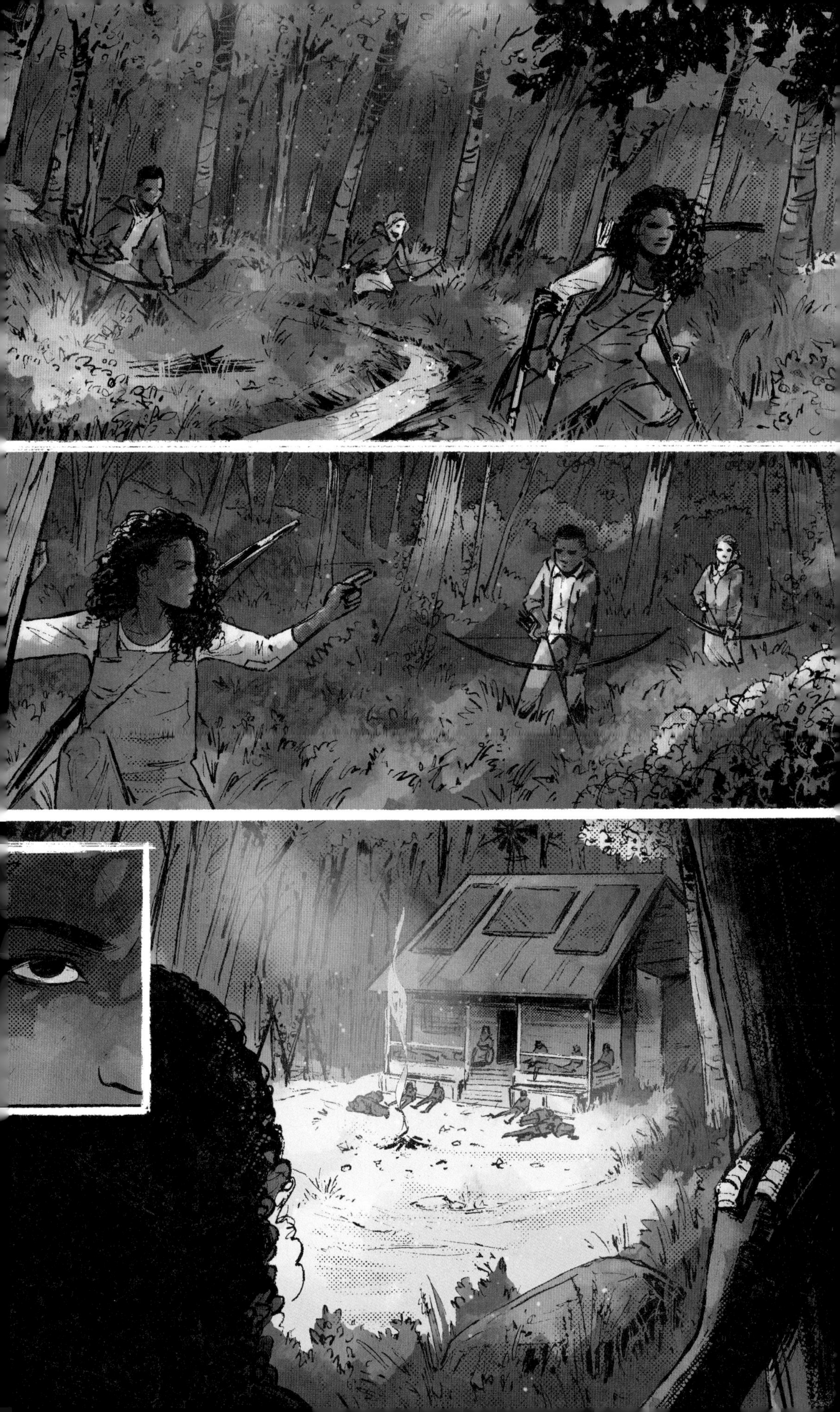

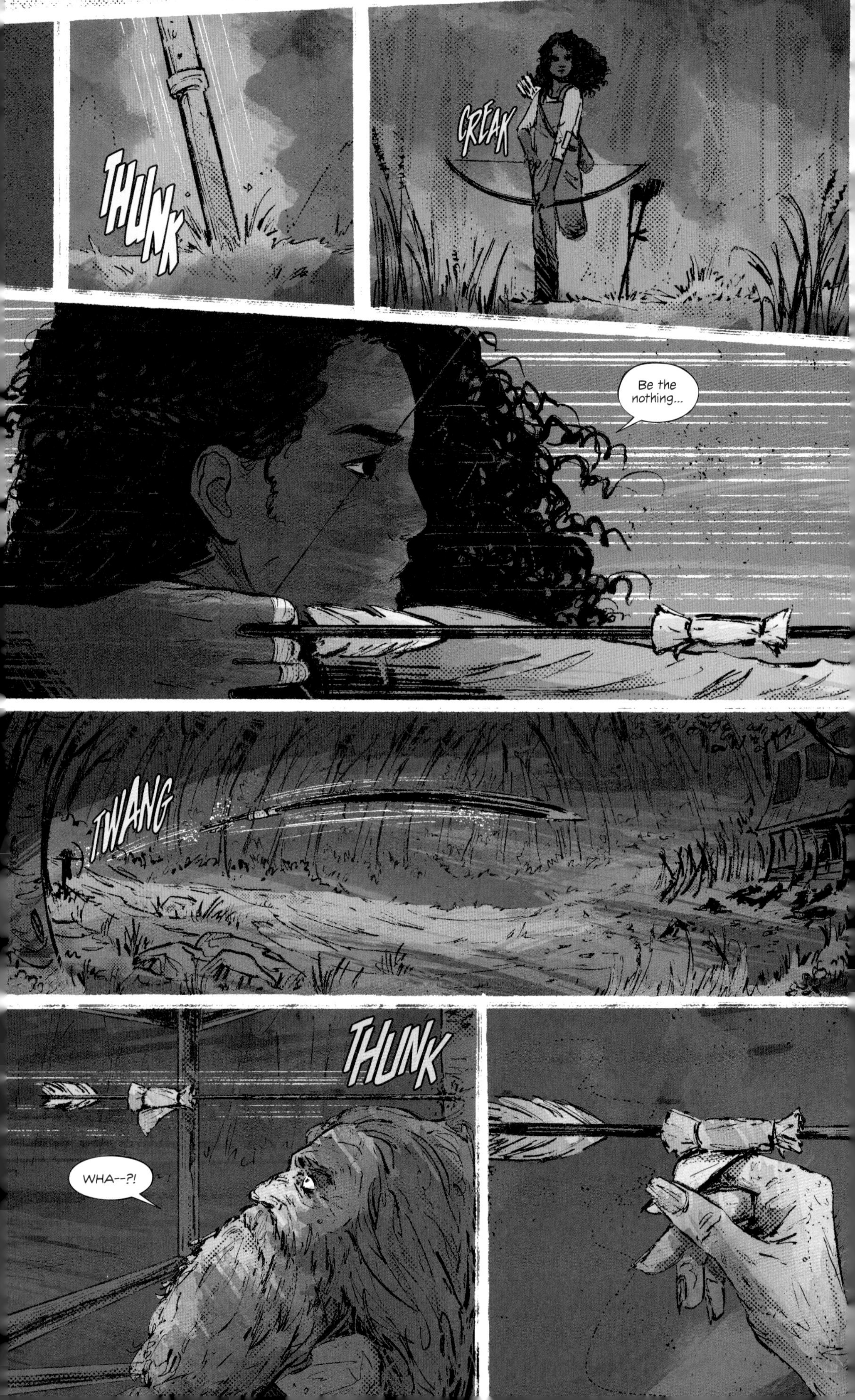
THUNK
CREAK
Be the nothing...
TWANG
THUNK
WHA--?!

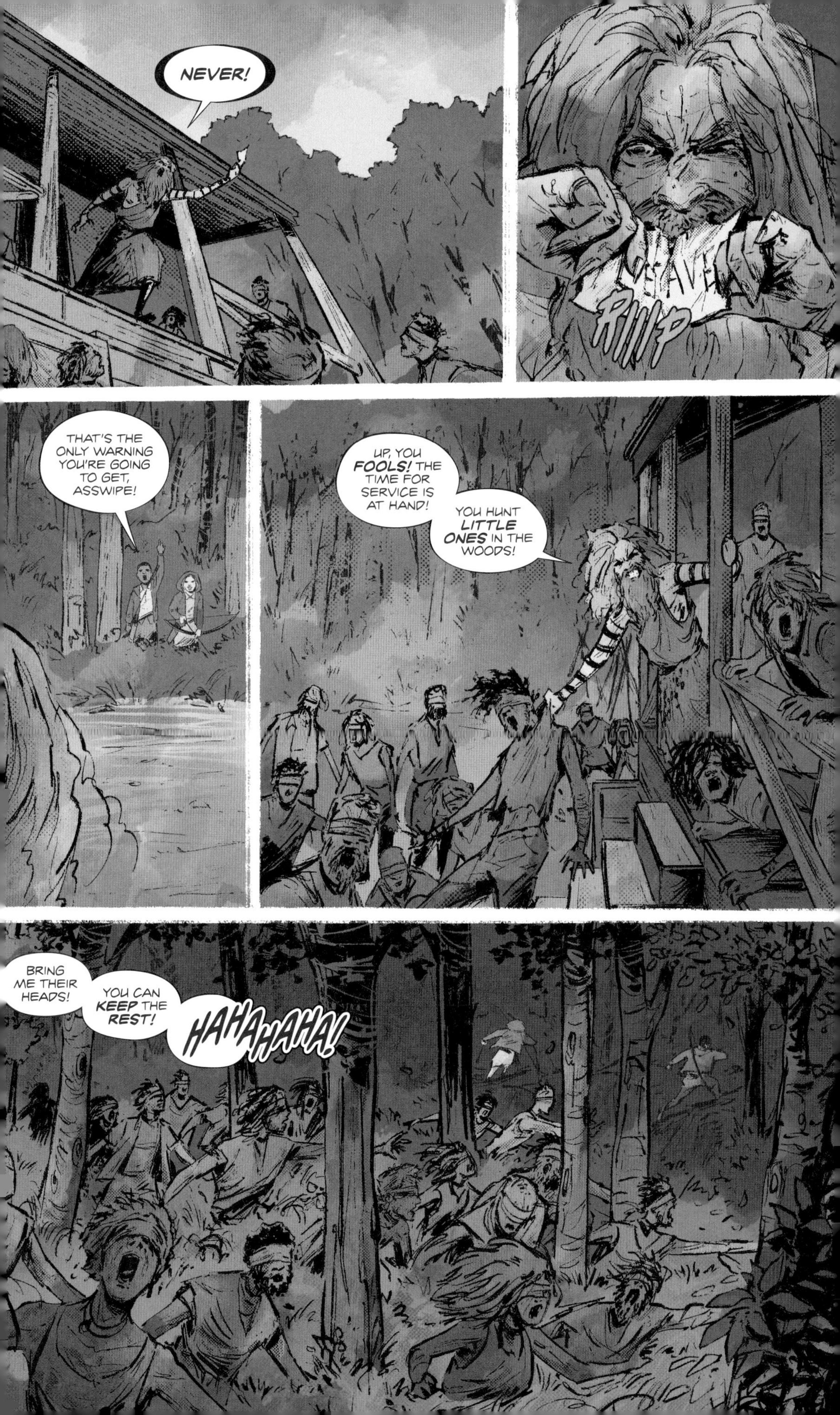

NEVER!
LEAVE
RIIIP
THAT'S THE ONLY WARNING YOU'RE GOING TO GET, ASSWIPE!
UP, YOU FOOLS! THE TIME FOR SERVICE IS AT HAND!
YOU HUNT LITTLE ONES IN THE WOODS!
BRING ME THEIR HEADS!
YOU CAN KEEP THE REST!
HAHAHAHA!

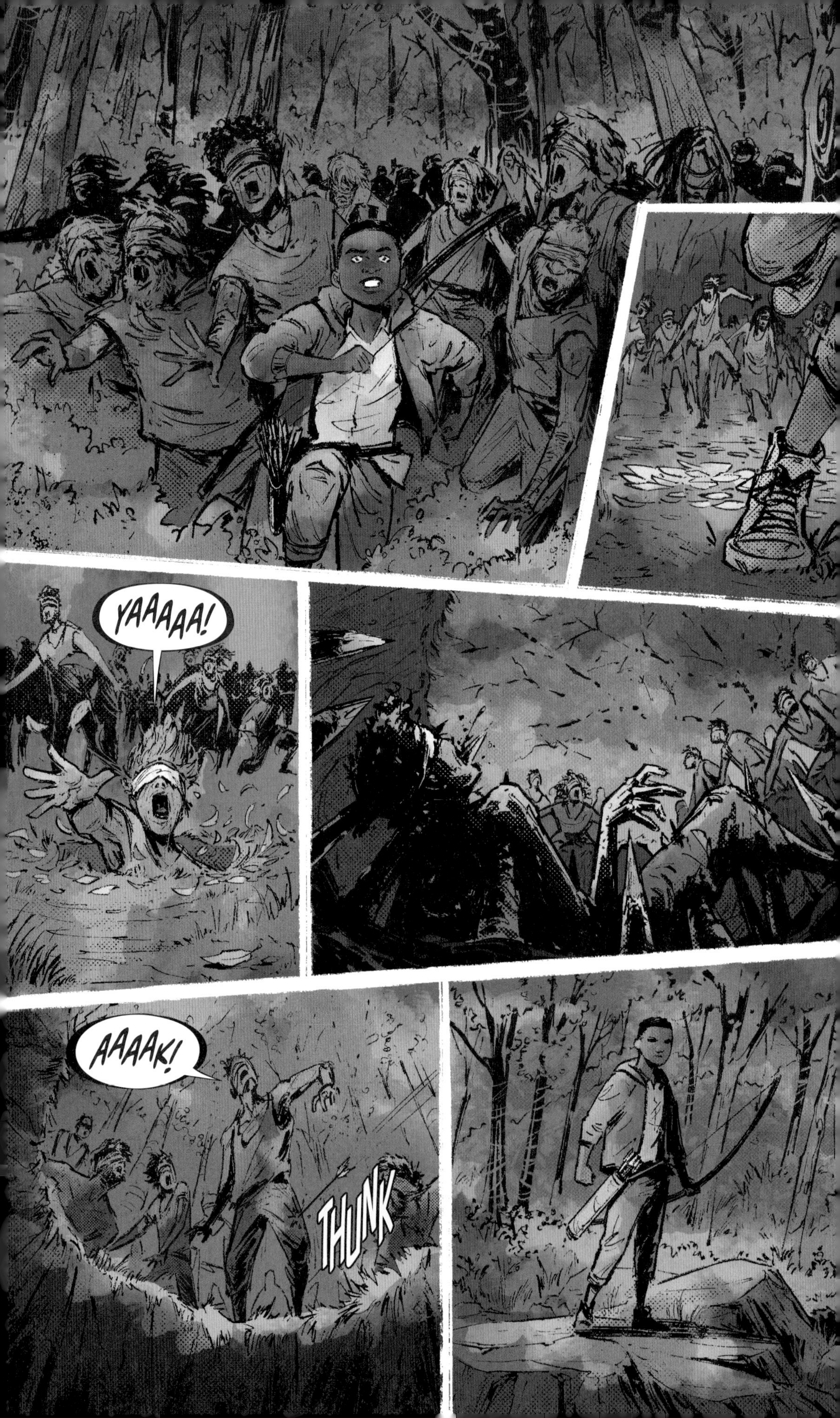
YAAAAA!
AAAAK!
THUNK

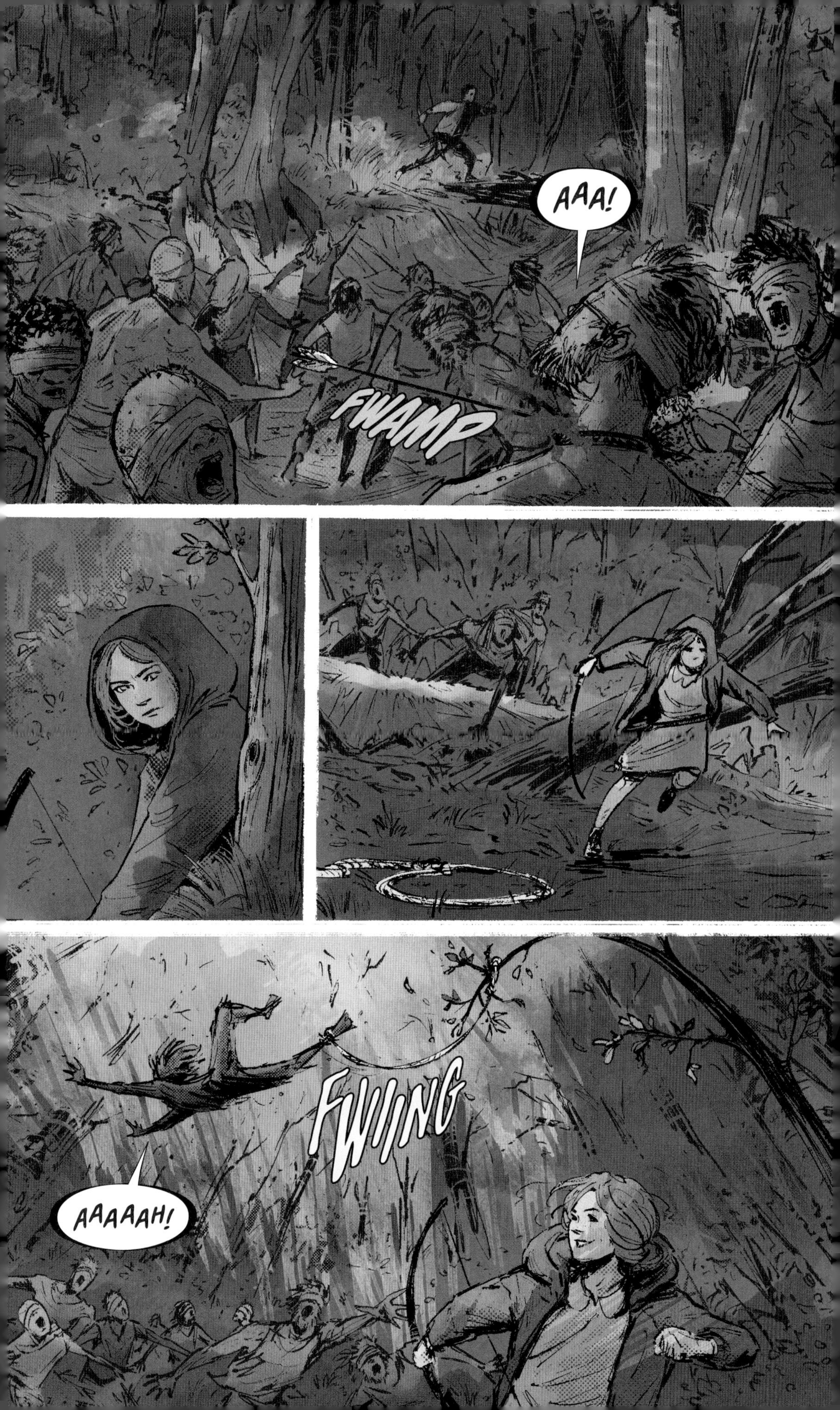
AAA!
FWAMP
FWIING
AAAAAH!

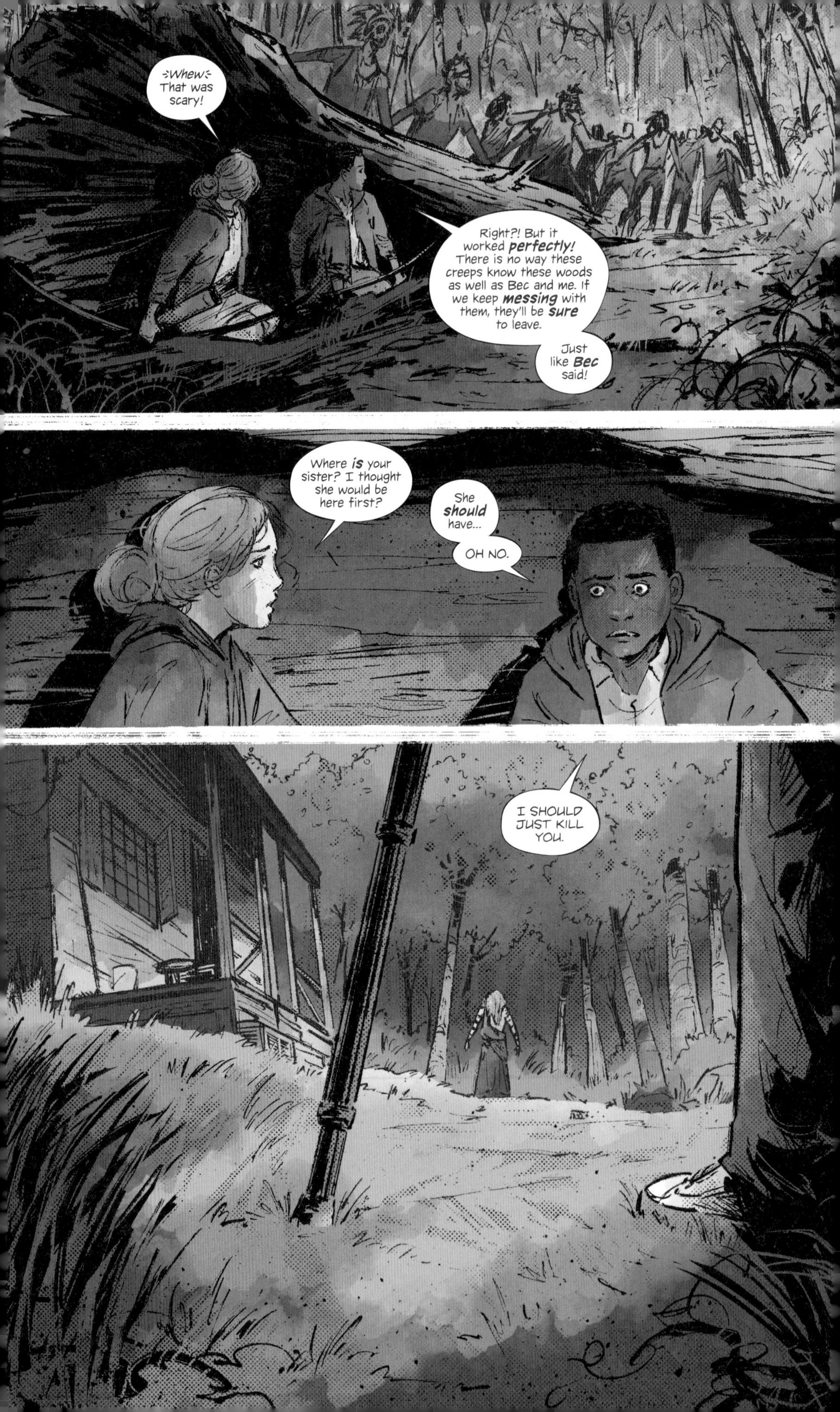
Whew That was scary!
Right?! But it worked perfectly! There is no way these creeps know these woods as well as Bec and me. If we keep messing with them, they'll be sure to leave.
Just like Bec said!
Where is your sister? I thought she would be here first?
She should have...
OH NO.
I SHOULD JUST KILL YOU.

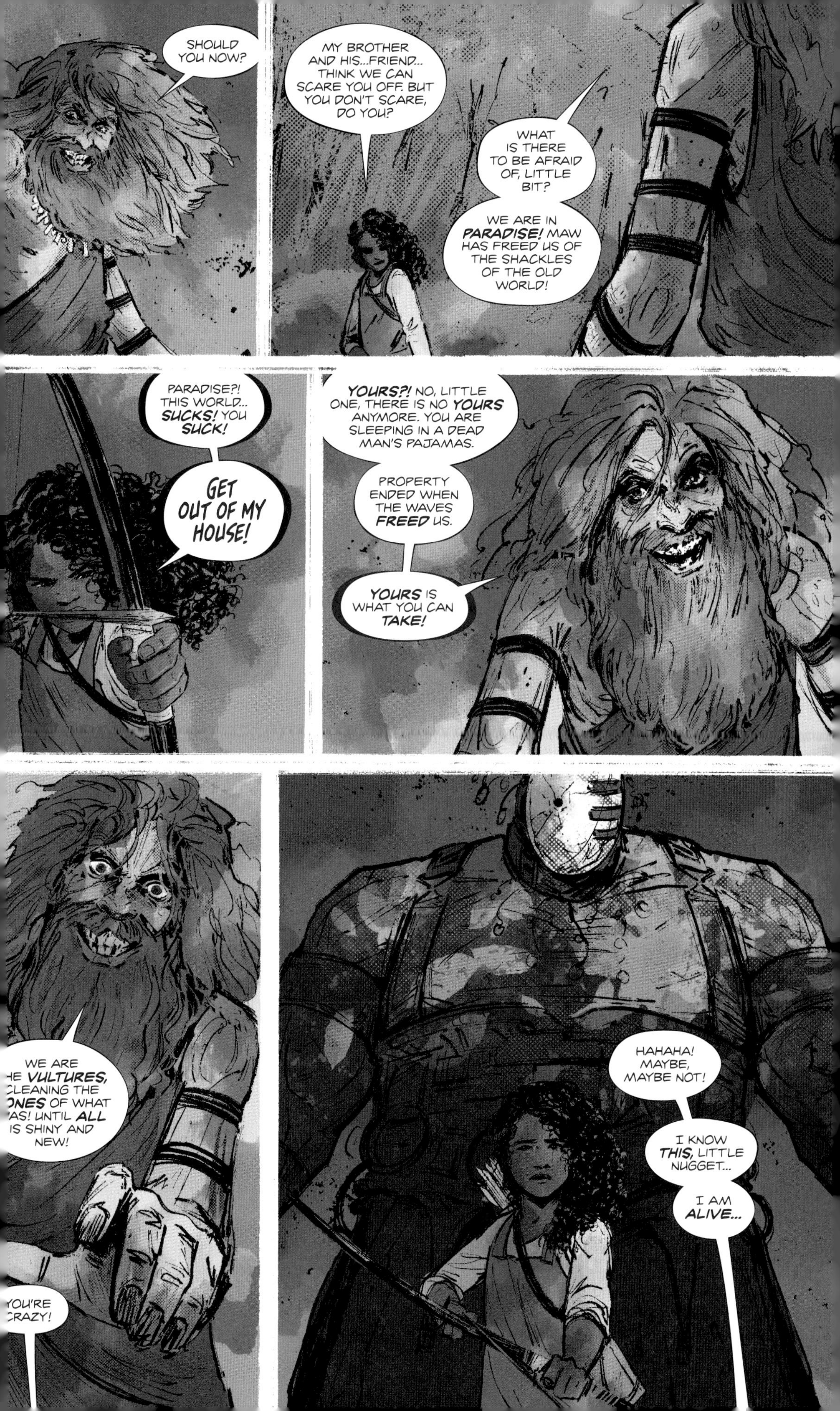

SHOULD YOU NOW?
MY BROTHER AND HIS...FRIEND... THINK WE CAN SCARE YOU OFF. BUT YOU DON'T SCARE, DO YOU?
WHAT IS THERE TO BE AFRAID OF, LITTLE BIT?
WE ARE IN **PARADISE!** MAW HAS FREED US OF THE SHACKLES OF THE OLD WORLD!
PARADISE?! THIS WORLD... **SUCKS!** YOU **SUCK!**
GET OUT OF MY HOUSE!
YOURS?! NO, LITTLE ONE, THERE IS NO **YOURS** ANYMORE. YOU ARE SLEEPING IN A DEAD MAN'S PAJAMAS.
PROPERTY ENDED WHEN THE WAVES **FREED** US.
YOURS IS WHAT YOU CAN **TAKE!**
WE ARE HE **VULTURES,** CLEANING THE ONES OF WHAT AS! UNTIL **ALL** IS SHINY AND NEW!
YOU'RE CRAZY!
HAHAHA! MAYBE, MAYBE NOT!
I KNOW **THIS,** LITTLE NUGGET...
I AM **ALIVE...**

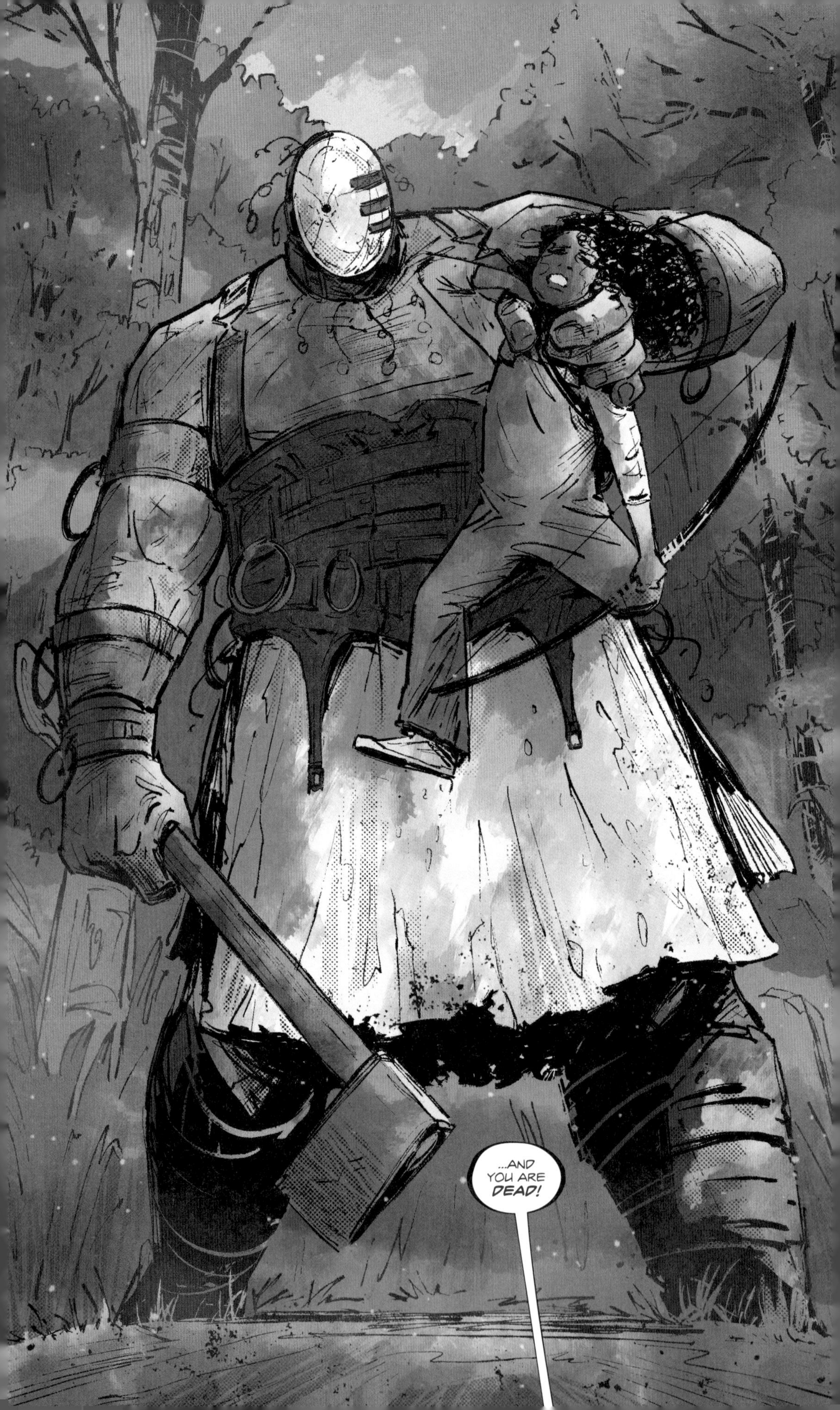
...AND YOU ARE DEAD!

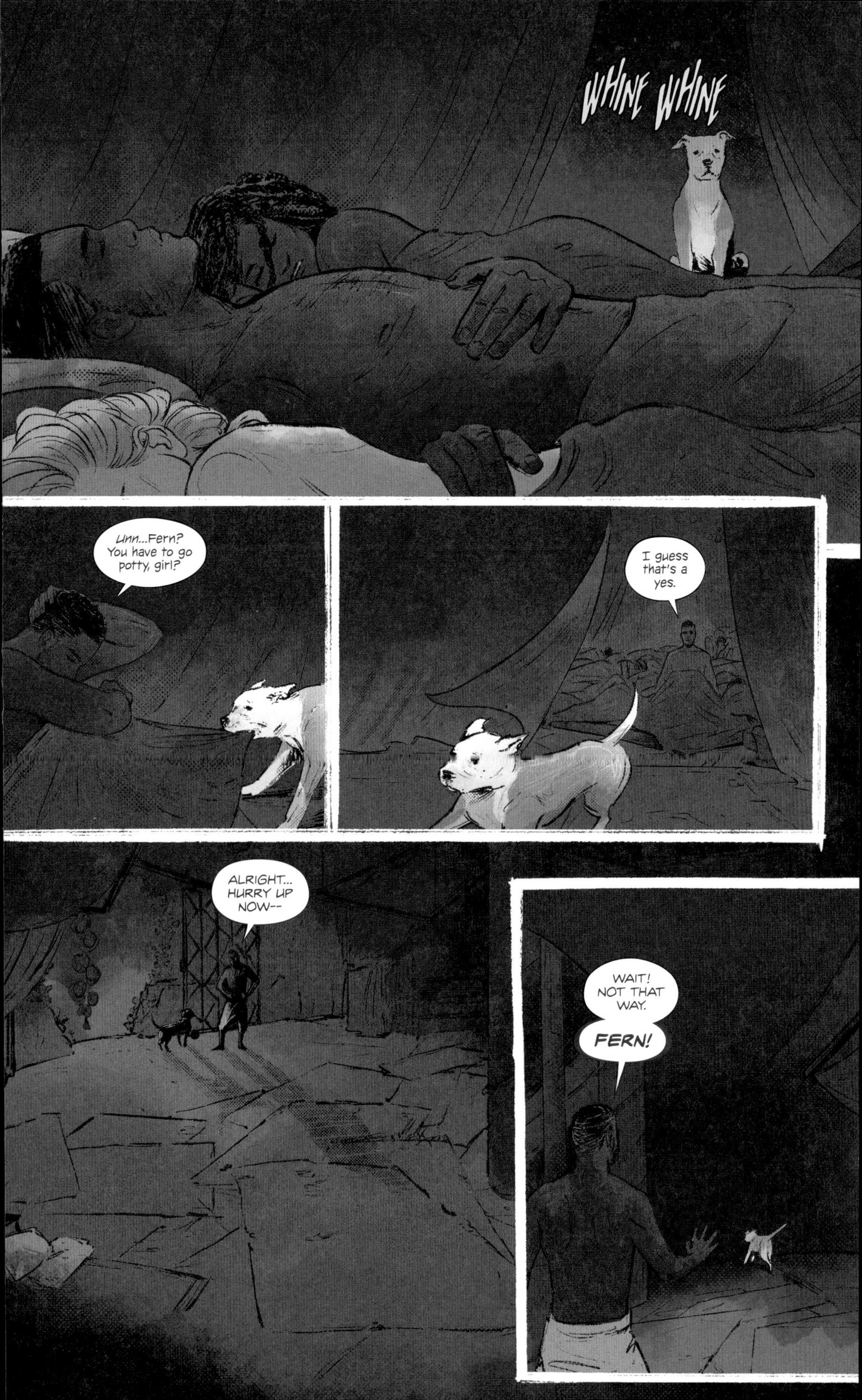
WHINE WHINE
Unn...Fern? You have to go potty, girl?
I guess that's a yes.
ALRIGHT... HURRY UP NOW--
WAIT! NOT THAT WAY.
FERN!

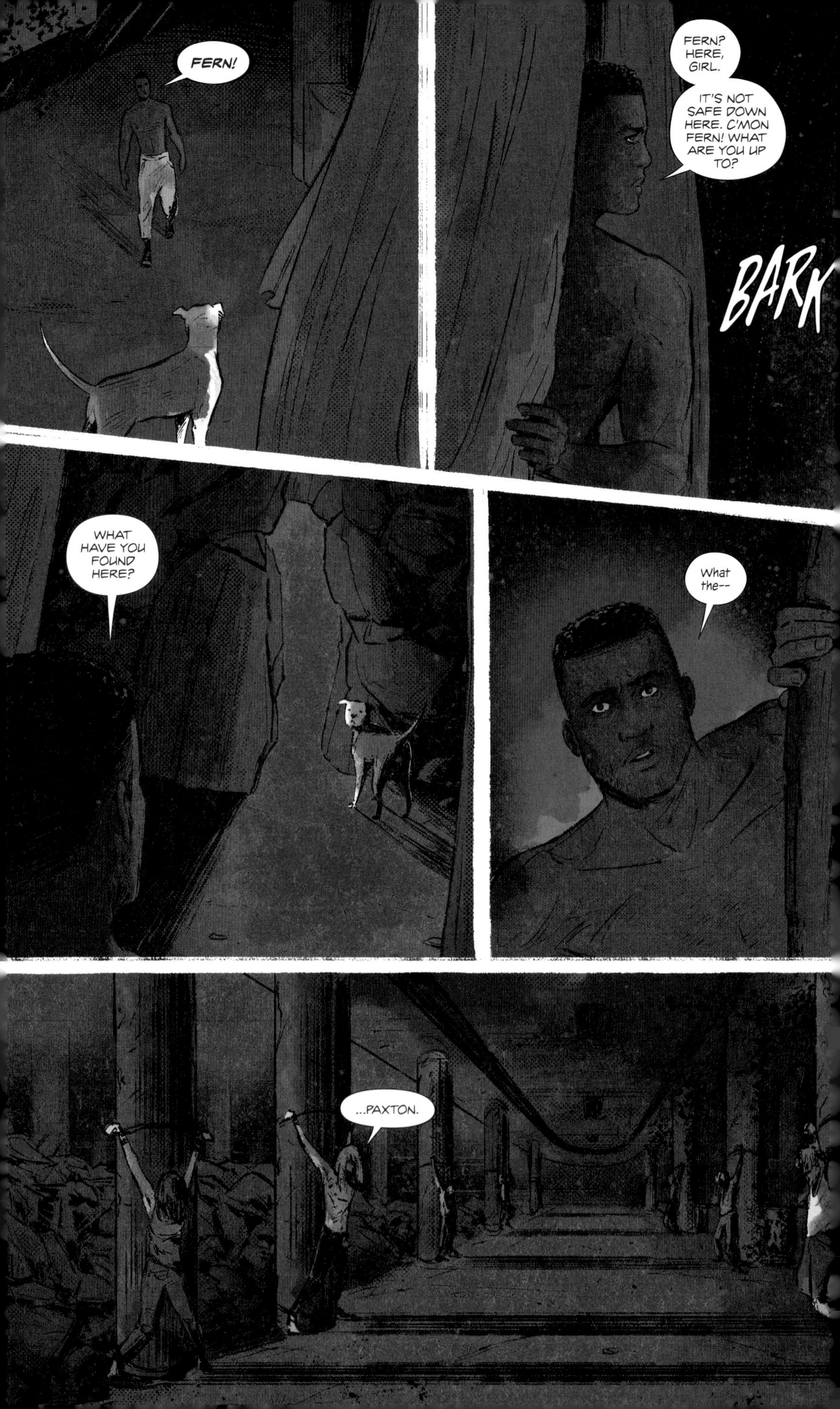
FERN!
FERN? HERE, GIRL.
IT'S NOT SAFE DOWN HERE. C'MON FERN! WHAT ARE YOU UP TO?
BARK
WHAT HAVE YOU FOUND HERE?
What the--
...PAXTON.

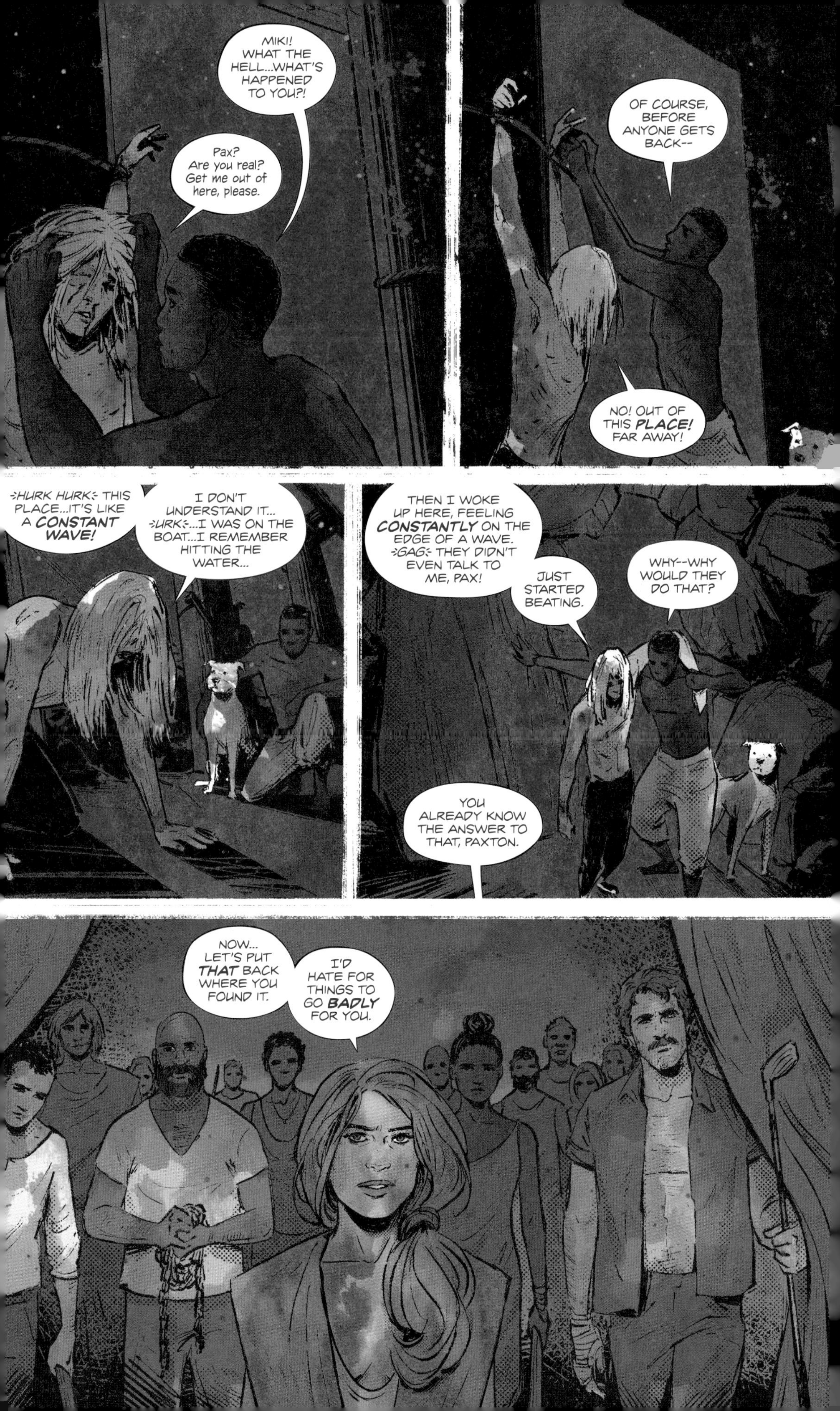
MIKI! WHAT THE HELL...WHAT'S HAPPENED TO YOU?!
Pax? Are you real? Get me out of here, please.
OF COURSE, BEFORE ANYONE GETS BACK--
NO! OUT OF THIS PLACE! FAR AWAY!
-HURK HURK- THIS PLACE...IT'S LIKE A CONSTANT WAVE!
I DON'T UNDERSTAND IT... -URK-...I WAS ON THE BOAT...I REMEMBER HITTING THE WATER...
THEN I WOKE UP HERE, FEELING CONSTANTLY ON THE EDGE OF A WAVE. -GAG- THEY DIDN'T EVEN TALK TO ME, PAX!
JUST STARTED BEATING.
WHY--WHY WOULD THEY DO THAT?
YOU ALREADY KNOW THE ANSWER TO THAT, PAXTON.
NOW... LET'S PUT THAT BACK WHERE YOU FOUND IT.
I'D HATE FOR THINGS TO GO BADLY FOR YOU.

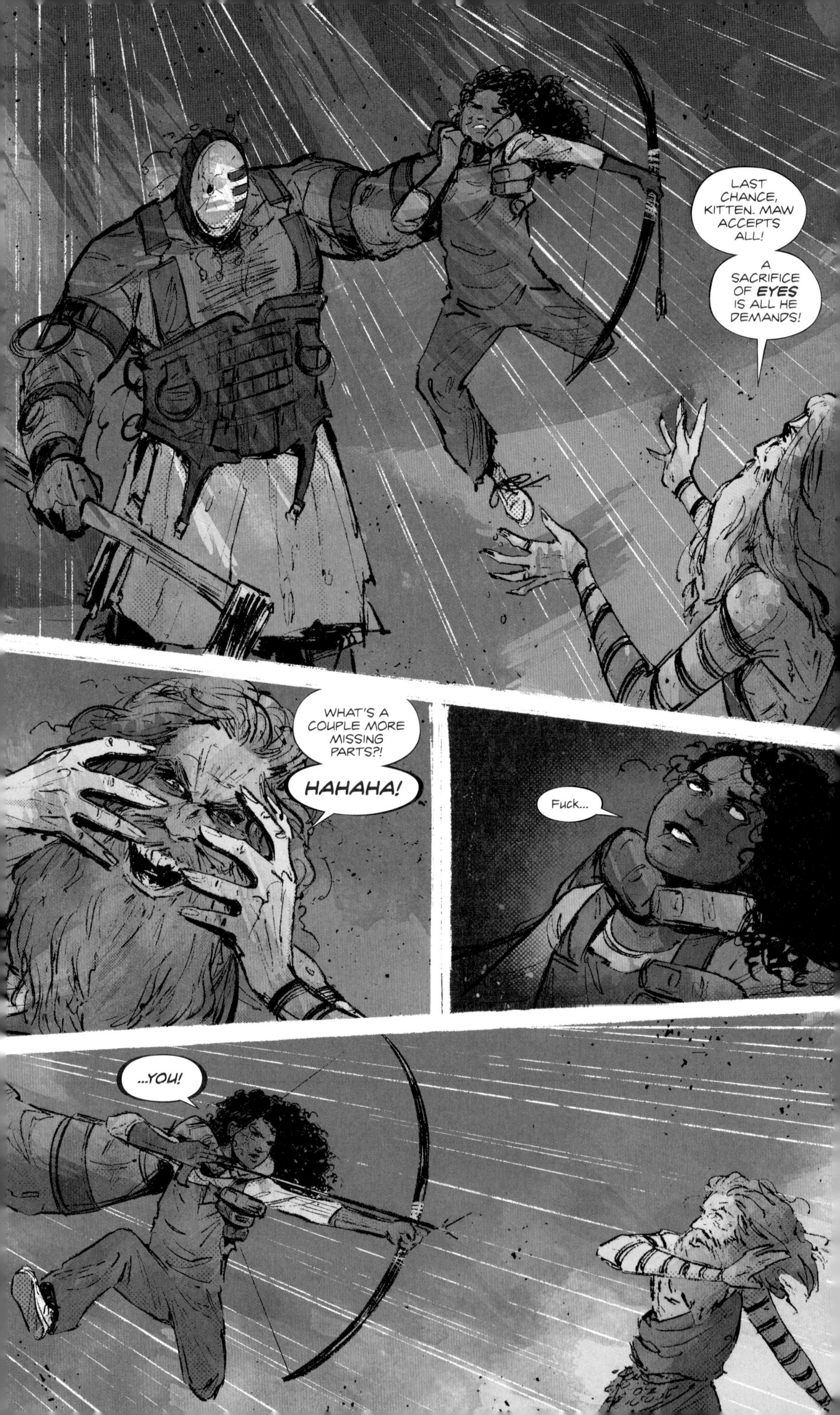
LAST CHANCE, KITTEN. MAW ACCEPTS ALL!
A SACRIFICE OF **EYES** IS ALL HE DEMANDS!
WHAT'S A COUPLE MORE MISSING PARTS?!
HAHAHA!
Fuck...
...YOU!

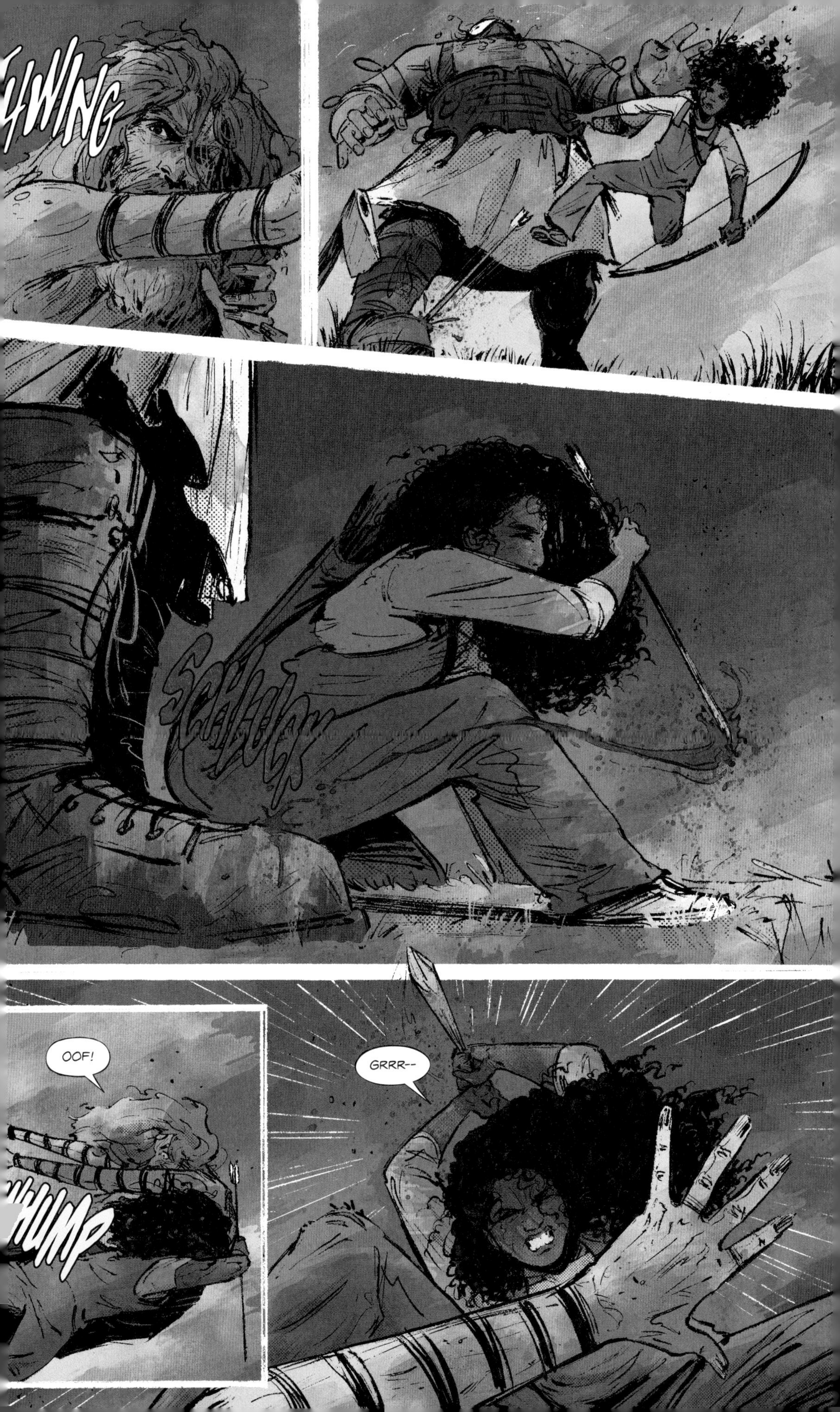
OOF!
GRRR--

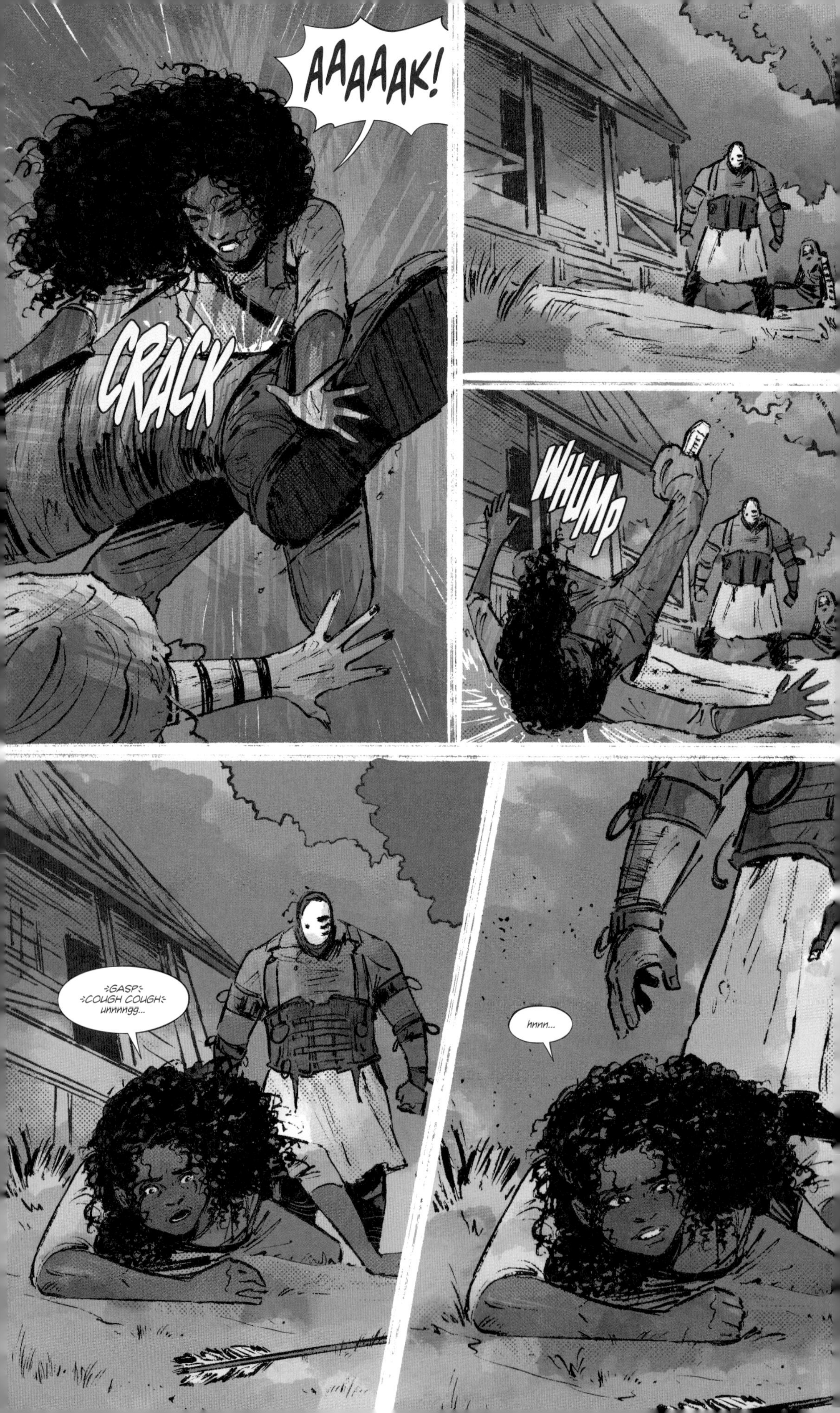
AAAAAK!
CRACK
WHUMP
GASP
COUGH COUGH
unnnngg...
hnnn...

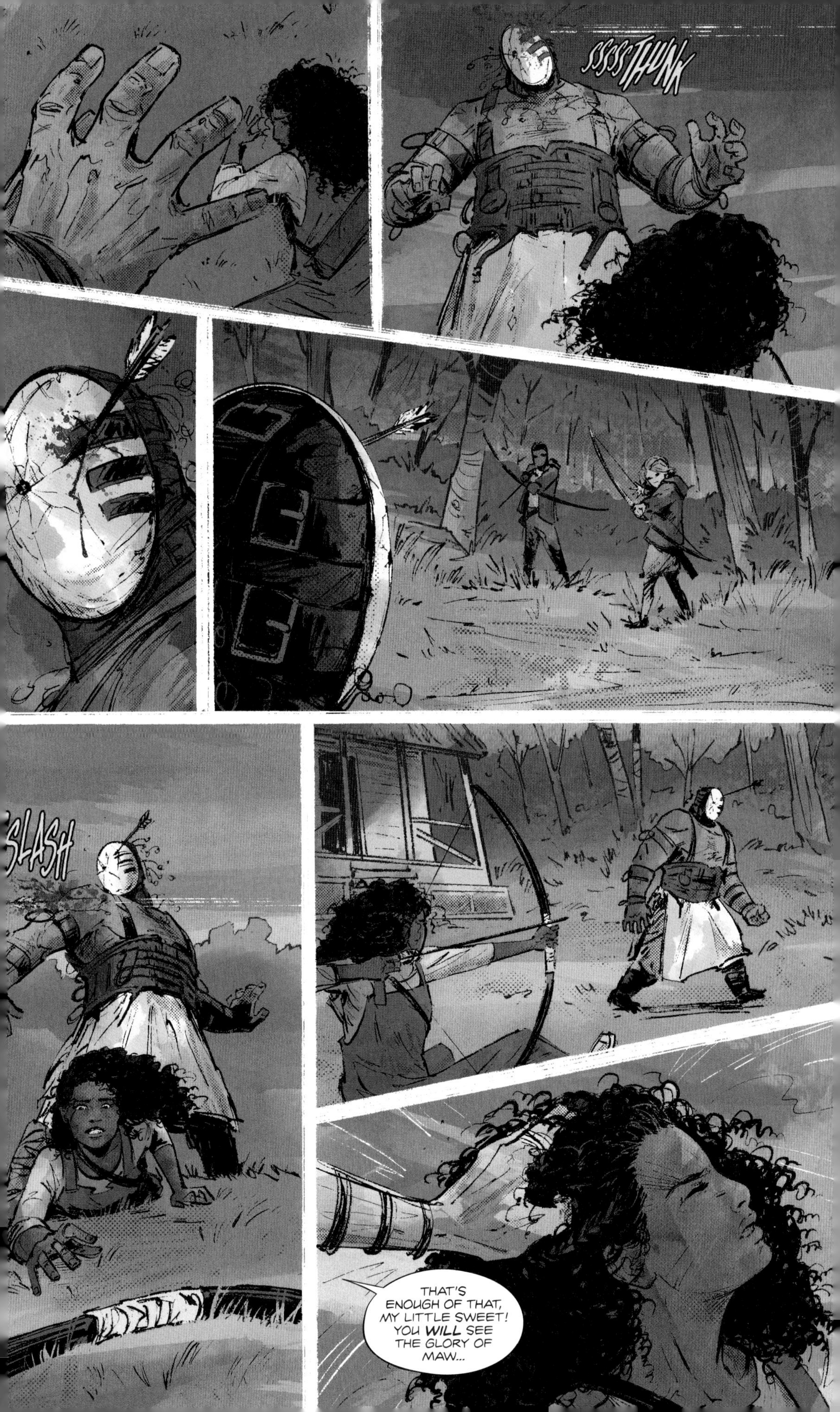
SSSSSTHUNK
SLASH
THAT'S ENOUGH OF THAT, MY LITTLE SWEET! YOU **WILL** SEE THE GLORY OF MAW...

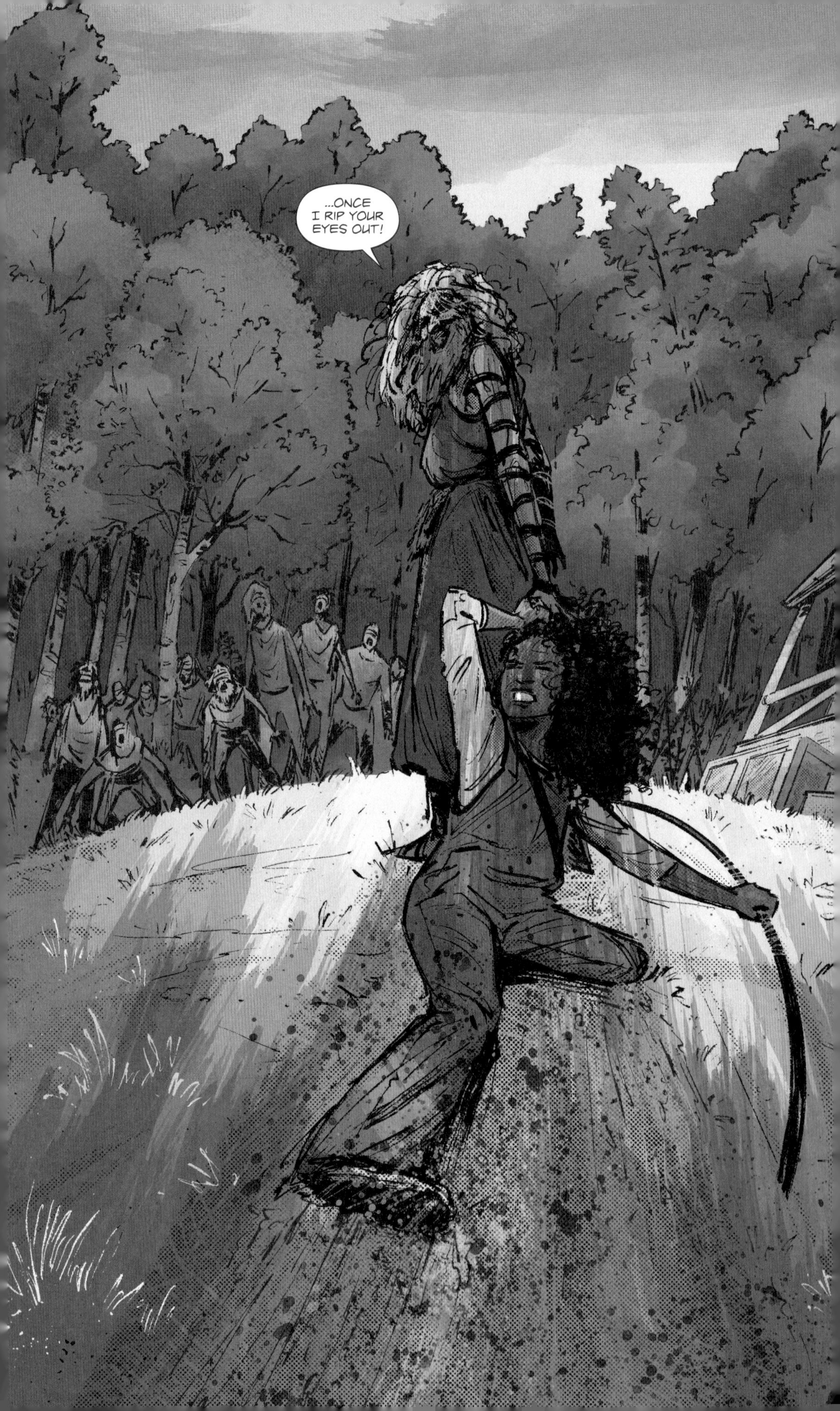
...ONCE I RIP YOUR EYES OUT!

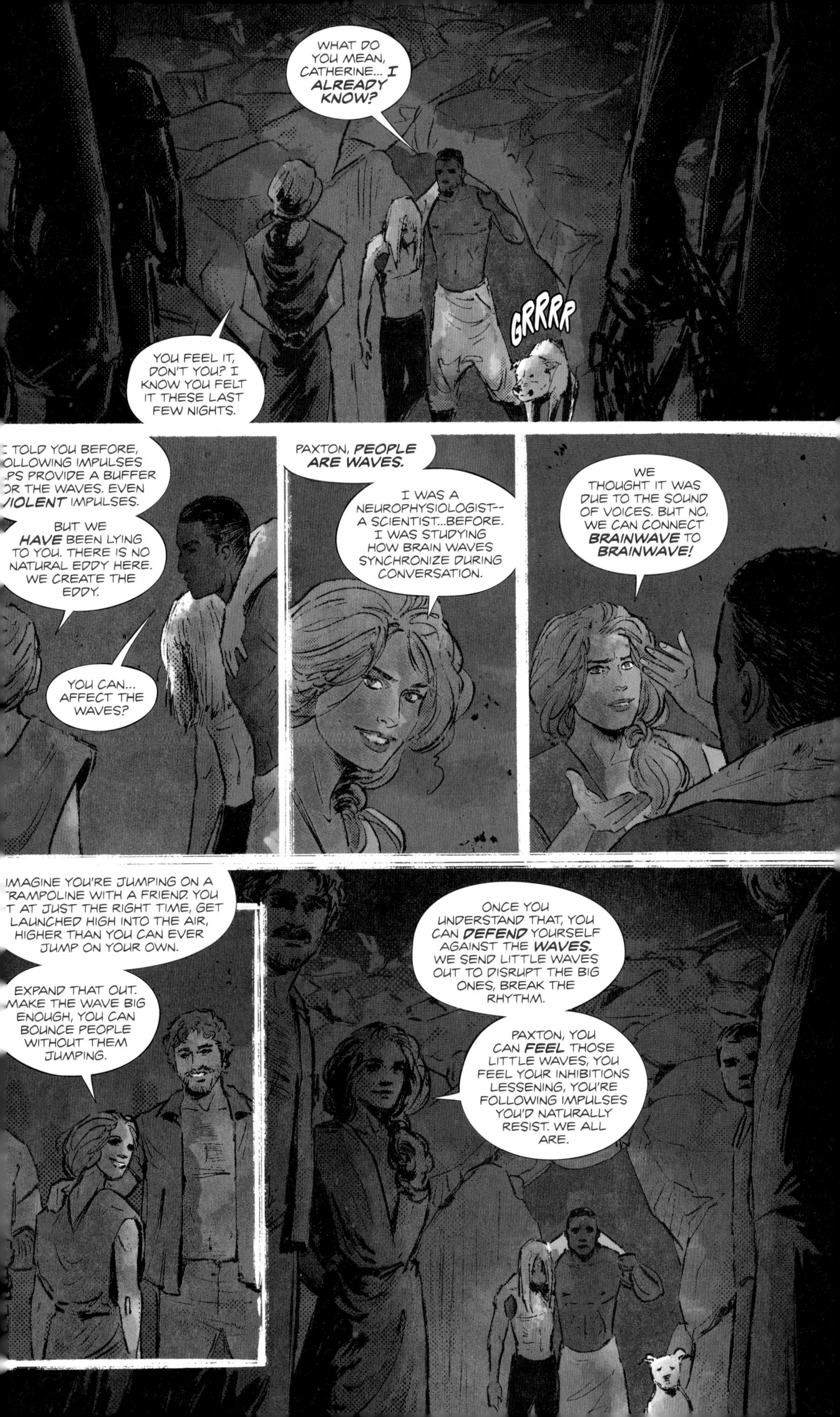
WHAT DO YOU MEAN, CATHERINE... I ALREADY KNOW?
GRRRR
YOU FEEL IT, DON'T YOU? I KNOW YOU FELT IT THESE LAST FEW NIGHTS.
TOLD YOU BEFORE, OLLOWING IMPULSES PS PROVIDE A BUFFER OR THE WAVES. EVEN VIOLENT IMPULSES.
BUT WE HAVE BEEN LYING TO YOU. THERE IS NO NATURAL EDDY HERE. WE CREATE THE EDDY.
YOU CAN... AFFECT THE WAVES?
PAXTON, PEOPLE ARE WAVES.
I WAS A NEUROPHYSIOLOGIST-- A SCIENTIST...BEFORE. I WAS STUDYING HOW BRAIN WAVES SYNCHRONIZE DURING CONVERSATION.
WE THOUGHT IT WAS DUE TO THE SOUND OF VOICES. BUT NO, WE CAN CONNECT BRAINWAVE TO BRAINWAVE!
IMAGINE YOU'RE JUMPING ON A TRAMPOLINE WITH A FRIEND. YOU T AT JUST THE RIGHT TIME, GET LAUNCHED HIGH INTO THE AIR, HIGHER THAN YOU CAN EVER JUMP ON YOUR OWN.
EXPAND THAT OUT. MAKE THE WAVE BIG ENOUGH, YOU CAN BOUNCE PEOPLE WITHOUT THEM JUMPING.
ONCE YOU UNDERSTAND THAT, YOU CAN DEFEND YOURSELF AGAINST THE WAVES. WE SEND LITTLE WAVES OUT TO DISRUPT THE BIG ONES, BREAK THE RHYTHM.
PAXTON, YOU CAN FEEL THOSE LITTLE WAVES, YOU FEEL YOUR INHIBITIONS LESSENING, YOU'RE FOLLOWING IMPULSES YOU'D NATURALLY RESIST. WE ALL ARE.

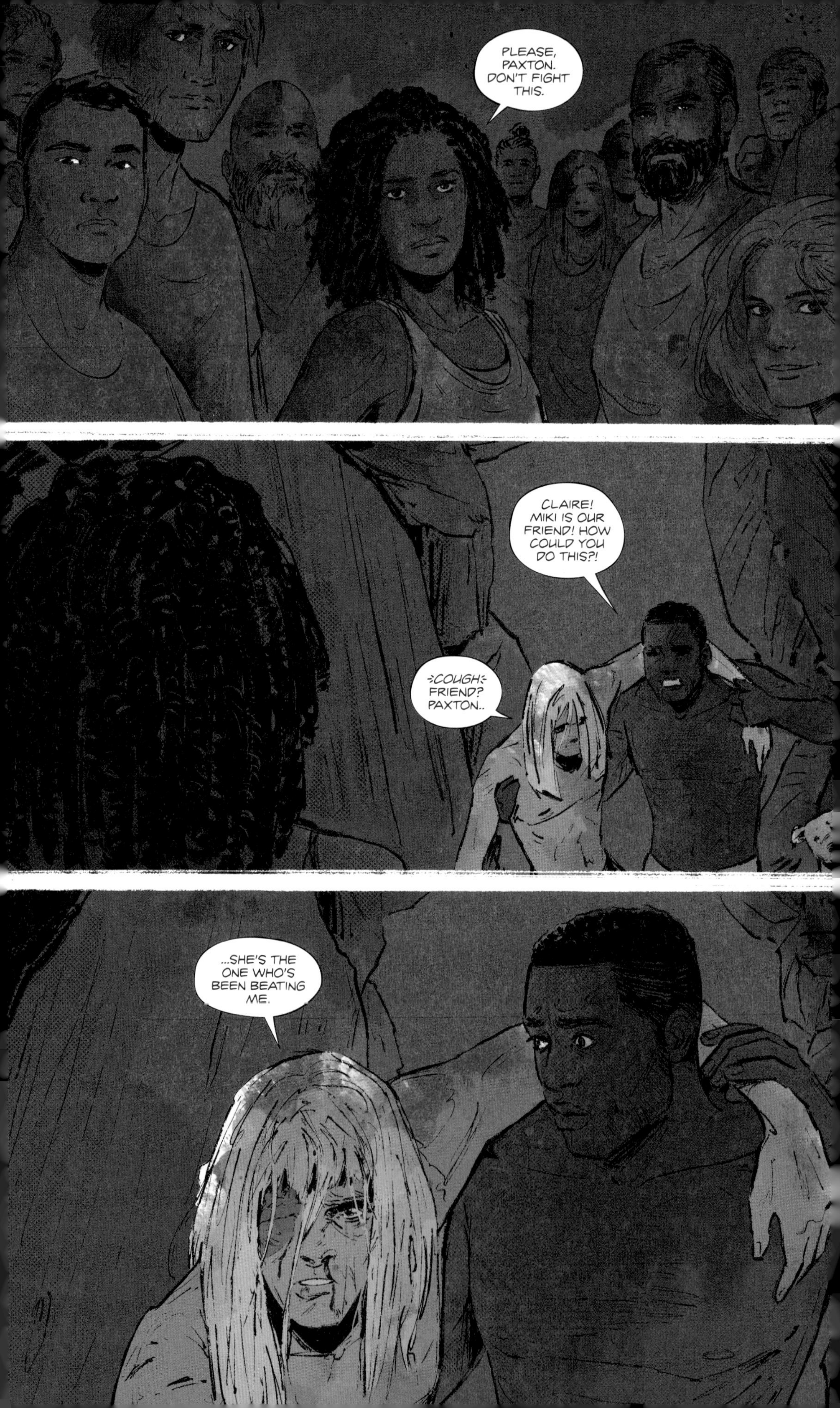
PLEASE, PAXTON. DON'T FIGHT THIS.
CLAIRE! MIKI IS OUR FRIEND! HOW COULD YOU DO THIS?!
-COUGH- FRIEND? PAXTON..
...SHE'S THE ONE WHO'S BEEN BEATING ME.

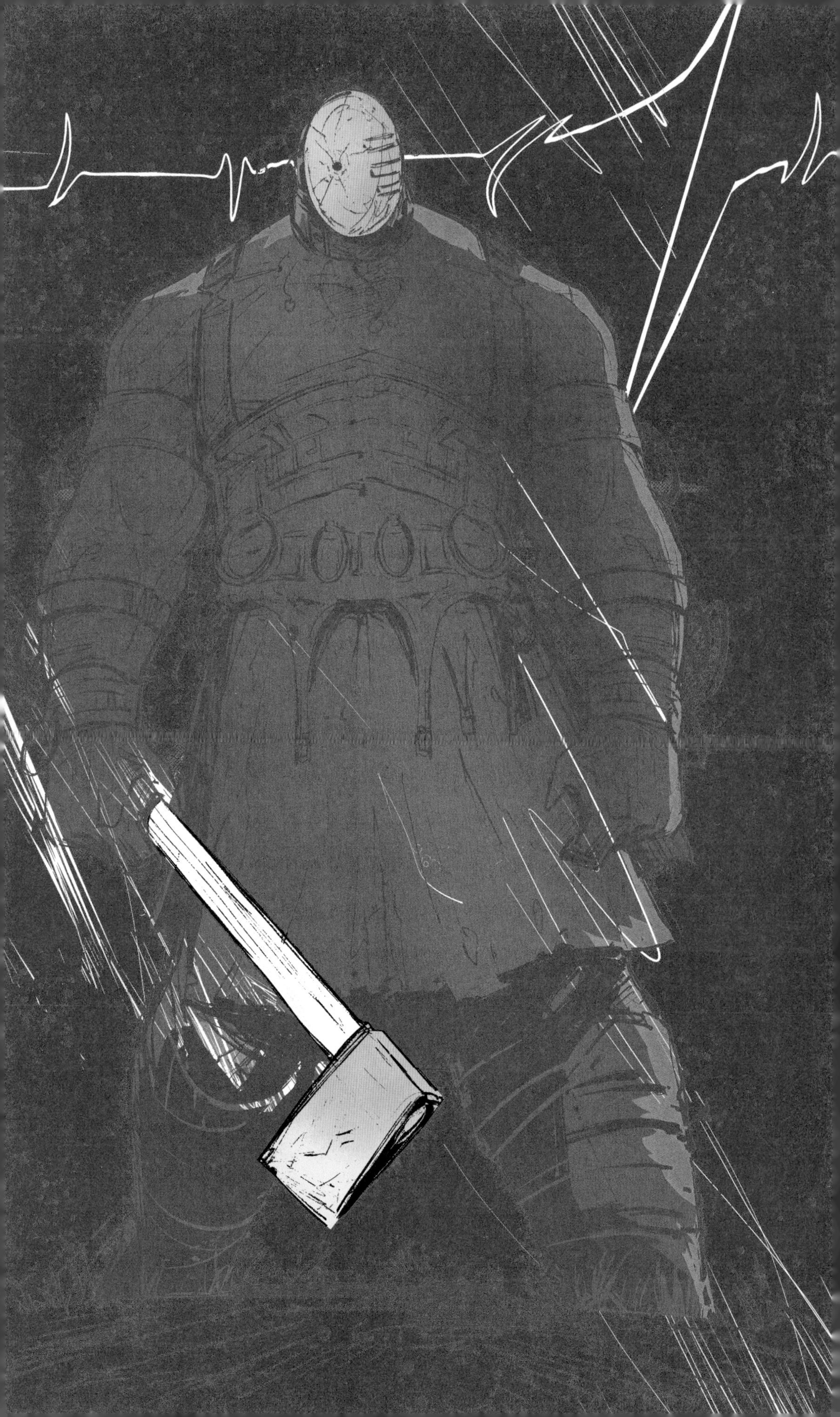

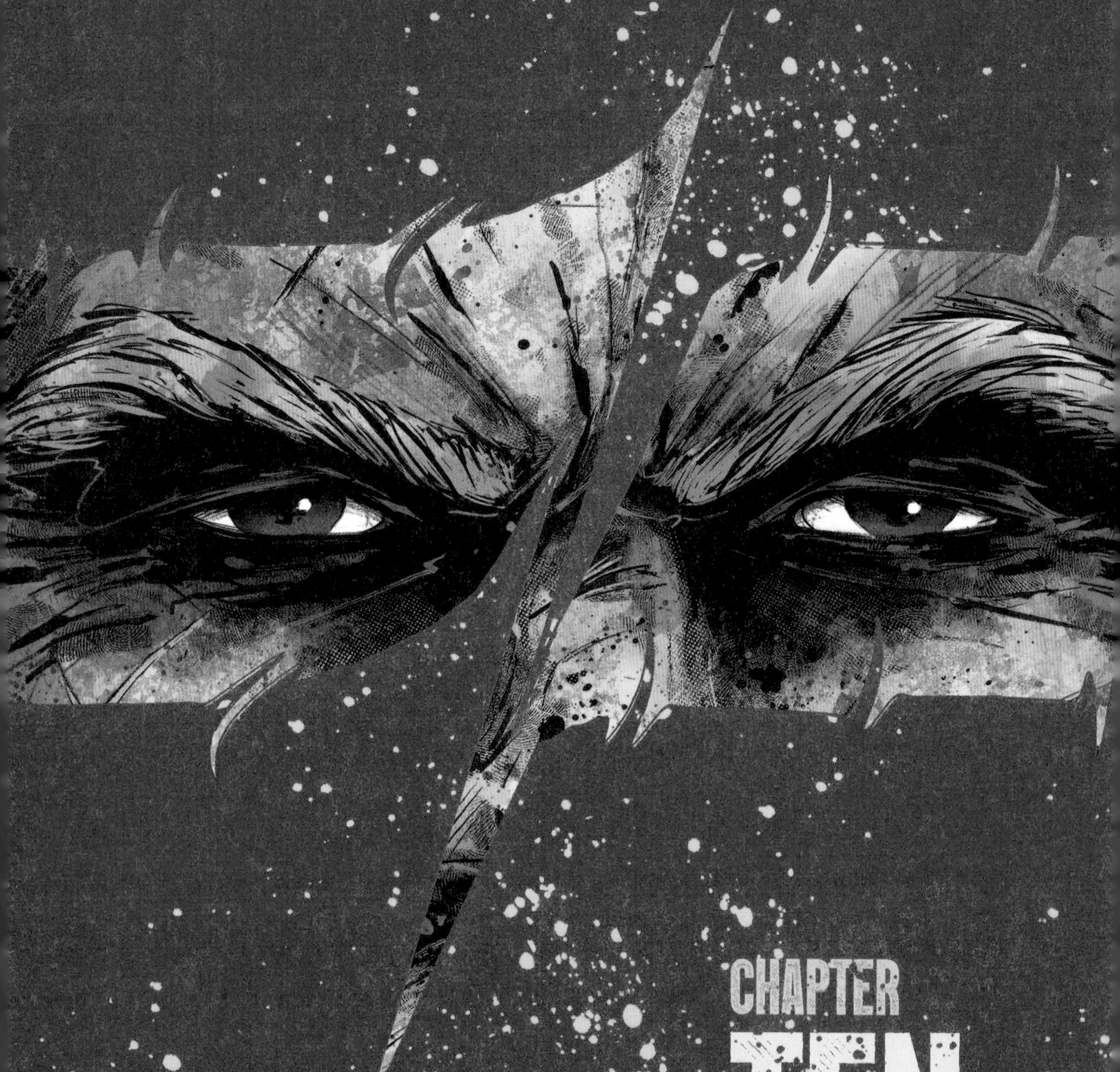

CHAPTER TEN

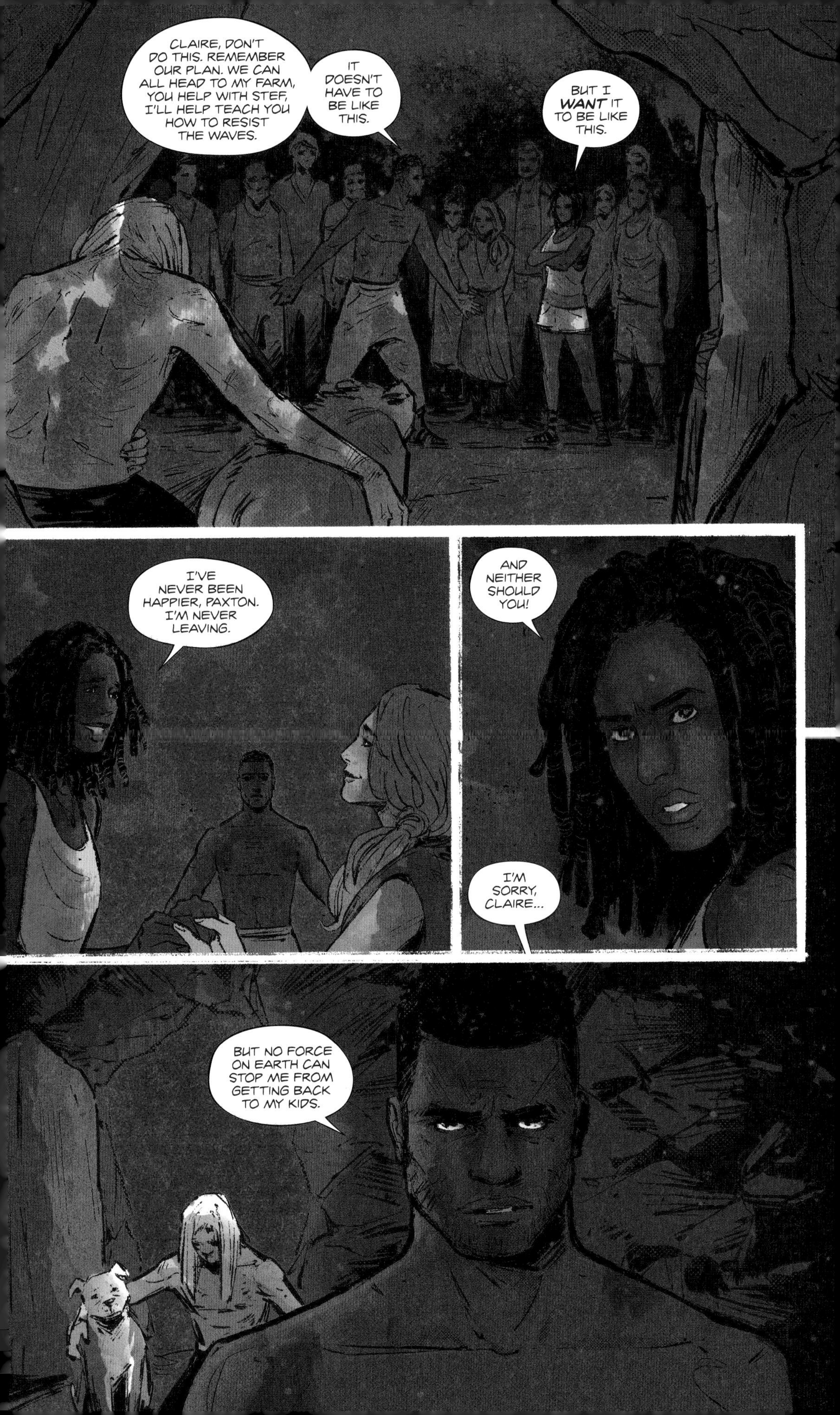
CLAIRE, DON'T DO THIS. REMEMBER OUR PLAN. WE CAN ALL HEAD TO MY FARM, YOU HELP WITH STEF, I'LL HELP TEACH YOU HOW TO RESIST THE WAVES.
IT DOESN'T HAVE TO BE LIKE THIS.
BUT I *WANT* IT TO BE LIKE THIS.
I'VE NEVER BEEN HAPPIER, PAXTON. I'M NEVER LEAVING.
AND NEITHER SHOULD YOU!
I'M SORRY, CLAIRE...
BUT NO FORCE ON EARTH CAN STOP ME FROM GETTING BACK TO MY KIDS.

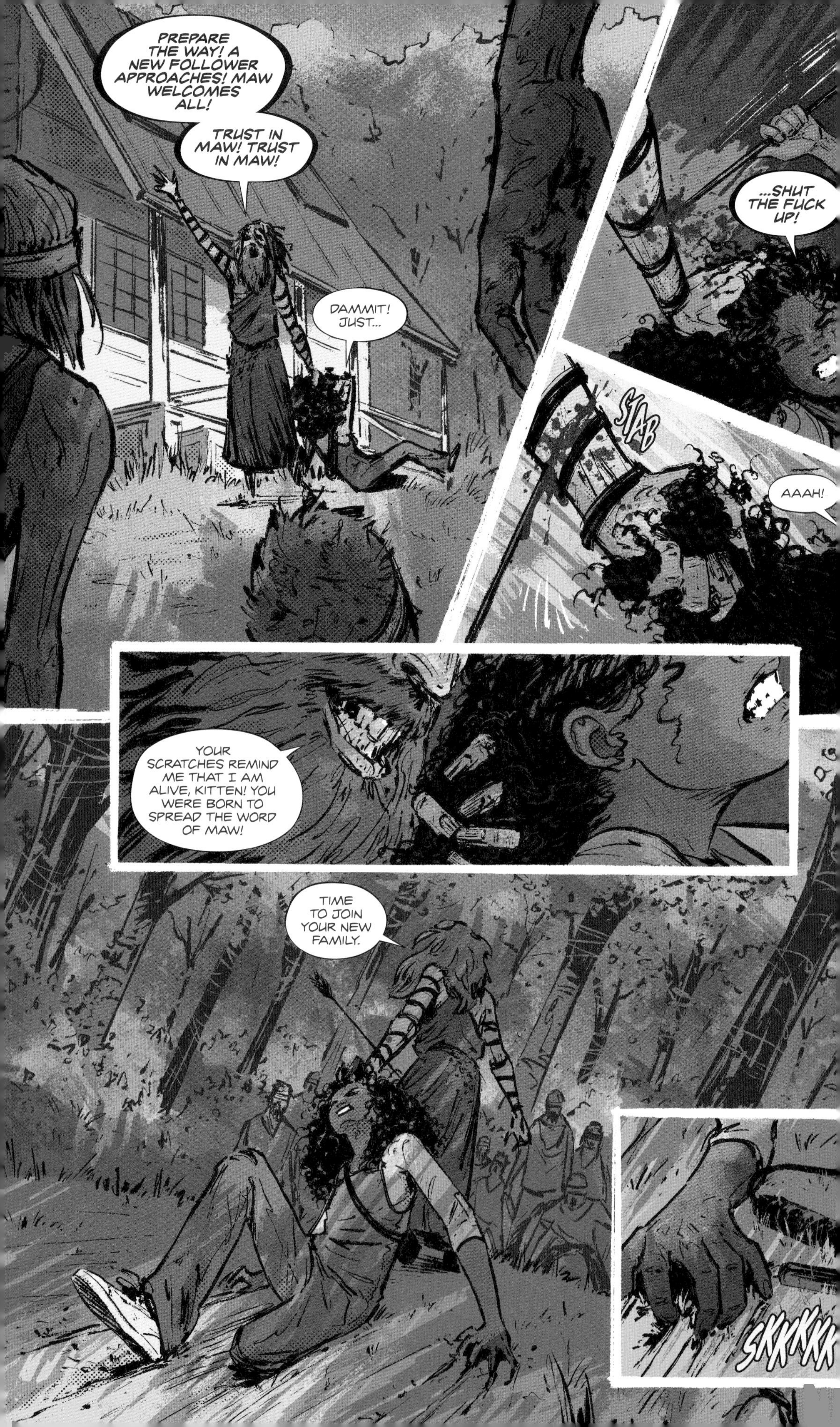
PREPARE THE WAY! A NEW FOLLOWER APPROACHES! MAW WELCOMES ALL!
TRUST IN MAW! TRUST IN MAW!
DAMMIT! JUST...
...SHUT THE FUCK UP!
STAB
AAAH!
YOUR SCRATCHES REMIND ME THAT I AM ALIVE, KITTEN! YOU WERE BORN TO SPREAD THE WORD OF MAW!
TIME TO JOIN YOUR NEW FAMILY.
SKKKKK

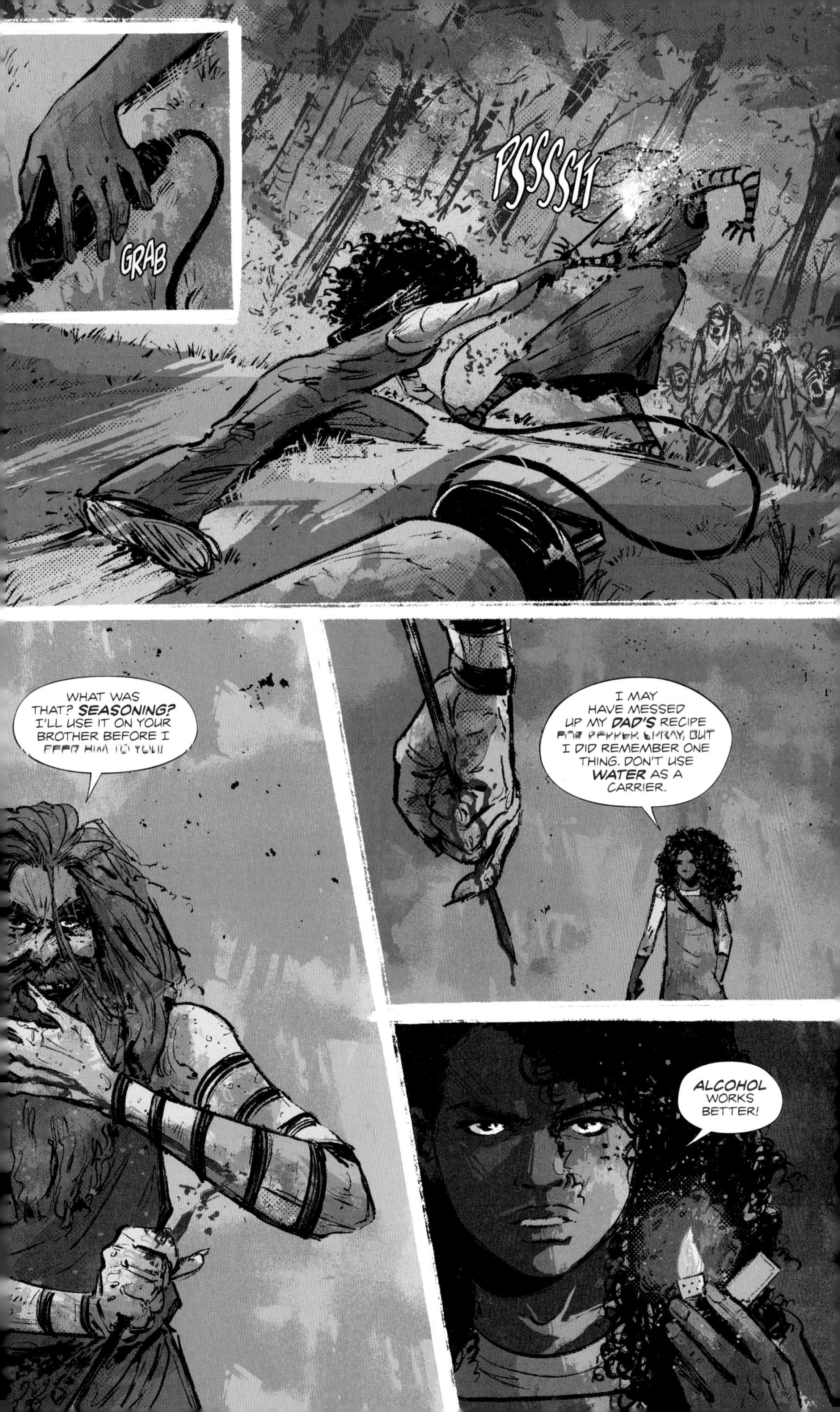
GRAB
PSSSST!
WHAT WAS THAT? **SEASONING?** I'LL USE IT ON YOUR BROTHER BEFORE I
I MAY HAVE MESSED UP MY **DAD'S** RECIPE … BUT I DID REMEMBER ONE THING. DON'T USE **WATER** AS A CARRIER.
ALCOHOL WORKS BETTER!

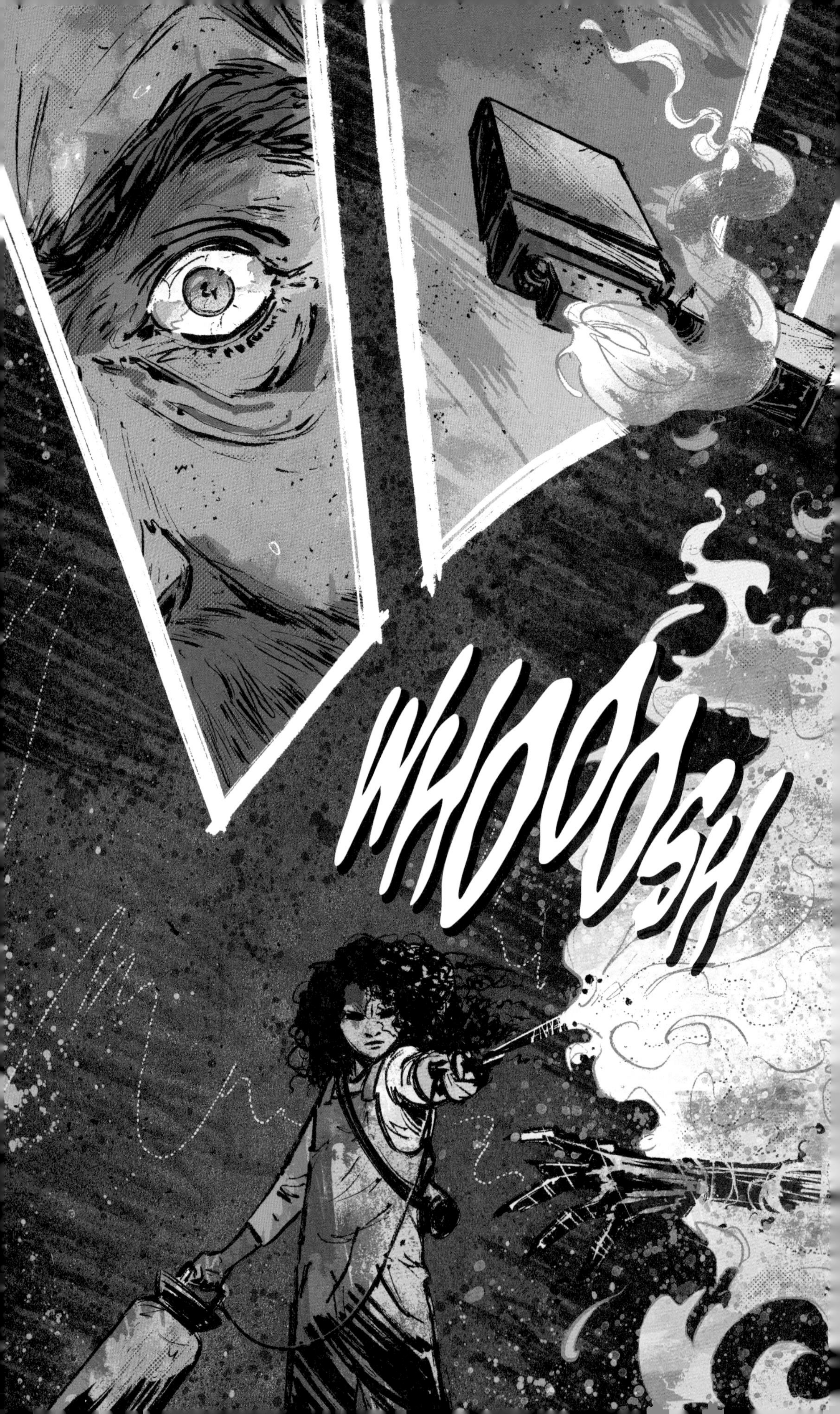
WHOOOSH

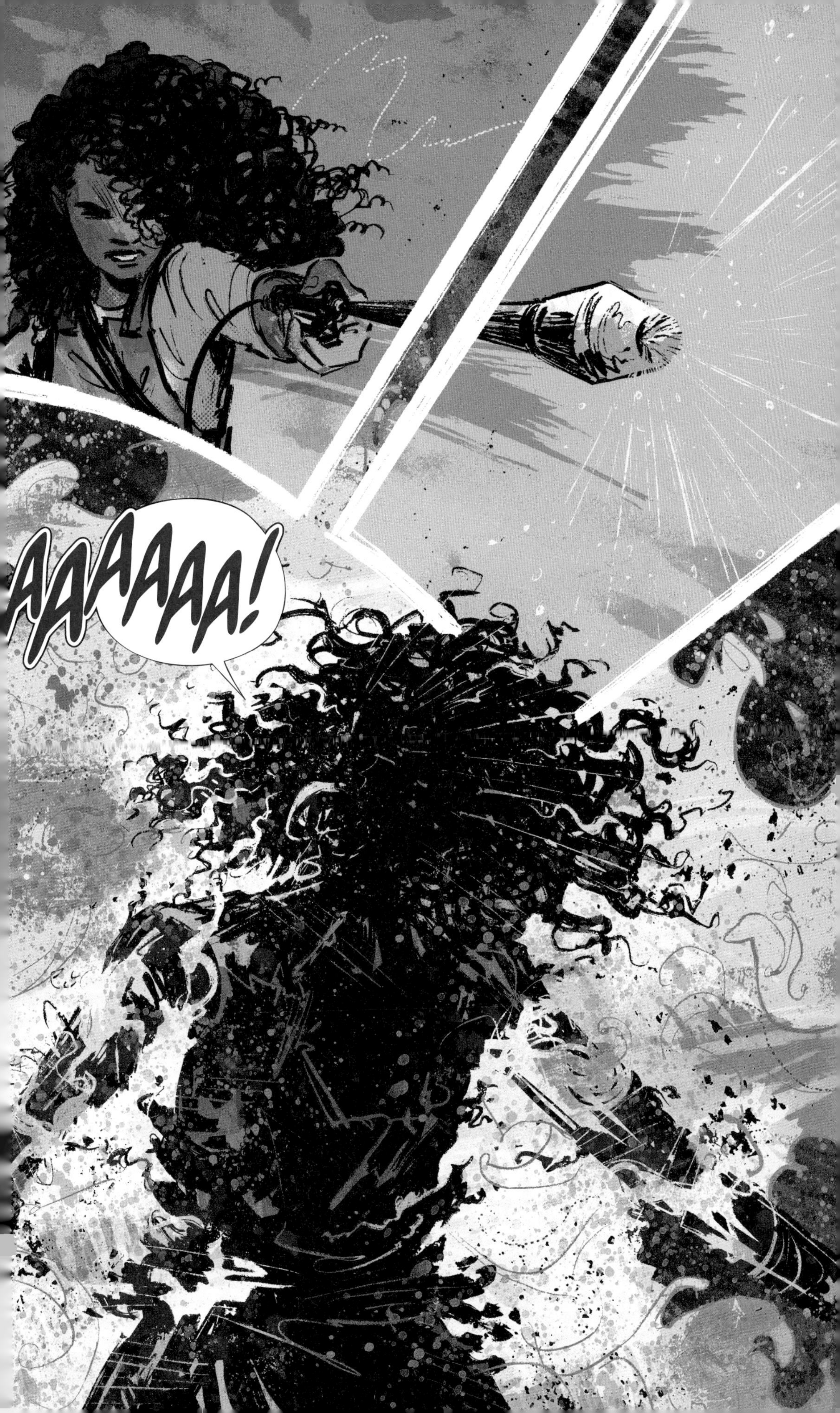
AAAAAA!

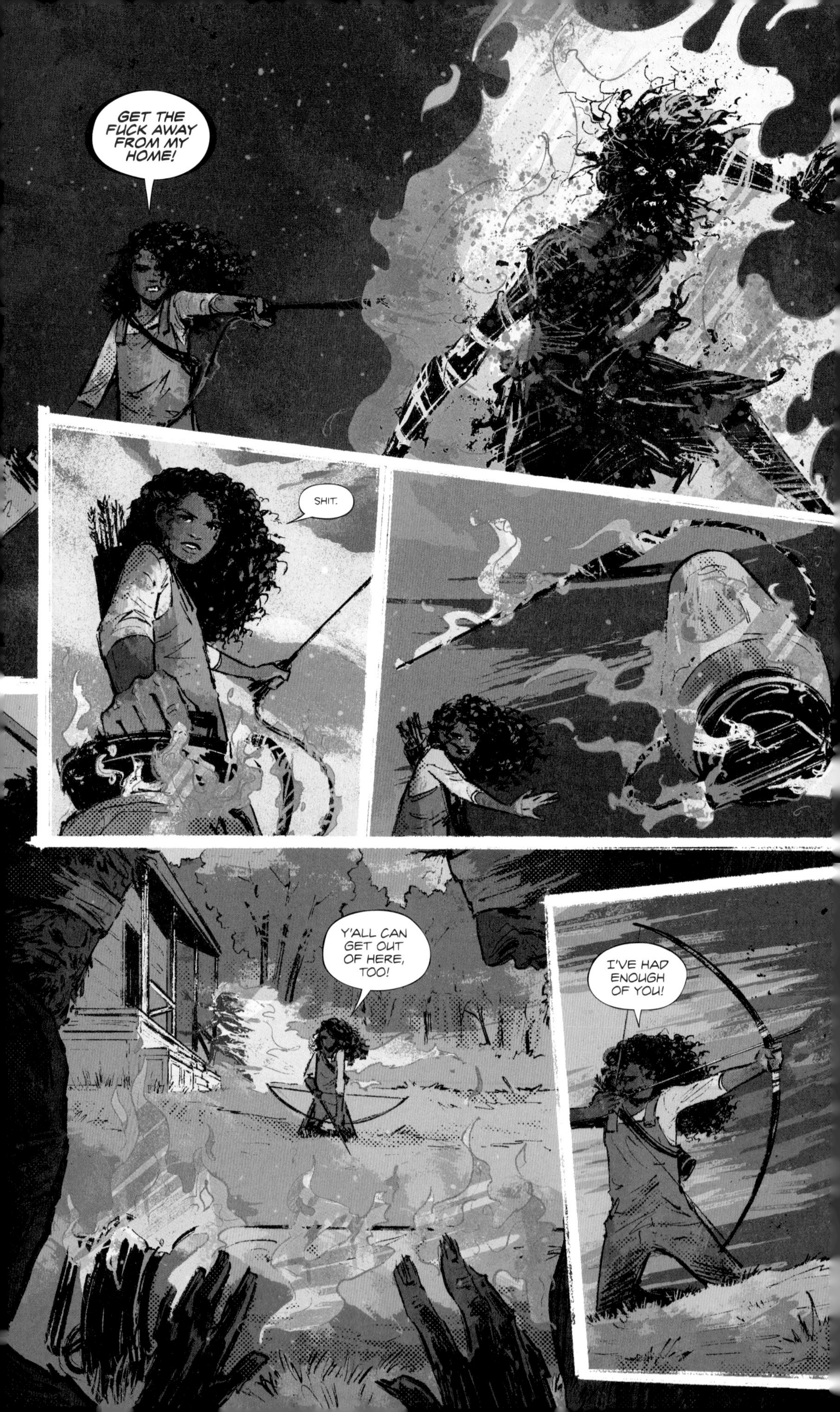
GET THE FUCK AWAY FROM MY HOME!
SHIT.
Y'ALL CAN GET OUT OF HERE, TOO!
I'VE HAD ENOUGH OF YOU!

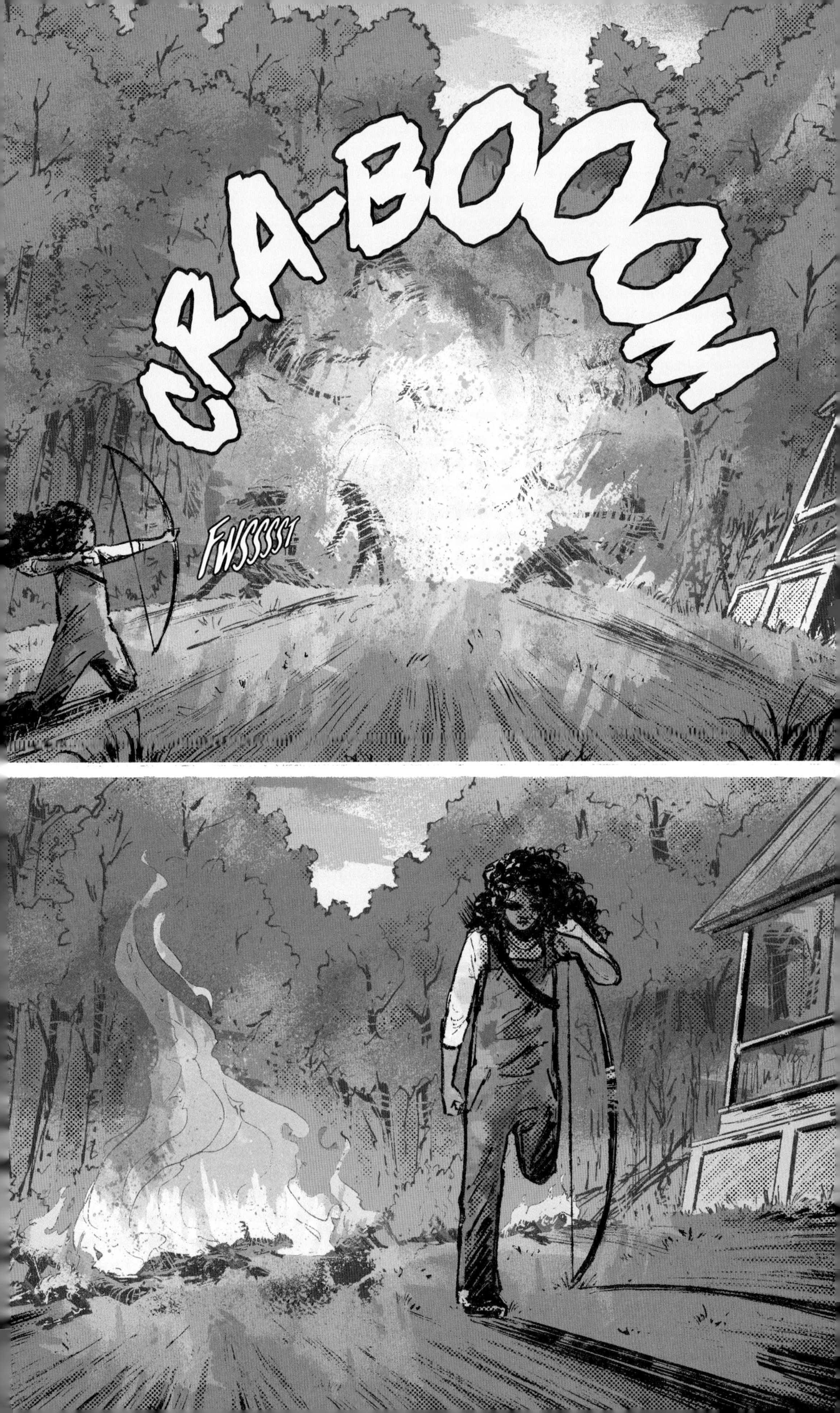
CRA-BOOOM
FWSSSST

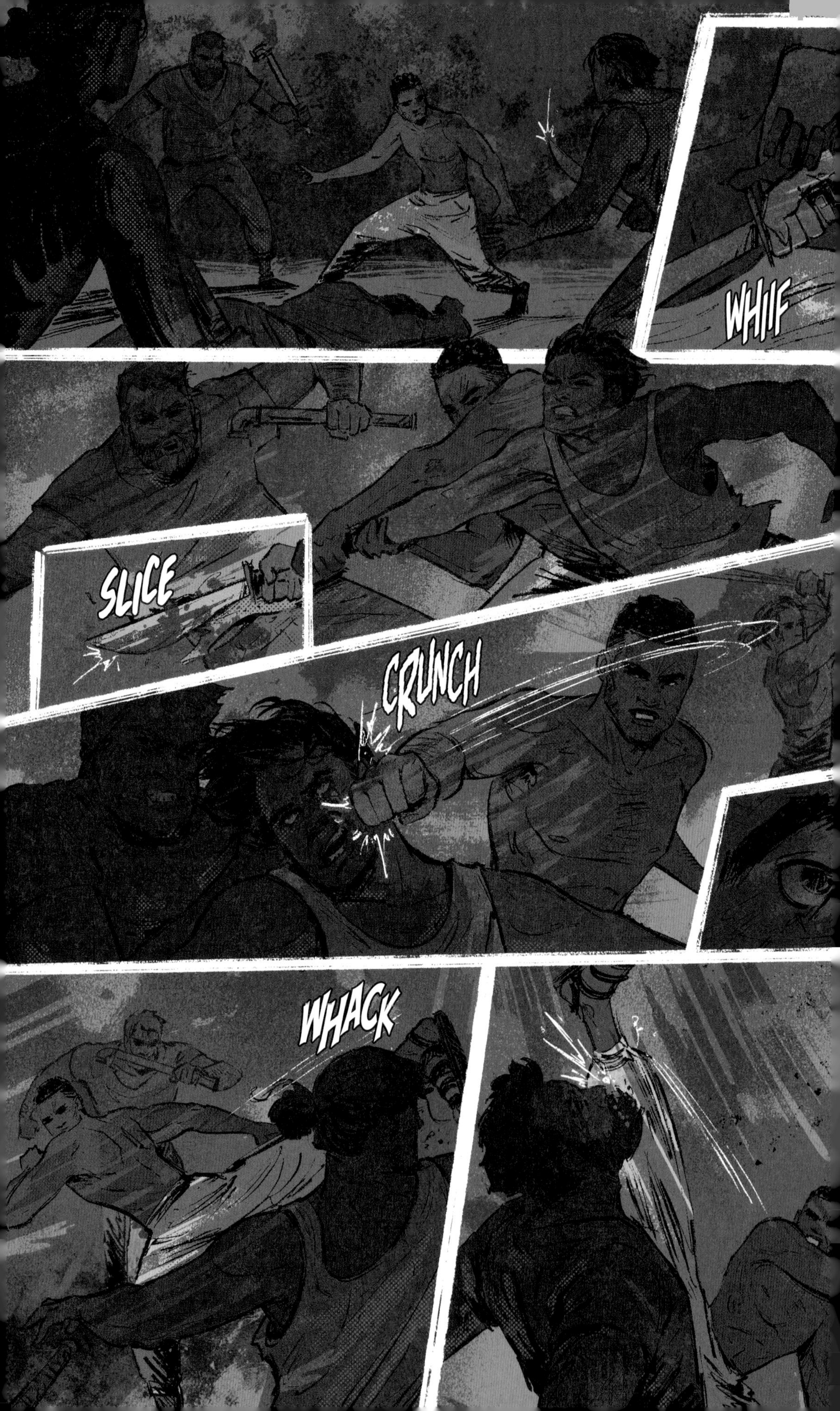
WHIF
SLICE
CRUNCH
WHACK

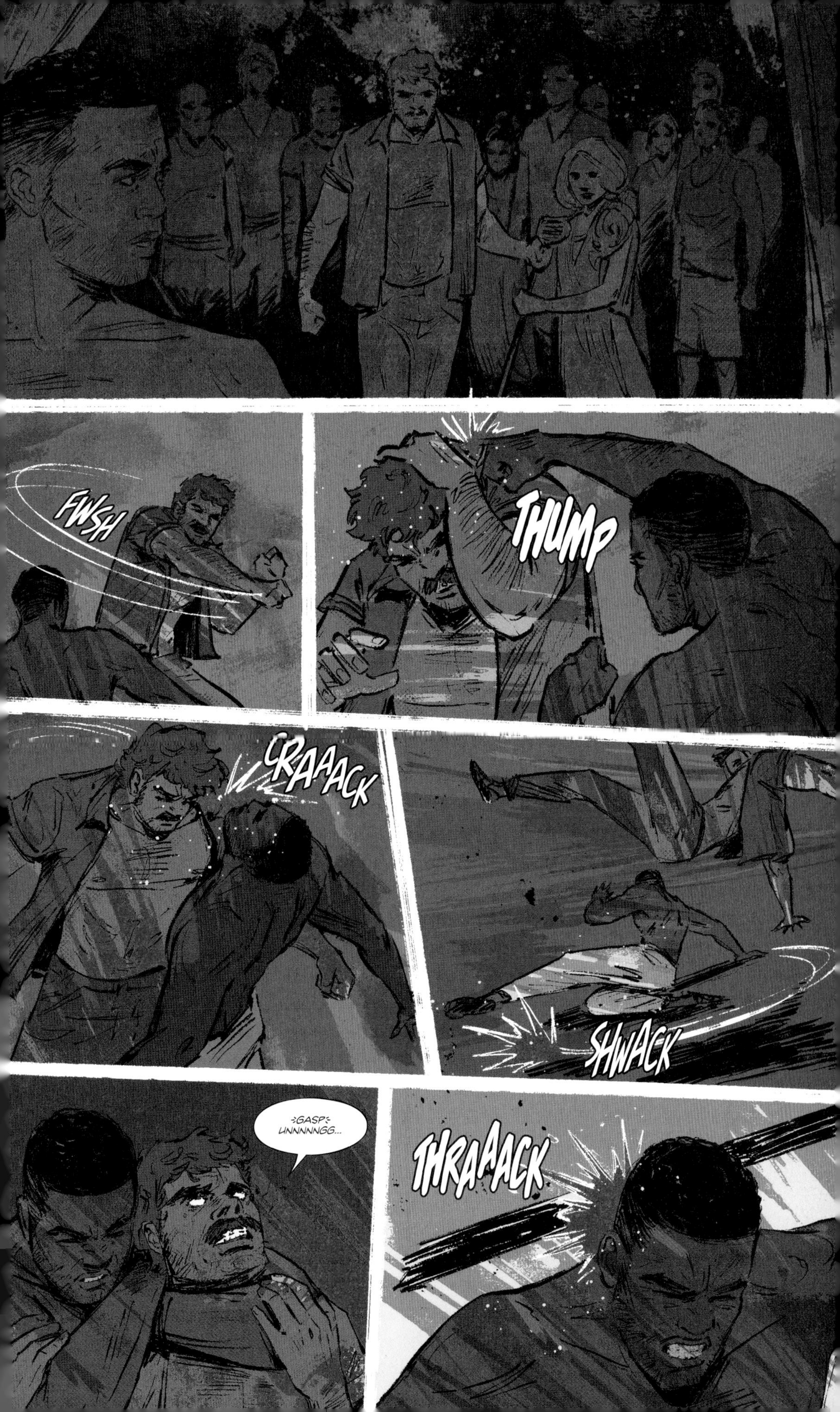
FWSH
THUMP
CRAAACK
SHWACK
GASP
UNNNNNGG...
THRAAACK

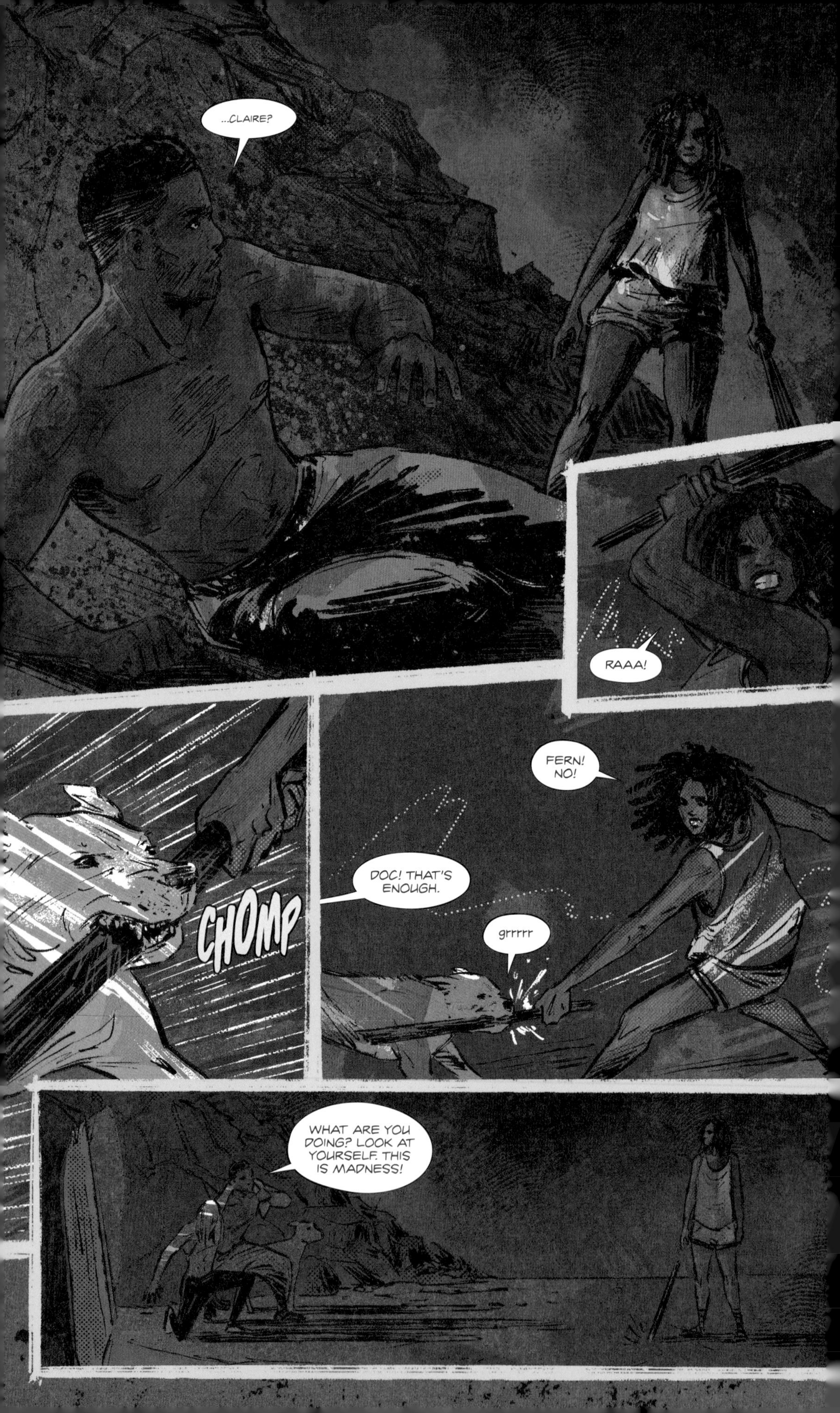
...CLAIRE?
RAAA!
CHOMP
DOC! THAT'S ENOUGH.
FERN! NO!
grrrrr
WHAT ARE YOU DOING? LOOK AT YOURSELF. THIS IS MADNESS!

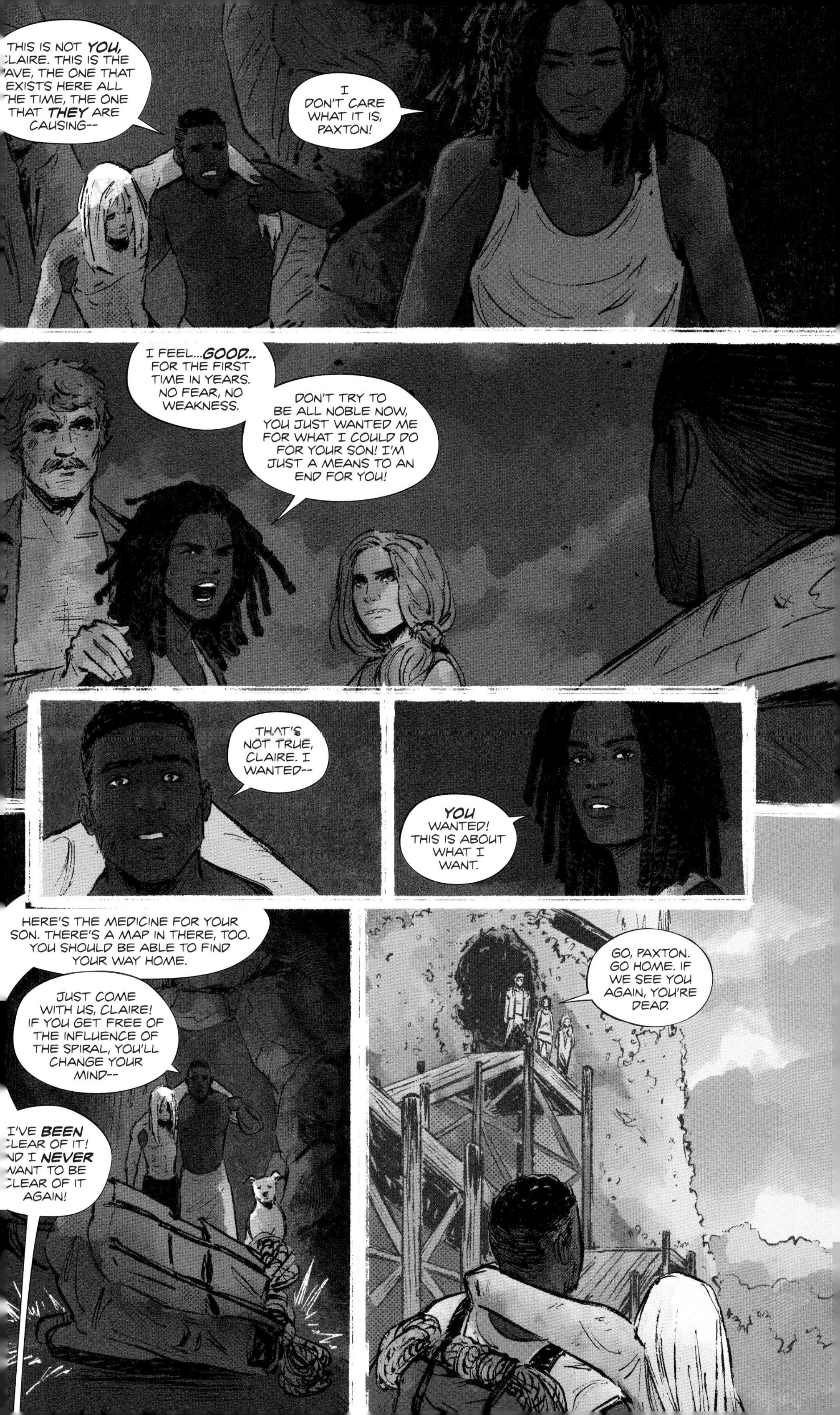
THIS IS NOT YOU, CLAIRE. THIS IS THE WAVE, THE ONE THAT EXISTS HERE ALL THE TIME, THE ONE THAT THEY ARE CAUSING--
I DON'T CARE WHAT IT IS, PAXTON!
I FEEL...GOOD... FOR THE FIRST TIME IN YEARS. NO FEAR, NO WEAKNESS.
DON'T TRY TO BE ALL NOBLE NOW, YOU JUST WANTED ME FOR WHAT I COULD DO FOR YOUR SON! I'M JUST A MEANS TO AN END FOR YOU!
THAT'S NOT TRUE, CLAIRE. I WANTED--
YOU WANTED! THIS IS ABOUT WHAT I WANT.
HERE'S THE MEDICINE FOR YOUR SON. THERE'S A MAP IN THERE, TOO. YOU SHOULD BE ABLE TO FIND YOUR WAY HOME.
JUST COME WITH US, CLAIRE! IF YOU GET FREE OF THE INFLUENCE OF THE SPIRAL, YOU'LL CHANGE YOUR MIND--
I'VE BEEN CLEAR OF IT! AND I NEVER WANT TO BE CLEAR OF IT AGAIN!
GO, PAXTON. GO HOME. IF WE SEE YOU AGAIN, YOU'RE DEAD.

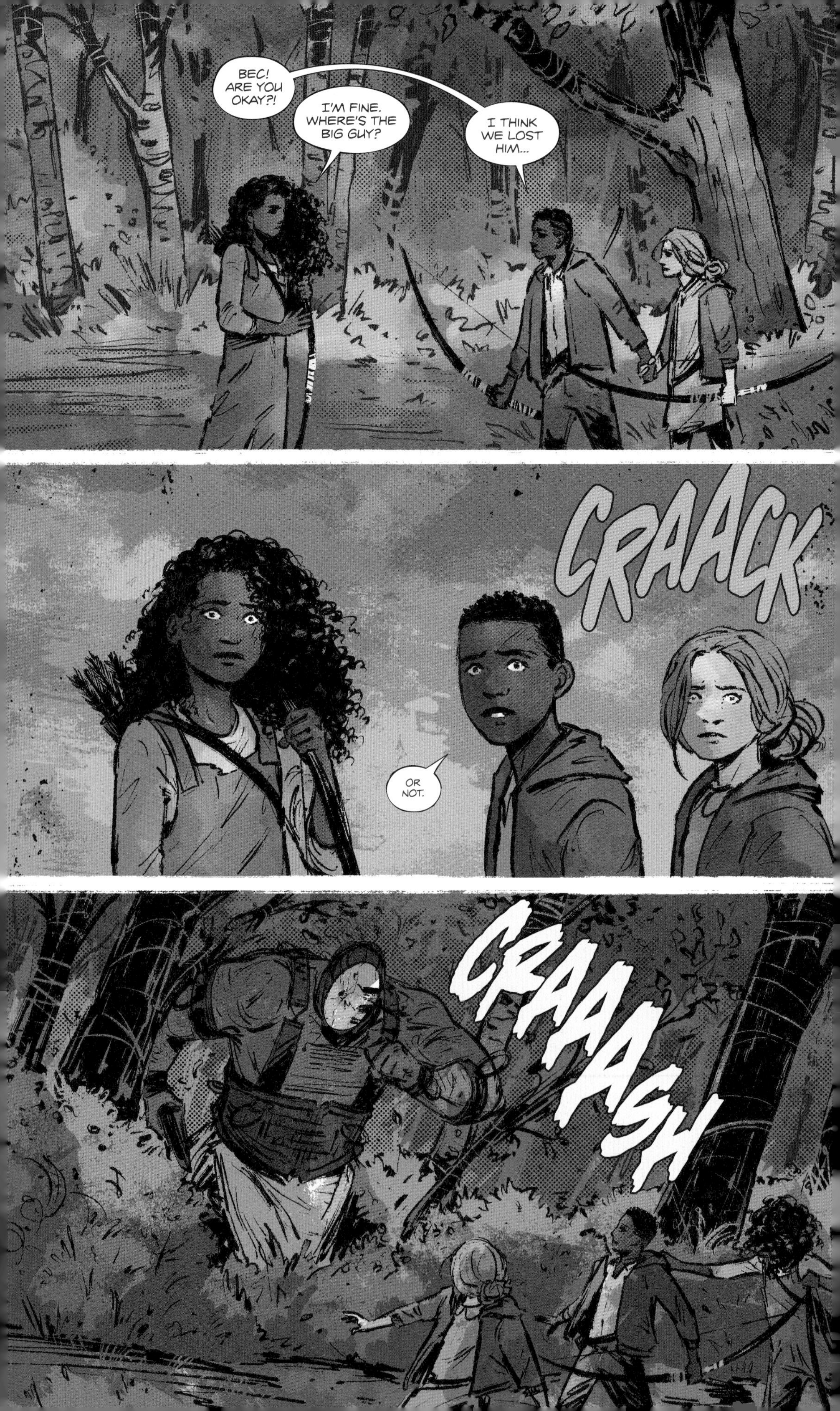
BEC! ARE YOU OKAY?!
I'M FINE. WHERE'S THE BIG GUY?
I THINK WE LOST HIM...
CRAACK
OR NOT.
CRAAAASH

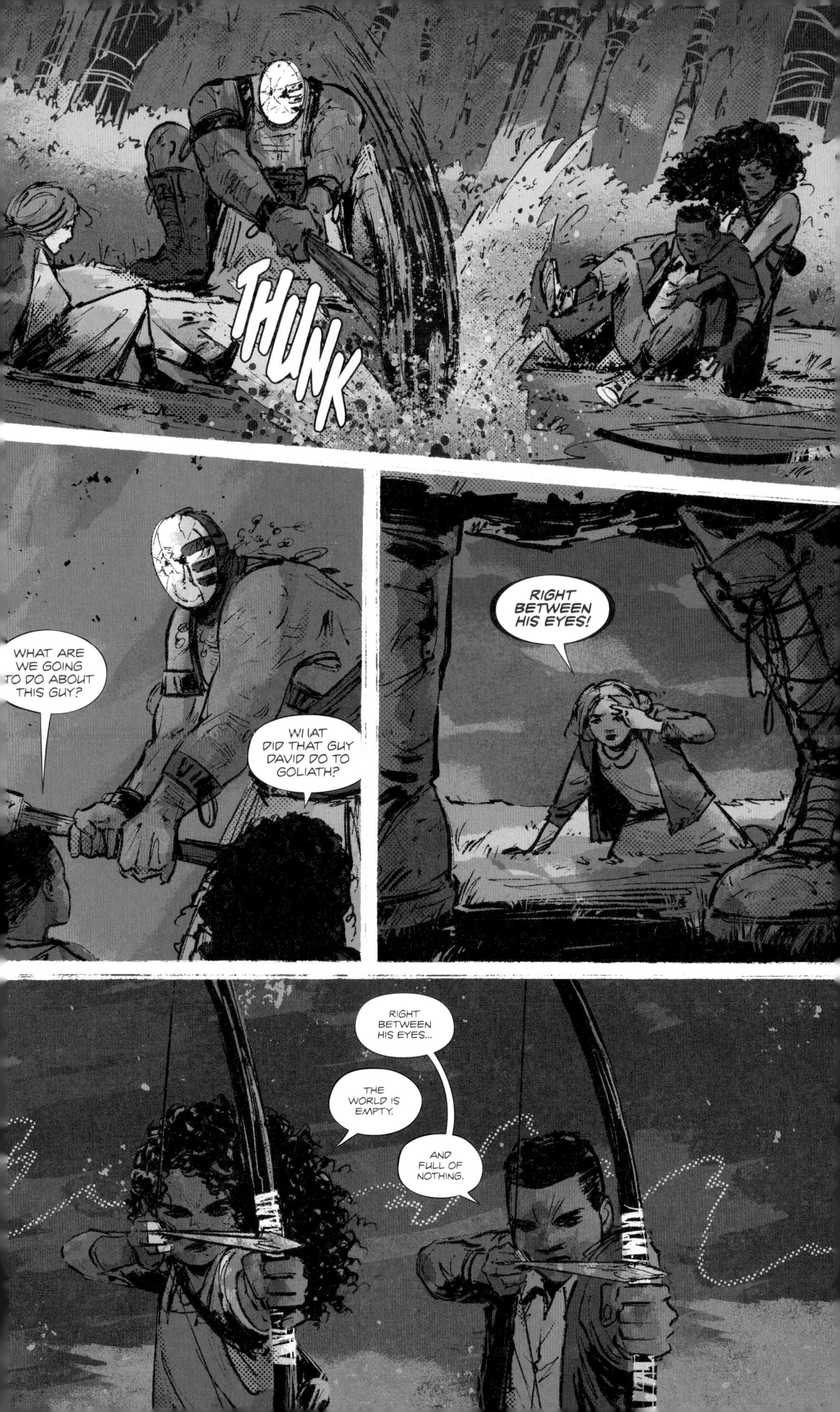
THUNK
WHAT ARE WE GOING TO DO ABOUT THIS GUY?
WHAT DID THAT GUY DAVID DO TO GOLIATH?
RIGHT BETWEEN HIS EYES!
RIGHT BETWEEN HIS EYES...
THE WORLD IS EMPTY.
AND FULL OF NOTHING.

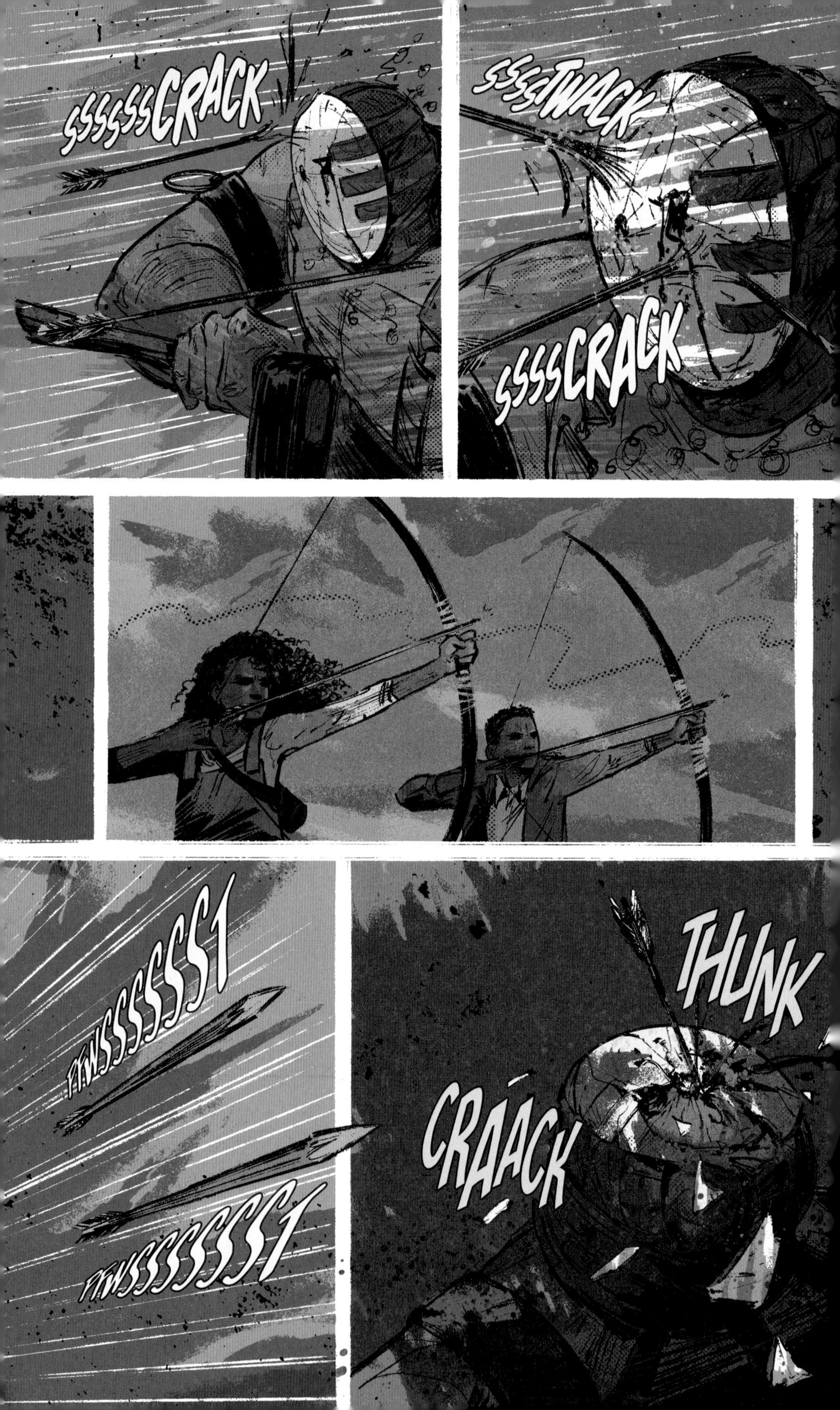
SSSSSSCRACK
SSSSTWACK
SSSSCRACK
PTWSSSSSSST
PTWSSSSSSST
THUNK
CRAACK

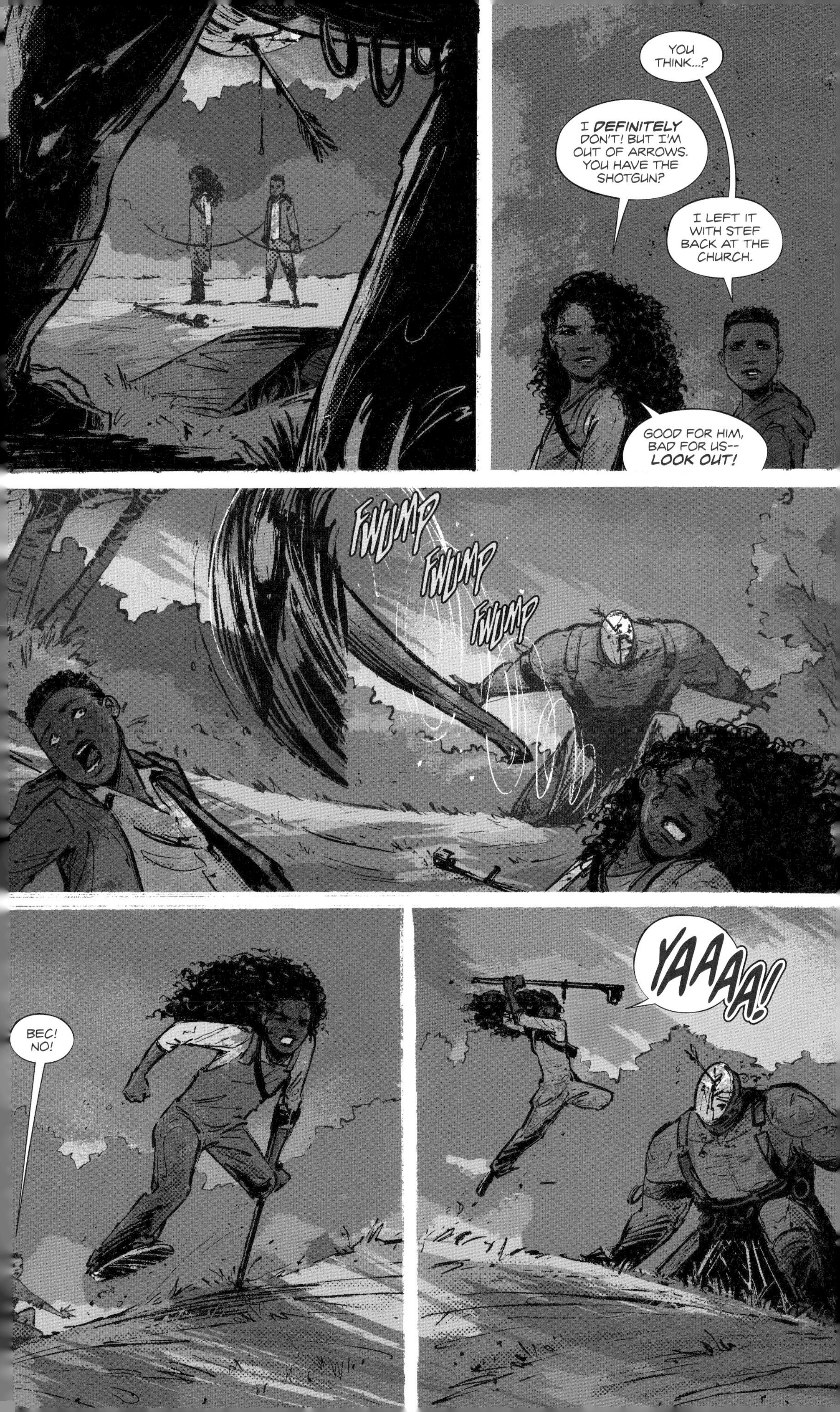
YOU THINK...?
I DEFINITELY DON'T! BUT I'M OUT OF ARROWS. YOU HAVE THE SHOTGUN?
I LEFT IT WITH STEF BACK AT THE CHURCH.
GOOD FOR HIM, BAD FOR US-- LOOK OUT!
FWUMP
FWUMP
FWUMP
BEC! NO!
YAAAA!

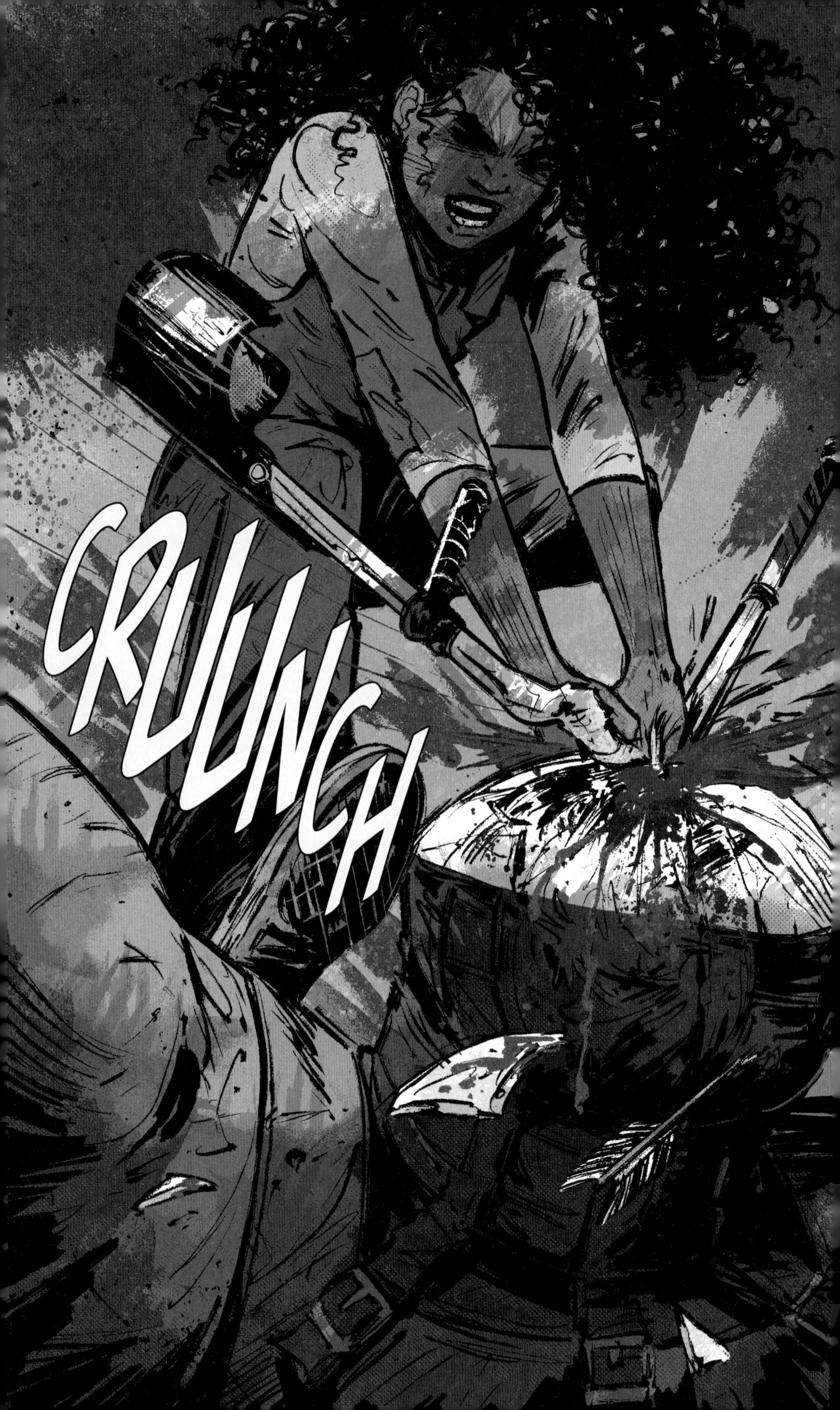
CRUNCH

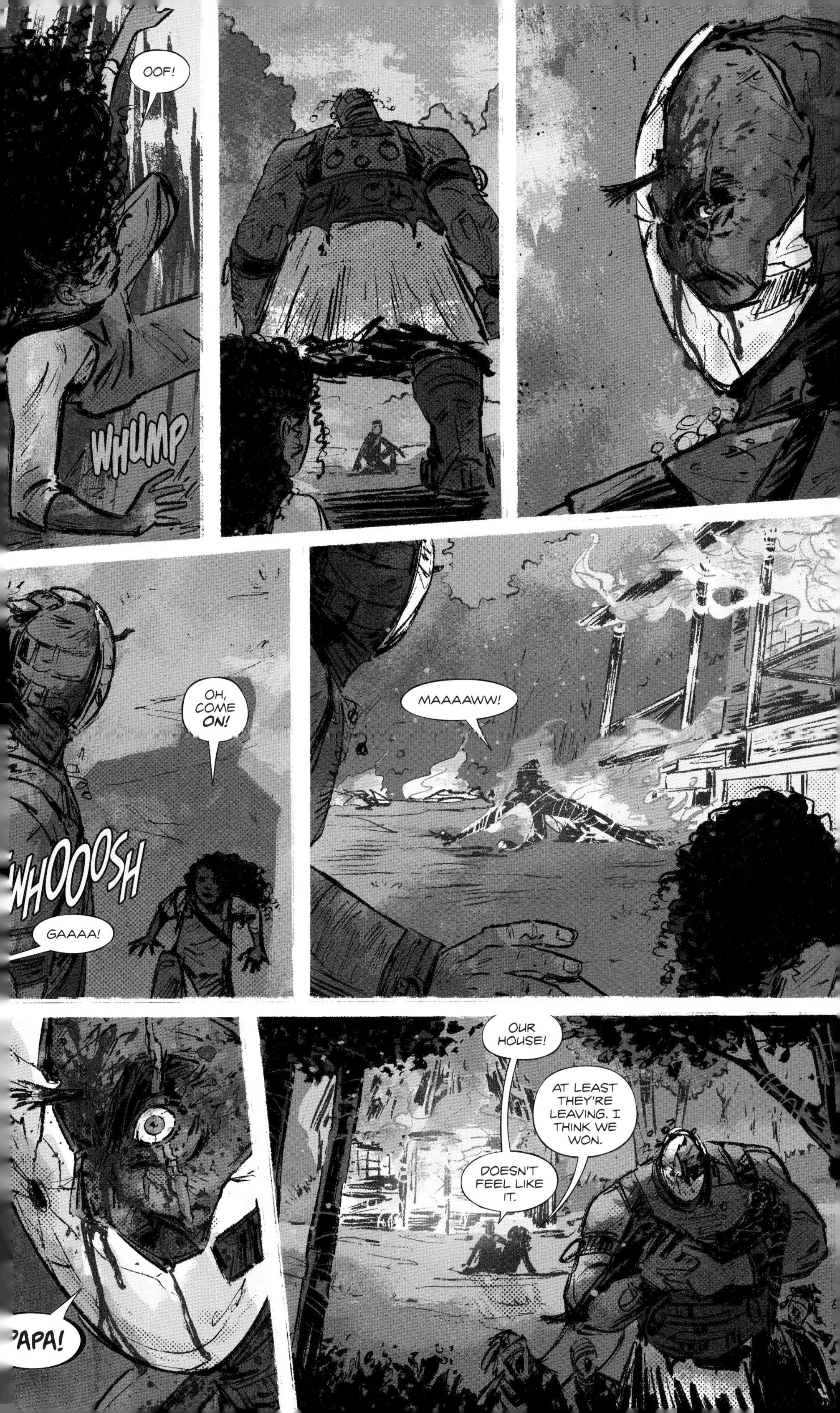
OOF!
WHUMP
OH, COME ON!
WHOOOSH
GAAAA!
MAAAAWW!
PAPA!
OUR HOUSE!
DOESN'T FEEL LIKE IT.
AT LEAST THEY'RE LEAVING. I THINK WE WON.

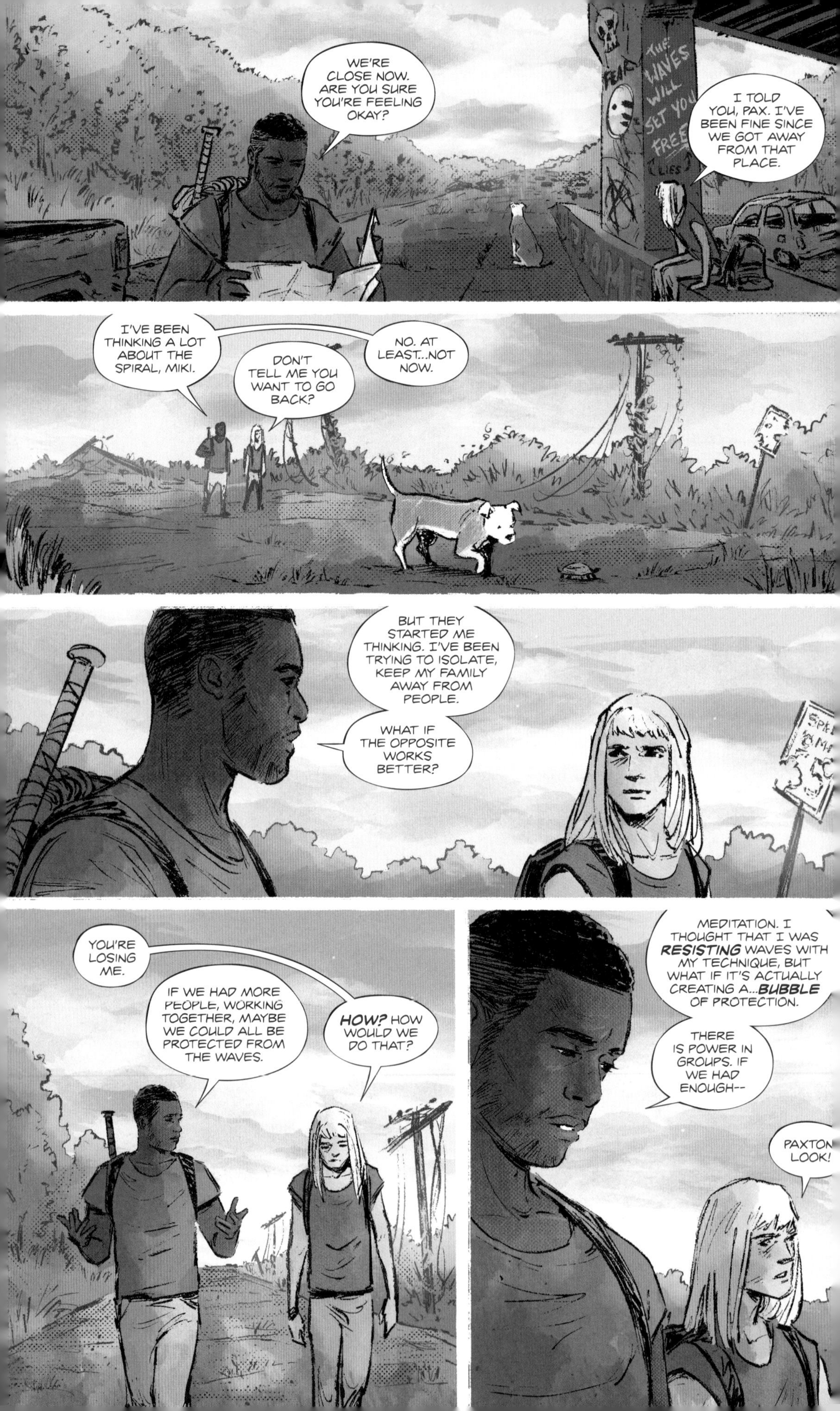
WE'RE CLOSE NOW. ARE YOU SURE YOU'RE FEELING OKAY?
FEAR
THE WAVES WILL SET YOU FREE
LIES
I TOLD YOU, PAX. I'VE BEEN FINE SINCE WE GOT AWAY FROM THAT PLACE.
I'VE BEEN THINKING A LOT ABOUT THE SPIRAL, MIKI.
DON'T TELL ME YOU WANT TO GO BACK?
NO. AT LEAST...NOT NOW.
BUT THEY STARTED ME THINKING. I'VE BEEN TRYING TO ISOLATE, KEEP MY FAMILY AWAY FROM PEOPLE.
WHAT IF THE OPPOSITE WORKS BETTER?
YOU'RE LOSING ME.
IF WE HAD MORE PEOPLE, WORKING TOGETHER, MAYBE WE COULD ALL BE PROTECTED FROM THE WAVES.
HOW? HOW WOULD WE DO THAT?
MEDITATION. I THOUGHT THAT I WAS RESISTING WAVES WITH MY TECHNIQUE, BUT WHAT IF IT'S ACTUALLY CREATING A...BUBBLE OF PROTECTION.
THERE IS POWER IN GROUPS. IF WE HAD ENOUGH--
PAXTON LOOK!

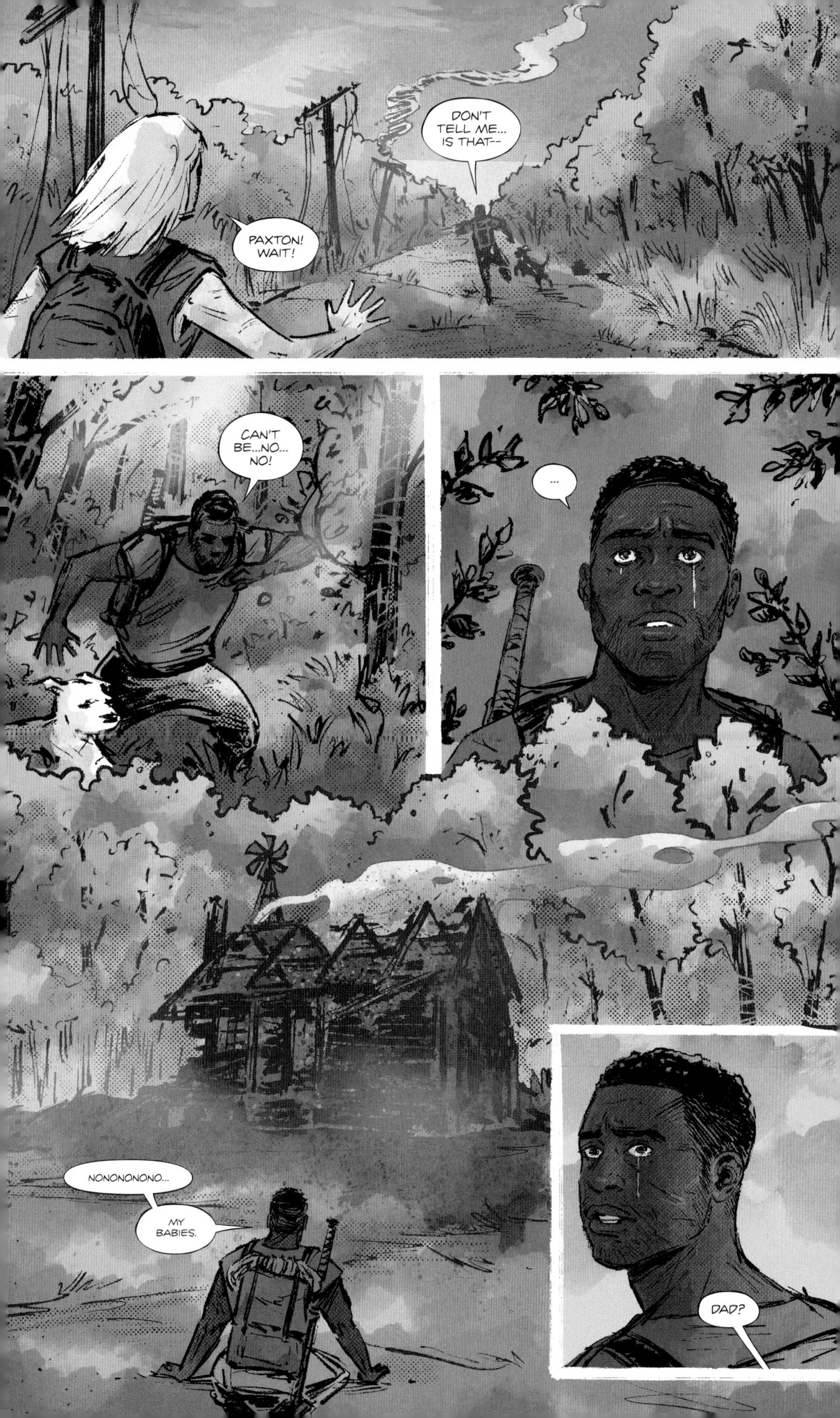
DON'T TELL ME... IS THAT--
PAXTON! WAIT!
CAN'T BE...NO... NO!
...
NONONONONO...
MY BABIES.
DAD?

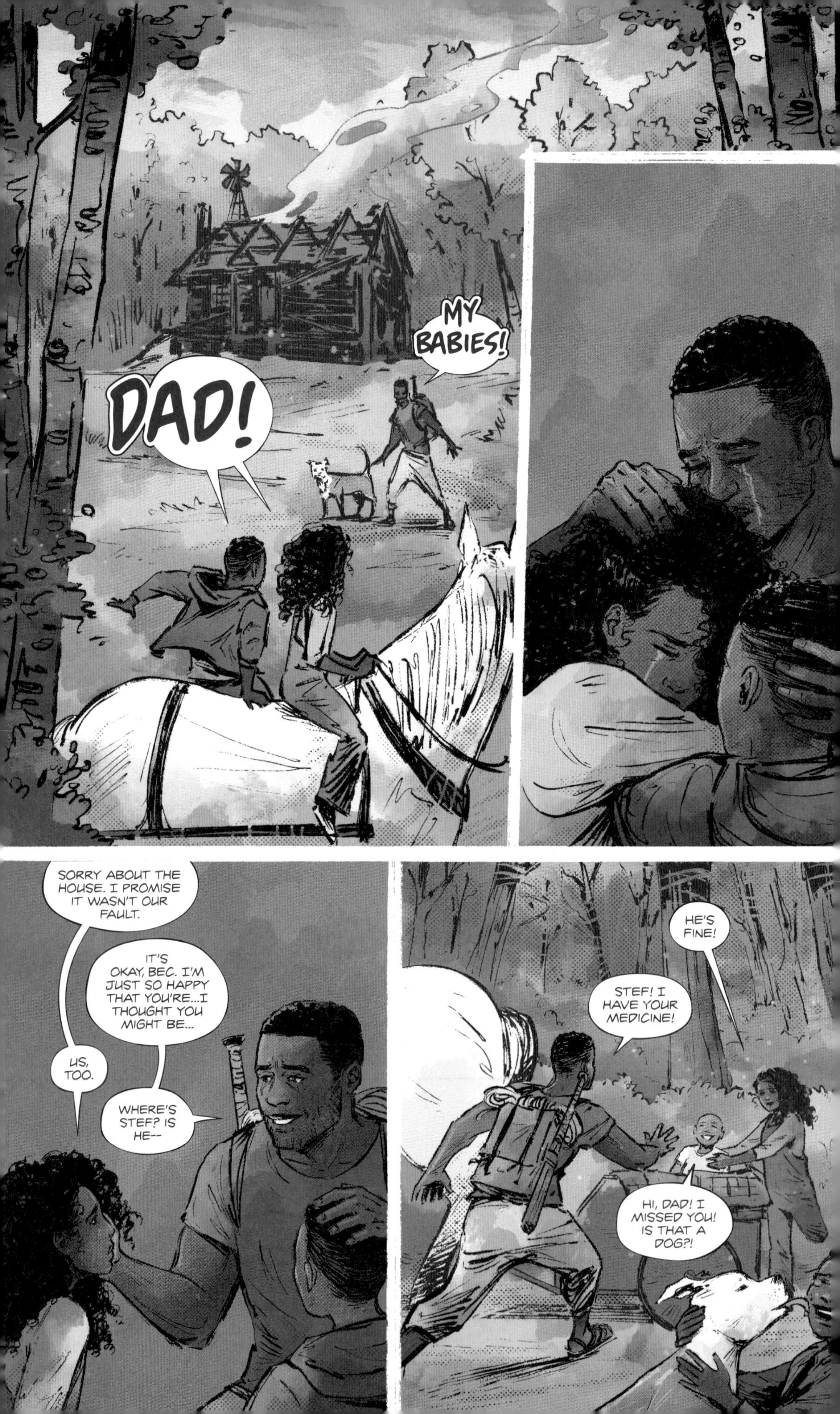
MY BABIES!
DAD!
SORRY ABOUT THE HOUSE. I PROMISE IT WASN'T OUR FAULT.
IT'S OKAY, BEC. I'M JUST SO HAPPY THAT YOU'RE...I THOUGHT YOU MIGHT BE...
US, TOO.
WHERE'S STEF? IS HE--
HE'S FINE!
STEF! I HAVE YOUR MEDICINE!
HI, DAD! I MISSED YOU! IS THAT A DOG?!

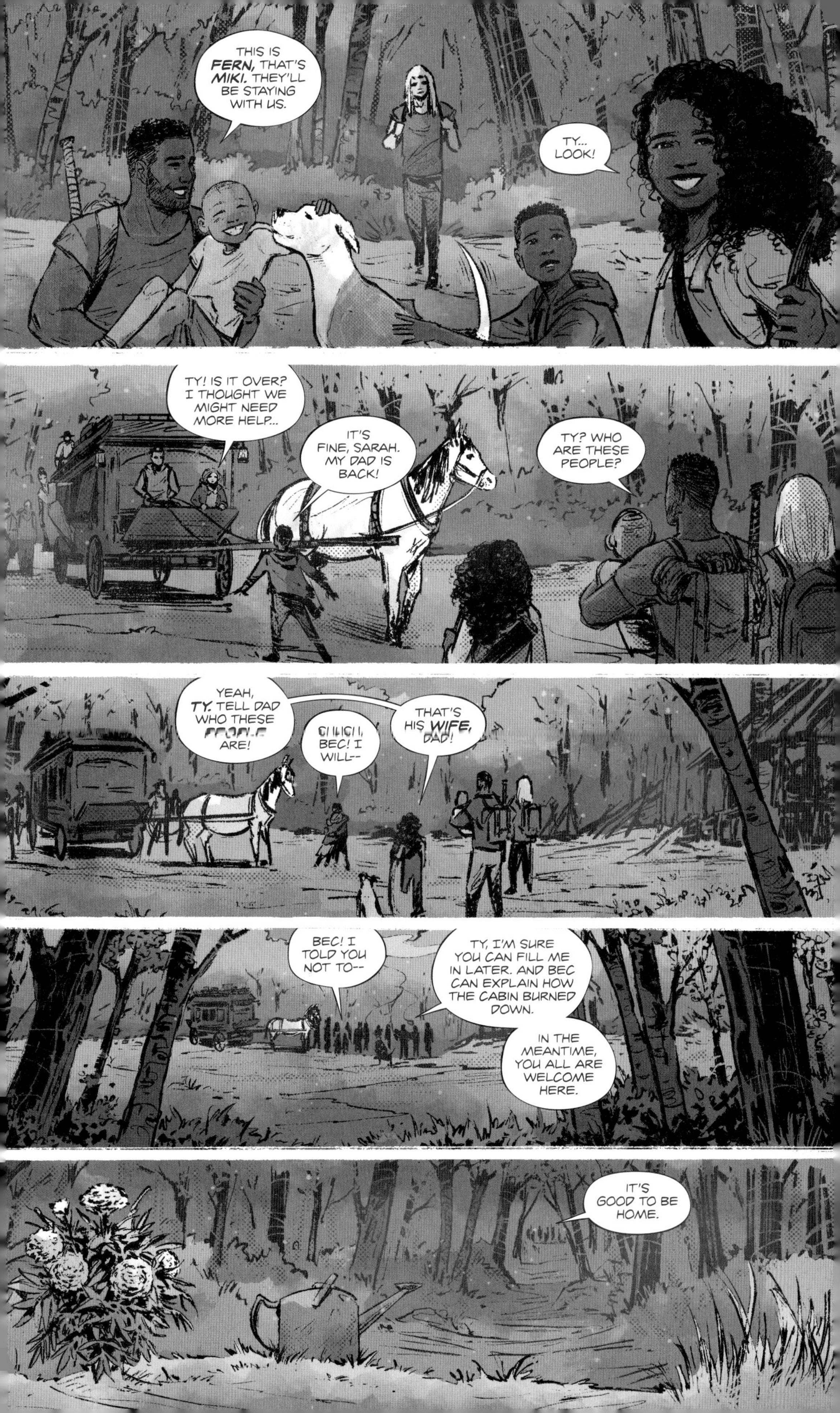
THIS IS FERN, THAT'S MIKI. THEY'LL BE STAYING WITH US.
TY... LOOK!
TY! IS IT OVER? I THOUGHT WE MIGHT NEED MORE HELP...
IT'S FINE, SARAH. MY DAD IS BACK!
TY? WHO ARE THESE PEOPLE?
YEAH, TY. TELL DAD WHO THESE
ARE!
BEC! I WILL--
THAT'S HIS WIFE, DAD!
BEC! I TOLD YOU NOT TO--
TY, I'M SURE YOU CAN FILL ME IN LATER. AND BEC CAN EXPLAIN HOW THE CABIN BURNED DOWN.
IN THE MEANTIME, YOU ALL ARE WELCOME HERE.
IT'S GOOD TO BE HOME.

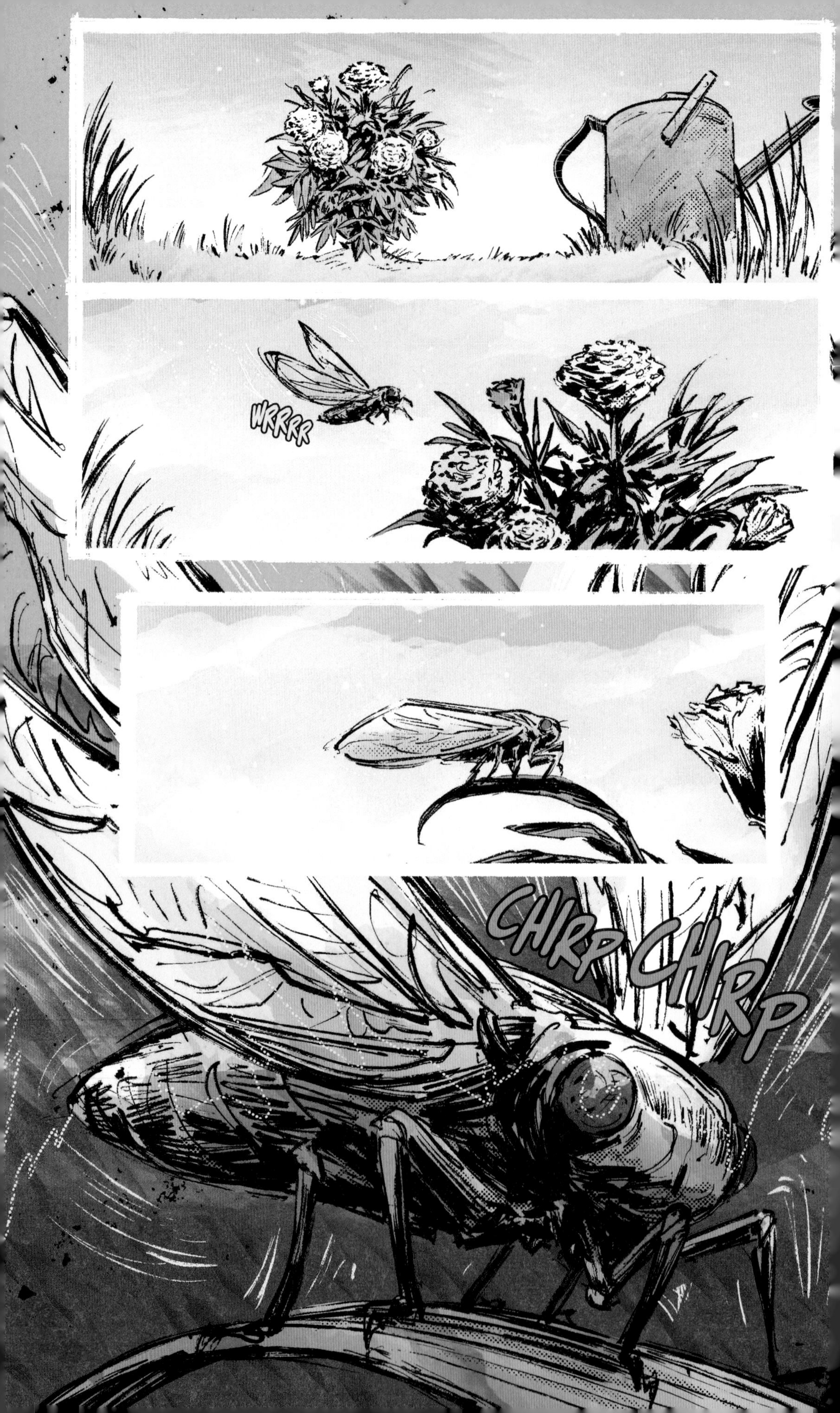
WRRRR
CHIRP CHIRP

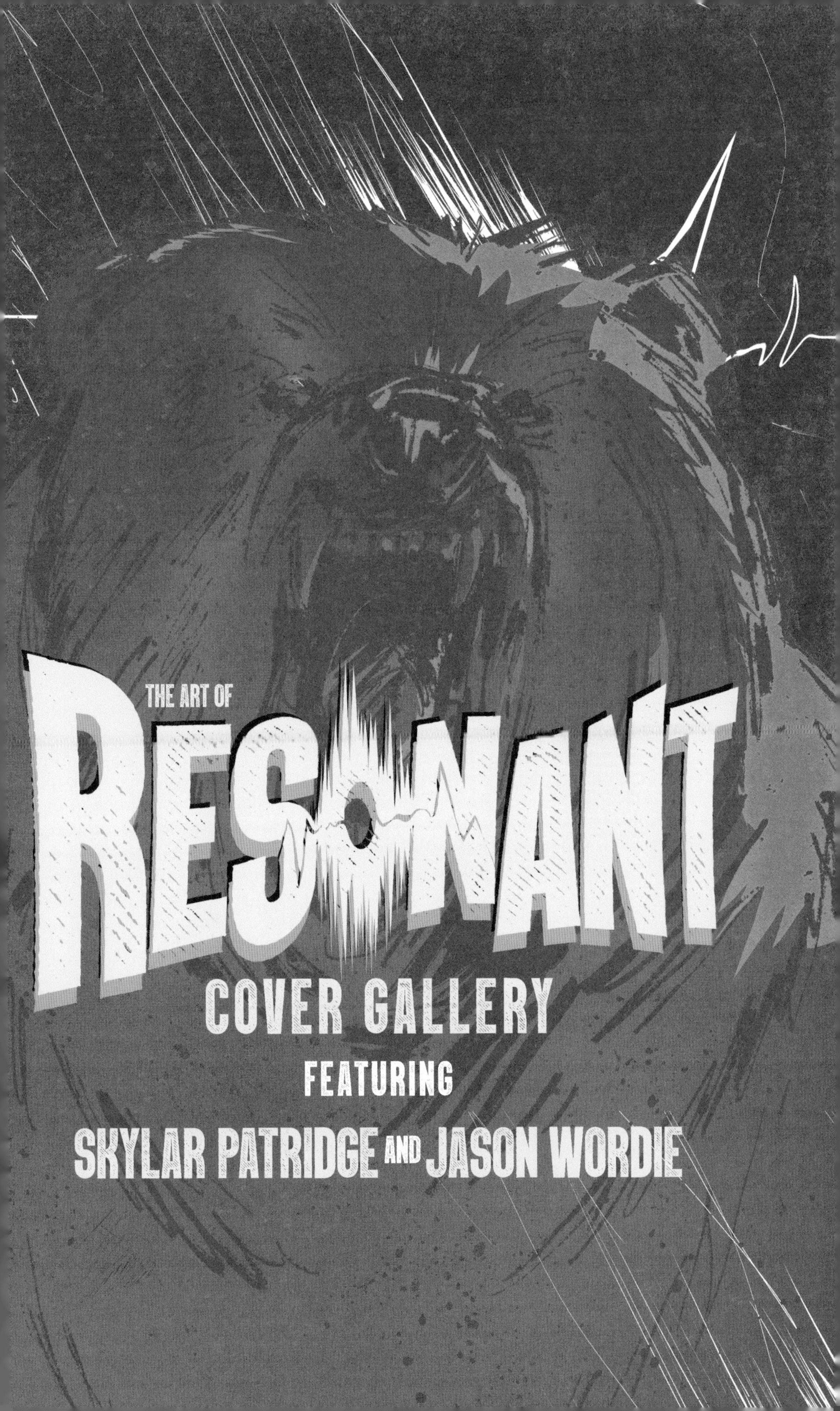
THE ART OF
RESONANT
COVER GALLERY
FEATURING
SKYLAR PATRIDGE AND JASON WORDIE

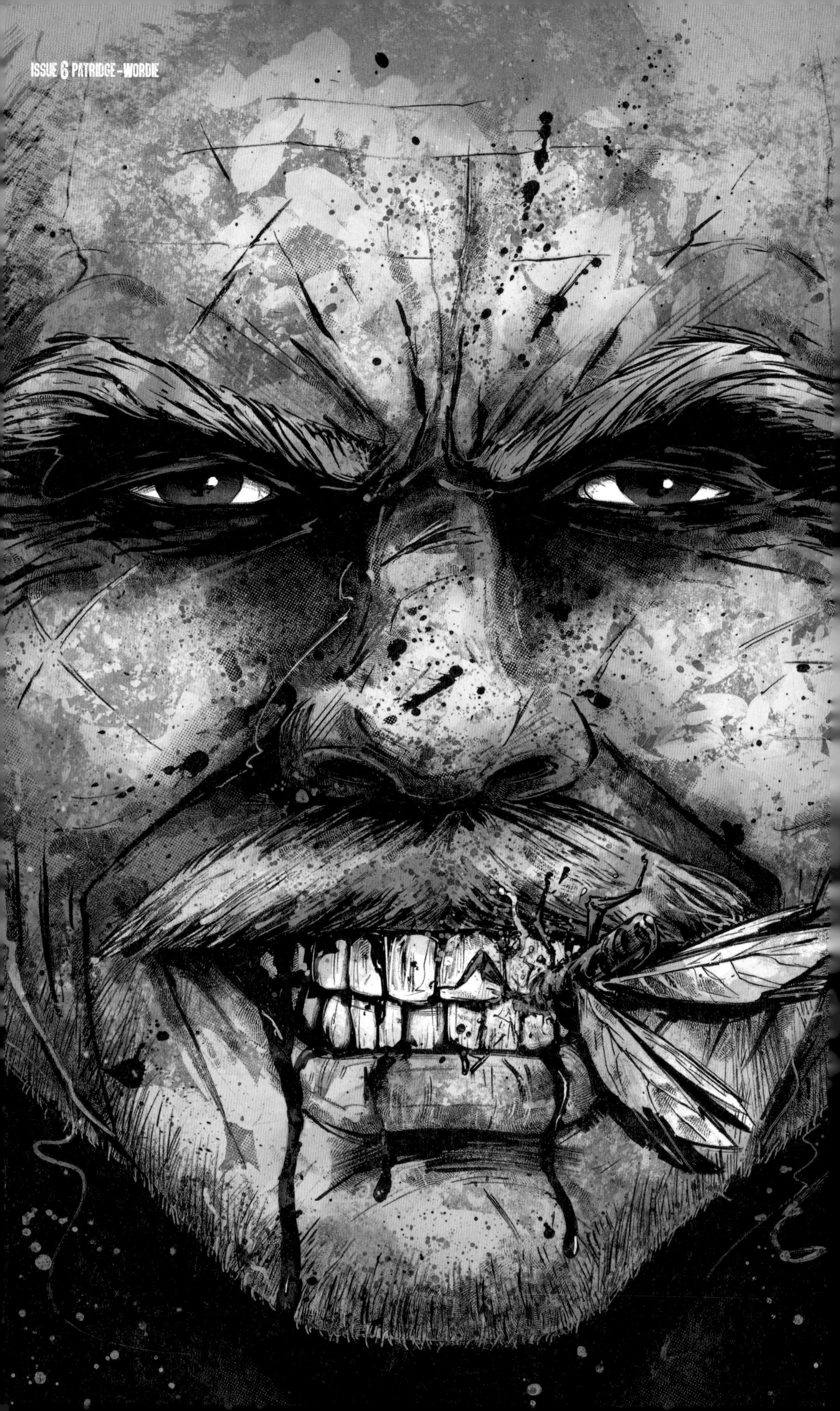
ISSUE 6 PATRIDGE-WORDIE

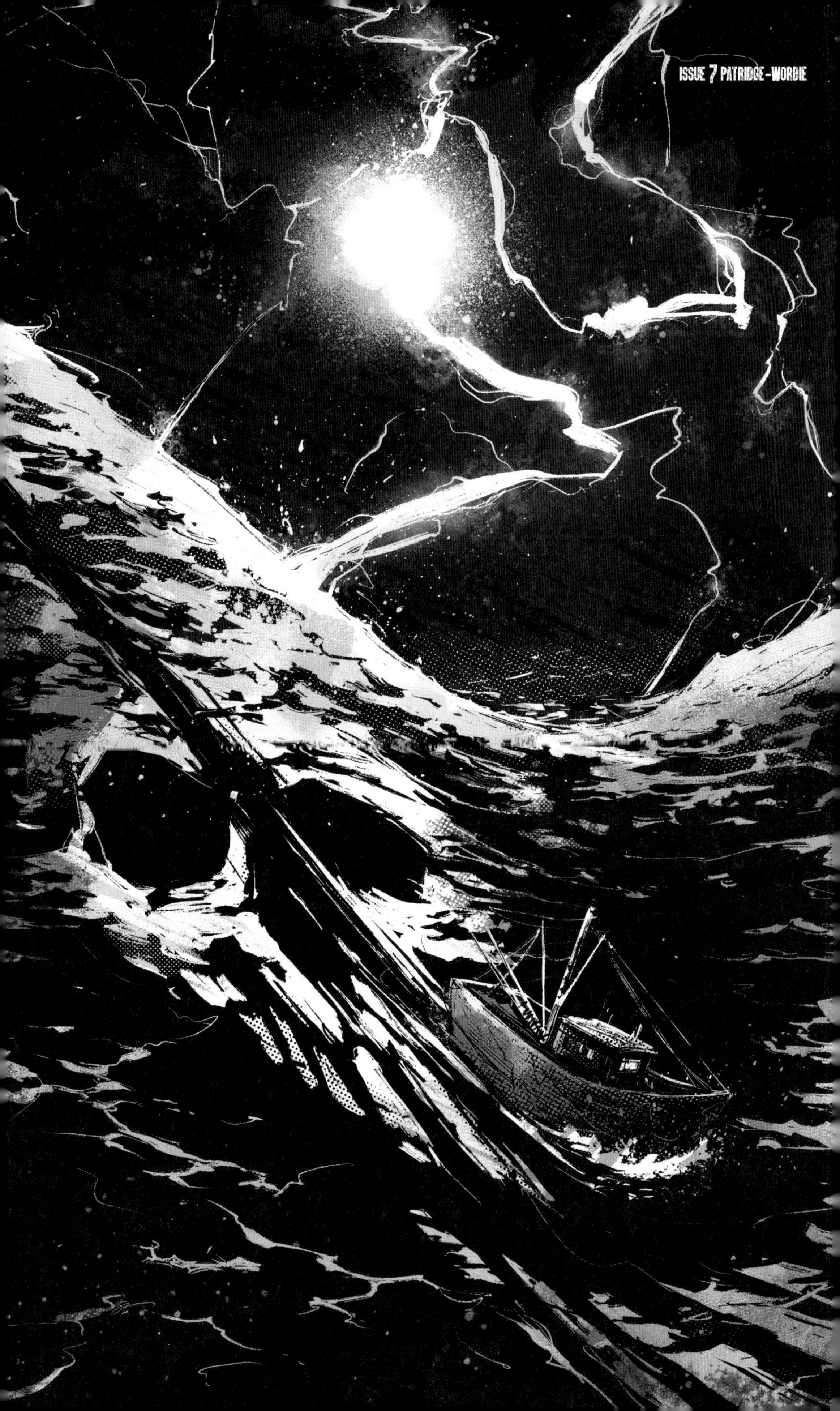

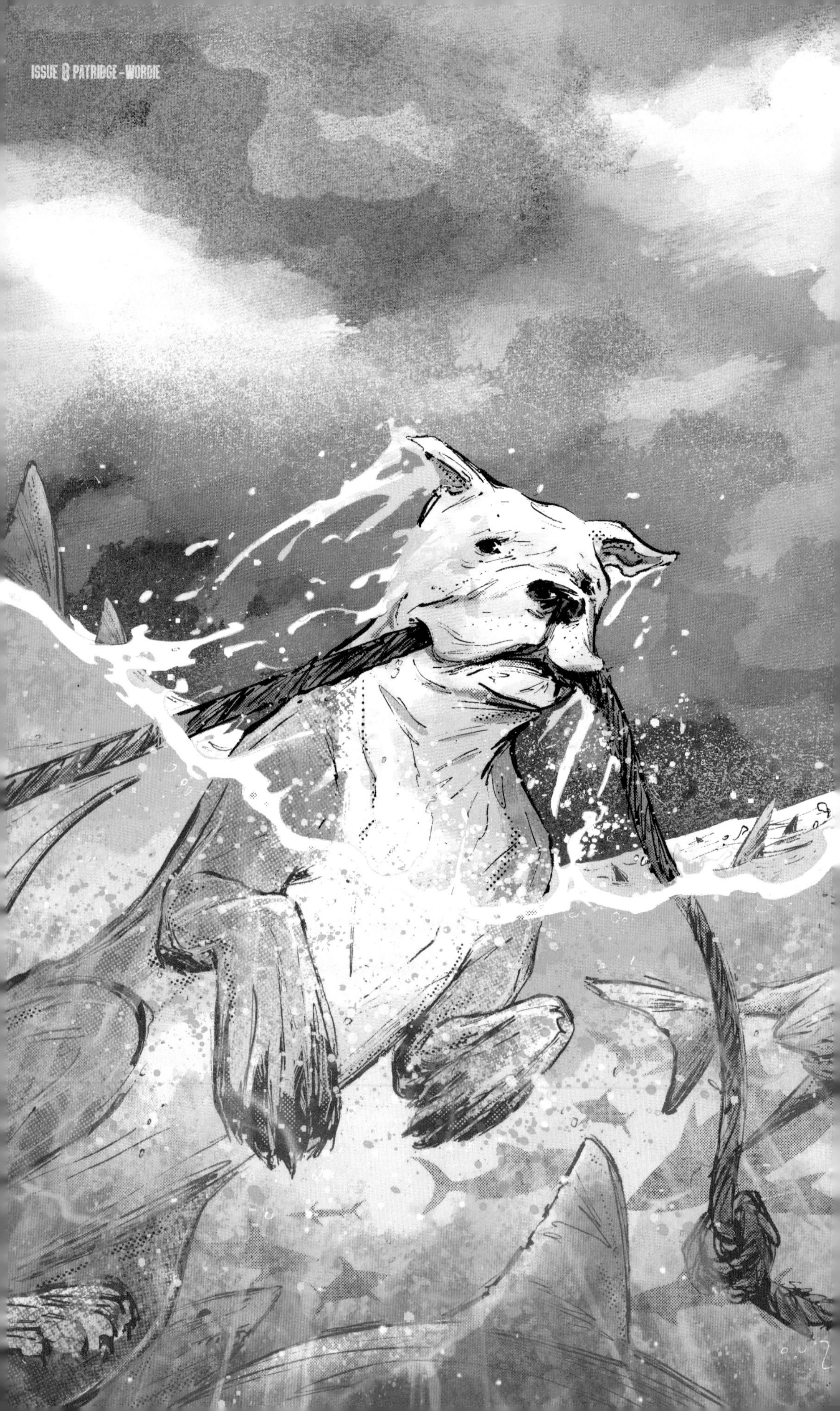
ISSUE 8 PATRIDGE - WORDIE

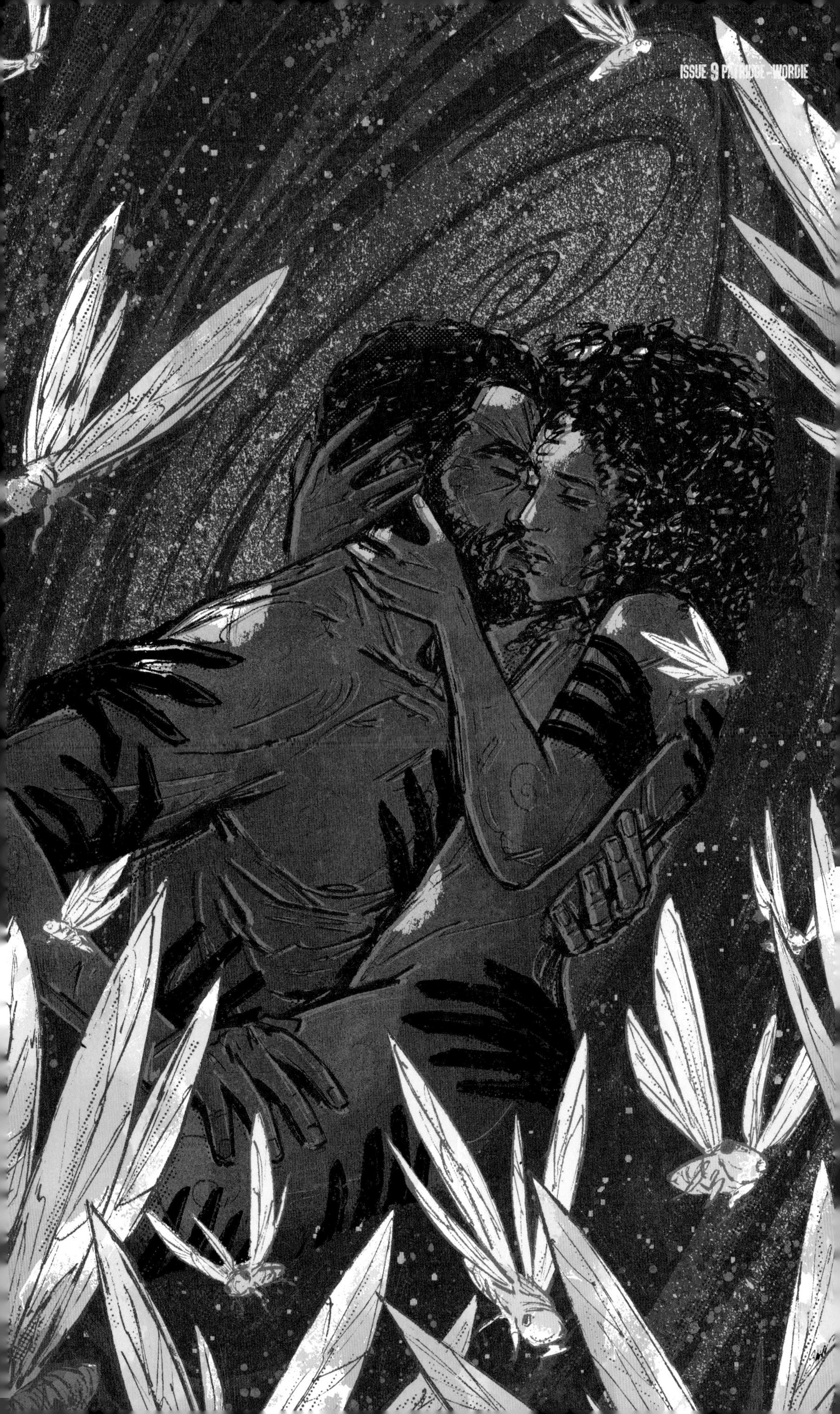
ISSUE 9
WORDIE

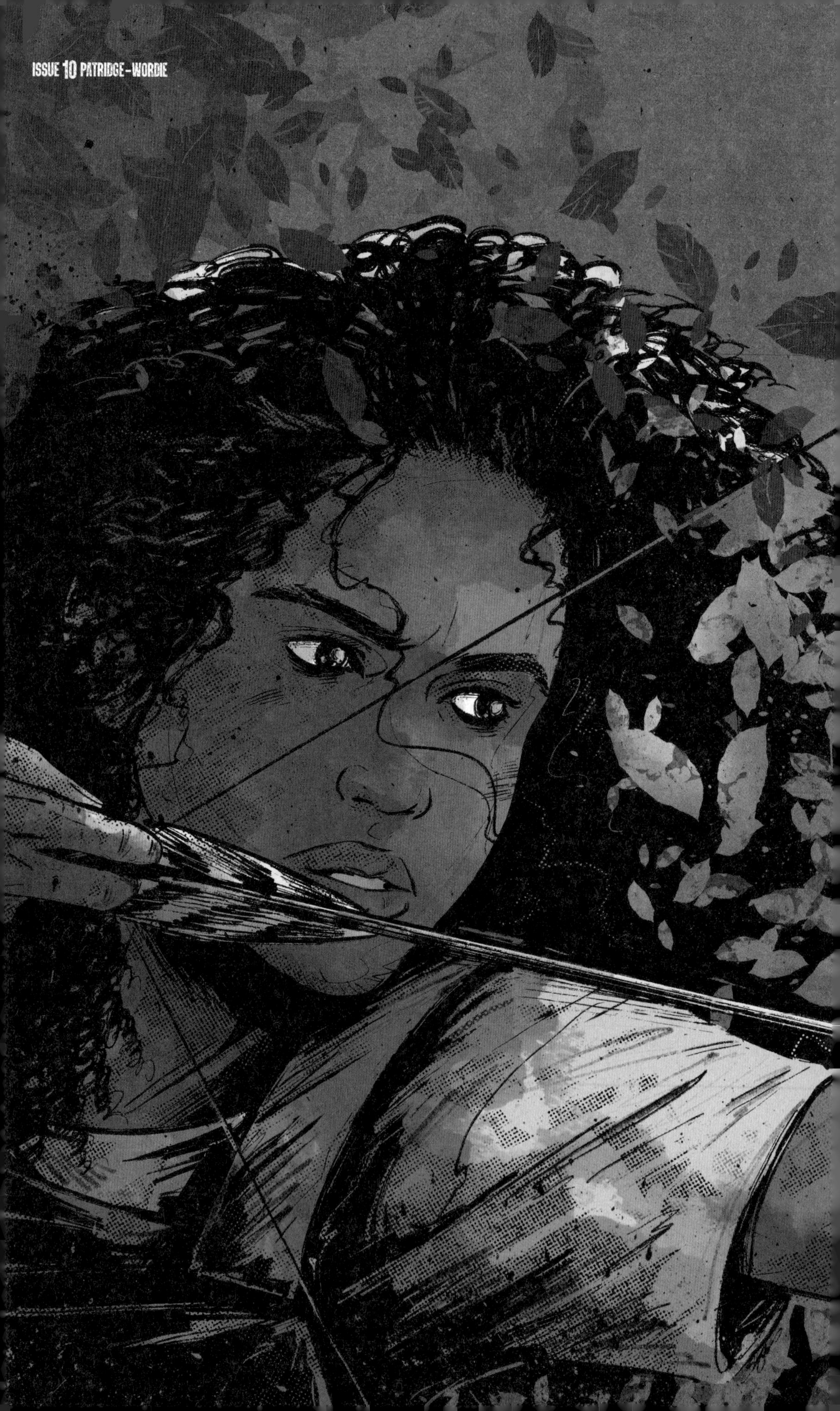
ISSUE 10 PATRIDGE-WORDIE